TENNYSON

Alfred, Lord Tennyson, 1859.
By G. F. Watts, R A.

TENNYSON

HIS HOMES
HIS FRIENDS
AND
HIS WORK

BY

ELISABETH L·CARY

ILLUSTRATED

SECOND IMPRESSION

G·P·PUTNAM'S SONS
The Knickerbocker Press
NEW YORK AND LONDON
· 1898 ·

The Knickerbocker Press, New York

PREFACE.

IN preparing this volume, I have included, in addition to the simple outline of the chief incidents in Tennyson's life, a selection of certain critical estimates of his work which impressed me as presenting most accurately his poetic quality with its limitations and its tendencies. Among these estimates are several, translated from French and German sources, which, so far as I know, have not before come into print in any of the various books about Tennyson. I was so fortunate also as to find in the *Massachusetts Quarterly* a review of *The Princess* by James Russell Lowell. I am indebted to Mr. Charles Eliot Norton for an unpublished letter concerning Tennyson's introduction to this country, and I wish to acknowledge the valuable assistance rendered in the collection of my material by the Librarians of the Brooklyn Mercantile Library and of the Brooklyn Historical Library.

While the result of my somewhat circumscribed researches can offer little if anything of original importance for the Tennyson specialist, I trust that for the general reader I have succeeded in giving a fair view of the life and work of the Laureate, a view possibly somewhat more detached and varied than that which may be gained from the official *Life* or from books written during the poet's lifetime.

E. L. C.

New York, Sept. 15, 1898.

CONTENTS.

ILLUSTRATIONS.

A portion of these illustrations were reproduced from the following English books : *Alfred, Lord Tennyson, and His Friends : A series of Portraits in photogravure from negatives*, by Julia Margaret Cameron and H. H. H. Cameron ; *The Laureate's Country*, by Professor Alfred J. Church ; *Tennyson and His Pre-Raphaelite Illustrators*, by George Somes Layard.

TENNYSON

CHAPTER I.

SOMERSBY AND LOUTH.

ALFRED TENNYSON belongs to the class of poets who strike their roots deep into their native soil. Not Virgil on the banks of the Mincio, or Wordsworth among the English Lakes, was more content with the scene at his door; and the Lincolnshire Wolds are interesting to us, as readers of Tennyson, less for their curious geologic formation and varied history of Roman and Danish occupation, than for the place given to their streams and trees and village gardens in the poems now read throughout the English-speaking world.

Lincolnshire was long known as a county of rabbits, and geese, and sheep "of whitest lock and magnitude of fleece," a county moist enough to suggest Herodian's description of the marshy places in Britain "over which the inhabitants will swim and walk, though up to the middle in water," but as dry now, thanks to an excellent system of drainage, as any part of England. The vast stretches of level land are richly cultivated, pleasant under the great waste of sky, and played upon by the winds. The

Wolds are the chalk hills that run from Spilsby to the southern shore of the Humber, and on a lower slope of these hills lies the little village of Somersby ; "an agreeable village," as the old guide-books describe it, with bowery lanes, a mere handful of inhabitants (in 1821 there were 62), a small sandstone church about which grows the wall-rue, and a low, white Rectory in which on the 6th of August, 1809, Alfred Tennyson was born.

Tennyson's father, the Rev. George Clayton Tennyson, held the two benefices of Somersby and Bag Enderby. He is described as a man of varied interests, something of a poet, something of an artist, much of a scholar and linguist, and of powerful physique. His wife was so tender-hearted a lady that a story is told of village roughs bringing their dogs beneath her window to beat them, knowing that she would buy them off from their cruelty.[1]

There were twelve children, eight of them sons, and it is not surprising that the Rector was obliged to add to his home a large room, which he built, after the fashion of ecclesiastical architecture, with mediæval windows. Here the large family were in the habit of gathering for evening games.

The Rectory, now no longer the Rectory, approached from Horncastle, stands on the right of the road and is separated from it by a narrow drive. The place has not been well kept up, and to see it as it was with the old garden and the lost view, we

---

[1] Waugh's *Alfred, Lord Tennyson.*

Somersby Rectory.

must turn to the "Ode to Memory" among Tennyson's early poems.   There we find

> " —— a garden bower'd close
>   With plaited alleys of the trailing rose,
>   Long alleys falling down to twilight grots,
>   Or opening upon level plots
>   Of crowned lilies, standing near
>   Purple-spiked lavender."

In the same poem we have further glimpses of
the fair visible world that intruded importunately
upon the lad's alert consciousness ; of "woods that
belt the grey hillside," of the "seven elms and pop-
lars four," and "the towering sycamore" behind the
house, of which group only the elms now remain,
and of the "ridgèd wolds" upon which bleated
"thick-fleeced sheep" in "wattled folds."   The
flowers in the Rectory garden inspired Tennyson's
first attempt at poetry, and Mrs. Ritchie's pretty story
of the boy of five, caught by the strong Lincolnshire
wind and whirled down the garden path, calling
out, "I hear a voice that's speaking in the wind,"
has gone the rounds with his biographers.   Another
favourite story connected with his early days is that
of the visitant owl.   Hearing one of these nocturnal
birds hoot or "snore" outside the window of the
little gable room in which he studied and wrote, he
responded with what must have been a clever imitation of the cry, for the owl flew in, made friends,
and remained as one of the family.   This episode,
no doubt, inspired the later poem "To the Owl,"

which so pleased the fancy of the genial Christopher North that he wrote in *Blackwood's :* " Alfred is as an owl ; all that he wants is to be shot, stuffed, and stuck into a glass case, to be made immortal in a museum."

Near the Rectory stands the old " Manor Farm," which in the change of years has been divided into labourers' dwellings. This dark old place owed its existence to an inexpert architectural mind, and furnished the Tennyson children with an admirable background for their singular games of joust and tournament, and one may easily picture Alfred, brown and strong and full of imaginative heat, taking much satisfaction in its " embattled parapet " ; but the story identifying it with the " Moated Grange," the home of weary Mariana, is altogether erroneous.

Somersby Church, of which Tennyson's father was Rector, underwent, in 1833, repairs that must have interfered with whatever quaintness the interior may have had in earlier days, and quite destroyed its atmosphere of delicate age. A fine Gothic window in the face of the tower was removed and one of crude taste was substituted ; the heavy high benches were replaced by new, open seats, and the rough uneven flagging gave way to encaustic tiles ; in general, a devastating spirit of order prevailed. The churchyard has, however, retained its ancient charm. The Roman Preaching Cross that stands near the porch on the south side of the building has escaped not only the ravages of time but the destructive tastes of the Commonwealth iconoclasts. It is about fifteen feet high with an octagonal shaft, and is decorated with a capital from which rises the cross, ornamented on its south face with the representation of the Crucifixion, and on the north face with the image of the Virgin and Child. Over the south porch is a sun-dial with the inscription "Time Passeth," and on the north side is a holy-water stoup. To the west of the tower is the tomb of the poet's father, who died at the early age of fifty-two.

Not far from the home of the Tennysons is a wooded place, unique in the landscape, deep and shady and wild, enclosing a well that furnishes the name of Holywell Glen. On one of the sandstone rocks at the upper end of this glen, the boy wrote his famous inscription "Byron is Dead," in his profound youthful grief, when the news penetrated to the Lincolnshire village; for him the "Byron and Bulwer age" began early!

At the lower end of the glen flows the Somersby brook, cool and dark, but *not* the stream that "comes from haunts of coot and hern" and with whose cheerful course we are all familiar. It might fairly enough boast of "hazel covers" and "sweet forget-me-nots" and "willow-weed and mallow," but it could not in honesty refer to "here and there a greyling." According to a very careful authority, the greyling is not a Lincolnshire fish, and the delicate verity of Tennyson's habit of mind—so reverenced by some, while others can only "endure to be told" of it—would not permit him to launch a foreign fish in one of his Lincolnshire brooks.[1] The "Brook" of which Edmund Aylmer sang is quite imaginary, while the little Somersby stream slips along in the "Ode to Memory,"

> " —— the brook that loves
>   To purl o'er matted cress and ribbed sand,
>   Or dimple in the dark of rushy coves,
>   Drawing into his narrow earthern urn
>   In every elbow and turn
>   The filtered tribute of the rough woodland,"

and shows its graver aspect in the poem beginning "Flow on, cold rivulet, to the sea."

In 1816, when Tennyson was only seven years old, he was sent to Louth, his mother's birthplace, and distinguished for a somewhat remarkable grammar-school in which he studied during four miserable years. The early part of the century seems to have been a dark period for the little grammar-school boys of Great Britain. Carlyle, who was sturdy enough about enduring physical hardship, never admired his master, and wrote of him, later in life, that " he knew syntax enough, and of the human soul thus much— that it had a faculty called memory, and could be acted on through the muscular integument by appliance of birch rods." Edward Irving, who had the same master as Carlyle, often had his ears pinched until they bled. The Reverend J. Waite, who was at the head of the Louth school when Tennyson was

---

[1] Professor Church's *The Laureate's Country*.

there, and long afterward, is described as having the character ascribed by Horace to his own teacher, being *plagosus*, fond of blows.[1]

Professor Hales, in his lively account of the Louth grammar-school,[2] writes with bitter humour of the conviction of the masters that "nothing could be taught that was not emphasised with the cane," but he adds quite pluckily : "Will it seem inconsistent to say that this old grammar-school is dear to my memory ? Even the house of bondage may have its charms. One may find most pleasant companions amongst one's fellow-captives. There may be fair views from the windows that inspire forgetfulness of the grievances of the interior. The taskmasters may be not without amiable features. And after all what is a good thrashing now and then if one's digestion is satisfactory ! What are all the syntaxes of the globe if only one sleeps well o' nights ! Then let us consider what excellent endurance our school taught us. What splendid training for martyrdom or any other suffering it provided ! We should have smiled benevolently at the stake, deemed the rack absolute repose, after our hardening experience."

Tennyson himself never rose to the height of this philosophy, and though the Louth school did its best to honour him in later years, he was not cajoled into forgetting that as a child he had hated it. It was natural enough that the little school, dull and aus-

[1] Professor Church's *The Laureate's Country*.
[2] *The Gentleman's Magazine*, 1892.

tere, as undoubtedly it was, and situated over a
sort of almshouse dedicated to the shelter of twelve
poor women, should have failed to leave jocund impressions on the mind of a sensitive, dreamy boy ;
but we will do it the justice to record that it held a
high place among the schools of Lincolnshire, boast-
ing the reputation of having educated more scholars
for the learned professions than any other school in
the county. Perhaps it justified in this way the inscription on the common-seal of the place : *Qui par-
cit virgæ odit filium* (Who spares the rod spoils the
child).

Although Tennyson wasted no affection upon the
Louth school, the town furnished him with at least
one moment of pure happiness. In 1827, Charles
and Alfred Tennyson made a collection of their verses
—already numerous—under the title *Poems by Two
Brothers*, and took the manuscript to Mr. J. Jackson,
a bookseller of Louth, who published the work and
paid twenty pounds for the copyright, a piece of
fortune that seems perhaps more surprising to us than
it did to the young authors.

There is a pleasant story that the "Two Brothers," on receipt of their money, hired a carriage and
drove fourteen or fifteen miles over the low hills and
marshy flats to Marblethorpe, with its sandy tracts
from which could be seen the "hollow ocean-ridges
roaring into cataracts." This coast is called by common consent tame and uninteresting ; but it is easy
to imagine the appeal made to a poetic mind by the

"wide-wing'd sunset of the misty marsh," by the "grey sand-banks" and dreary winds that drive the low clouds across the horizon, and by the infinite character of the sea.

This first lucky little volume is, very properly, not much dwelt upon by the critics of Tennyson's work. The authors wrote deprecatingly : "We have passed the Rubicon, and we leave the rest to fate ; though its edict may create a fruitless regret that we ever emerged from 'the shade' and courted notoriety." Notoriety came only in the shape of a little notice in *The Literary Chronicle and Weekly Review*, and the poems did not, certainly, deserve any more striking welcome.   Taking such lines as these :

> "Memory ! dear enchanter !
>   Why bring back to view
> Dreams of youth, which banter
>   All that e'er was true."

or these :

> "The vices of my life arise,
>   Pourtrayed in shapes, alas ! too true,
>   And not one beam of hope breaks through
> To cheer my old and aching eyes,"

we can readily concur with Stopford Brooke, who finds the boyish verses "without one trace of originality, force, or freshness—faded imitations of previous poets, chiefly of Byron ; or, where not imitative, full of the futile modesty of boyhood which would fain be vain but does not dare, made up partly of bald noise and partly of sentimentality, accurately true to the type of the English poetry between the death of Shelley and the publication of Tennyson's volume of 1830."[1]

It was, however, the natural failure of youth, delighted with the literature of its own day and inquisitive concerning it, without the power of turning life into similar treasure. Still "feeling after" poetry, the brothers, Charles and Alfred, went in 1828 to Cambridge, to get from its associations and atmosphere, if not from its teachings, much intellectual dignity and grace.

[1] Stopford Brooke's *Tennyson : His Art and Relation to Modern Life*.

CHAPTER II.

CAMBRIDGE AND NEW LIFE.

FOR reasons not altogether difficult of comprehension, Cambridge University has not been able to command a scrupulous devotion from its poets. Milton, early in the seventeenth century, described it as "a place quite incompatible with the votaries of Phœbus," and found himself so irresistibly in opposition to it that he was irritated even by the aspect of the innocent fields in its neighbourhood; fields on which, later, his "idle orbs" would fain have looked. Dryden, in his Prologue to the University of Oxford, let no formal loyalty to his own University restrain him, while Gray, who was both pupil and professor at Cambridge in the middle years of the eighteenth century, went so far as to say: "Surely it was of this place, now Cambridge, but formerly known by the name of Babylon, that the prophet spoke when he said: 'But wild beasts of the desert shall lie there; and their houses shall be full of doleful creatures; and owls shall dwell there, and satyrs shall dance there.'"[1] Byron, whose name

[1] Isaiah xiii., 21.

was still fresh in Trinity College when Tennyson went there, wrote in 1807 : "This place is wretched enough—a villainous chaos of din and drunkenness, nothing but hazard and Burgundy, mathematics and Newmarket, riot and racing"; and in 1808 : "Were reasoning, eloquence, or virtue the object of my search, Granta is not their metropolis, nor is the place of her situation an El Dorado, far less an Utopia. The intellects of her children are as stagnant as her Cam ; and their pursuits limited to the church, not of Christ, but of the nearest benefice."

It was then a natural sequence that Tennyson should have been at least indifferent to Cambridge as it was before the middle of the present century. Mathematics held possession of the place and were by no means pursued with the imagination and breadth of vision that, one may think, should have been awakened daily by the noble statue in the ante-chapel of Newton

> "—— with his prism and silent face ;
> The marble index of mind forever
> Voyaging through strange seas of thought alone."

The teaching was undoubtedly technical and sterile, formal and seldom illuminating. Only since 1822 had there been an annual voluntary classical examination, and the condition imposed on all candidates was that they should have obtained an honour at the mathematical examination of the preceding January.

The social life, moreover, was not harmoniously

blent. As far back as the sixteenth and seventeenth centuries there had been more opportunities for sympathy between tutor and pupil ; but as the numbers increased, the older men ceased to share their rooms with the undergraduates, ceremony and artificiality crept in, and these opportunities were curtailed. A spirit of "donnishness," incompatible with the finer essence of social intercourse, prevailed, and, doubtless, there was much extravagance and recklessness of living, although it may not have been so wild a spirit as dominated Oxford when Ruskin, at his first college supper, helped to carry away four fellow-students, "one of them the son of the head of a college, head-foremost, down-stairs and home."

Still there was the quickening influence of many men of many minds, and concerning this we can hardly do better than quote Carlyle's words on the side of Cambridge ; always the old Cambridge, be it remembered, before the leaven of modernity had begun to work. He writes :

"One benefit not to be dissevered from the most obsolete University still frequented by young, ingenuous, living souls, is that of manifold collision and communication with the said young souls ; which, to everyone of these coevals, is undoubtedly the most important branch of breeding for him. In this point, as the learned Huber has insisted, the two English Universities, their studies otherwise being granted to be nearly useless, and even ill done of their kind, —far excel all other Universities : so valuable are the rules of human behaviour which from of old have tacitly established themselves there ; so manful, with all its sad drawbacks, is the style of English character, 'frank, simple, rugged, and yet courteous,' which has tacitly but imperatively got itself sanctioned and prescribed there. Such, in full sight of Continental and other Universities, is Huber's opinion. . . . Another judge in whom I have confidence, declares further : That of these two Universities, Cambridge is decidedly the more Catholic (not Roman Catholic but Human Catholic) in its tendencies and habitudes ; and that, in fact, of all the miserable Schools and High Schools in the England of these years, he, if reduced to choose from them, would choose Cambridge as a place of culture for the young idea."[1]

Walter Bagehot had the same idea in estimating the value of college life. " Take an uncollegiate Englishman," he says, " and you will generally find that he has no *friends :* he has not the habit " ; and he adds : " The real plastic energy is not in tutors or lectures or in books ' got up,' but in Wordsworth and Shelley ; in the books that all read because all like, in what all talk of because all are interested, in the argumentative walk or disputatious lounge." This was precisely the debt that Tennyson owed to Cambridge, and one that he amply acknowledged in the very permanence and strength of the associations he formed there.

[1] Carlyle's *Life of John Sterling.*

Charles and Alfred Tennyson lodged together first at Rose Crescent, and afterwards in Trumpington Street. They are said to have been shy and taciturn lads, and for a moment they hesitated at the threshold of the untried world. But they were not long in finding their special circle, and it is interesting to know that Thackeray, in the same college at the same time, was apparently not included in it. We learn somewhat vaguely from *In Memoriam* of the little band that held debate

> " —— on mind and art
> And labour and the changing mart
> And all the framework of the land.
>
> When one would aim an arrow fair
> But send it slackly from the string,
> And one would pierce an outer ring
> And one an inner, here and there."

These were the "Twelve Apostles" as they were called, an association started in 1820, and limited to twelve members. The group may have been, as Mr. Swinburne has said, "very plausibly definable by nameless curs of letters as a 'mutual admiration society' artificially heated by the steam of reciprocal incense for the incubation of 'coterie glory'"[1]; but there must have been something of real worth in the ardent speculation and discussion that took place among such men as Richard Trench (afterwards Archbishop of Dublin), Richard Milnes (afterwards Lord Houghton), the humorous Brookfield, Thack-

[1] See article on "Tennyson and Musset."

eray's friend, Spedding, Sterling, and the rest.   There
was enough intellectual activity among them, at all
events, and a story is told of them that reflects almost
beyond credence upon the literary "atmosphere" of
Oxford at that time.   A deputation was sent by the
Cambridge Union, a literary club then recently organised, to the corresponding society at Oxford, to maintain the proposition that Shelley was a greater poet
than Byron.   Milnes, who was one of the representatives of Cambridge, writes of the expedition :

"The contrast from our lounging, shuffling, scrap-
ing, talking, ridiculous kind of assembly to a neat
little square room, with eighty or ninety young gentlemen sprucely dressed, sitting on chairs or lounging
about the fireplace, was enough to unnerve a more
confident person than myself.   Even the brazen Sun-
derland was somewhat awed and became tautologi-
cal, and spake what we should call an inferior speech,
but which dazzled his hearers.   Hallam, as being
among old friends, was bold and spake well.   I was
certainly nervous, but, I think, pleased my audience
better than I pleased myself."   The spruce young
gentlemen proved to be "wretched speakers," and
some of them believed that *Shenstone* was the poet
under discussion, and said they knew but one poem
by him, the one beginning

"My banks are all furnished with bees."[1]

The "Old Man of Highgate" was casting his pale

[1] See *Life of Lord Houghton* by Wemyss Reid.

metaphysical light over Cambridge at that moment, and Wordsworth was in possession of his fame. There was, too, a spirit stirring toward religious and social awakening. Newman at Oxford, Maurice at Cambridge, had ruffled the smooth surface of conventional thought in the two Universities; and Maurice, struggling with the eternal verities against the influence of what we may call a dogmatically liberal training, and pouring out eloquence that had slowly gathered intensity in the frightened silence of his home life, was a magical leader for the young "Apostles" of Tennyson's circle. Out of their fervour and disputation a certain amount of character was bound to develop, and Carlyle's glowing picture of the young Sterling may stand as the type of them all :

"—— a young, ardent soul looking with hope and joy into a world which was infinitely beautiful to him, though overhung with falsities and foul cobwebs as world never was before; overloaded, overclouded, to the zenith and nadir of it, by incredible uncredited traditions, solemnly sordid hypocrisies, and beggarly deliriums old and new; which latter class of objects it was clearly the part of every noble heart to expend all its lightnings and energies in burning up without delay, and sweeping into their native Chaos out of such a Cosmos as this. Which process it did not then seem to him could be very difficult; or attended with much other than heroic joy and enthusiasm of victory or of battle to the

gallant operator, in his part of it. This was, with
modifications such as might be, the humour and
creed of College Radicalism five and twenty years
ago.[1] Rather horrible at that time, seen to be not so
horrible now, at least to have grown very universal,
and to need no concealment now. The natural humour and attitude, we may well regret to say,—and
honourable, not dishonourable, for a brave young
soul such as Sterling's in those years in those local-
ities."

Tennyson, it would seem, was not so disputatious nor so fiery as many of his companions ; he
had always about him a saving—when not blighting
—grace of common-sense. The Reverend Stopford
Brooke takes him to task for this,[2] finding his theories of patriotism, progress, and so forth, unpoetic, and
wishing he had taken "the side of the rushers, of
the enthusiastic seekers, of the wild warriors, of the
sacrificers whom the world calls insane," of the indignant men whose speech and action he thought
were "blind hysterics of the Celt." One episode of
his youth, however, shows him deeply moved by
the necessities and sufferings of his human kind.
Carlyle speaks of certain weary groups of Spanish
exiles, "stately, tragic figures, in proud threadbare
cloaks," pacing Euston Square in London during the
winter of 1829–30. These were the political refugees,
awaiting their chance to overthrow the Government

[1] Written in 1851.
[2] *Tennyson: His Art and Relation to Modern Life.*

of Ferdinand VII., and hanging upon the counsel of the revolutionist, General Torrijos. The youth of England, or at all events the youth of Cambridge, impelled by fire and pity, made various attempts to help them, and the two friends, Arthur Hallam and Alfred Tennyson, went to the aid of certain refugees in hiding near the Pyrenees border. Very little information concerning this expedition, with its bravery of letters written in concealed ink and money donated to the " Cause," has reached us ; but it was probably its own reward, University life seldom providing for young exuberance an outlet at once so romantic and so virtuous.

Meanwhile, Tennyson was steadily developing his poetic talent. At twenty there is time for everything, and discussions, theatricals, not impossibly mathematics, were sooner neglected than the one absorbing occupation. The subject for the Chancellor's Prize Poem in 1829 was " Timbuctoo "—not very inspiring to the modern mind. Tennyson's father thought that his son's poetic faculty might here be turned to good account, and urged him to compete ; and he did so, apparently in a spirit of reckless indifference, as, in place of preparing a new poem, he furbished up an old one written in blank verse instead of in the orthodox heroic couplet, and sent it in. The result was quite a surprising success, the poem containing fine lines and spirited imagery, and Tennyson was awarded the medal over worthy competitors, of whom Hallam was one.

Milnes wrote to his father concerning it : "Tennyson's poem has made quite a sensation ; it is certainly equal to most parts of Milton ! "

A curious story attributes to Thackeray a parody on this prize poem containing these alluring lines :

> " In Africa—a quarter of the world—
> Men's skins are black, their hair is crisped and curled,
> And somewhere there, unknown to public view,
> A mighty city lies, called Timbuctoo."

Mr. Arthur Waugh very sensibly decides against the theory of parody on Thackeray's part, suggesting that he made merely a comic effort on the theme given out.

Beside "Timbuctoo," which did not, it is conceivable, deeply engage the poet's mind, Tennyson was hard at work upon his own themes. At night in his room he "crooned out his mellifluous music" to his friends, and, in 1830, he was ready for a wider public with a thin volume of *Poems, Chiefly Lyrical*. It was a noticeable flight, and gave contemporary critics some interesting work to do, for which they were obviously grateful. The *Westminster Review* devoted a number of pages to a grave and what now seems a pompous explanation of the virtues of the poems, and the dangers that lay in wait for their author. The reviewer, said to be John Stuart Mill, soliloquises as follows :

"A genuine poet has deep responsibilities to his country and the world, to the present and future generations, to earth and heaven. He of all men should have distinct and worthy objects before him, and consecrate himself to their promotion. It is thus that he best consults the glory of his art and his own lasting fame. Mr. Tennyson has a dangerous quality in that facility of impersonation on which we have remarked, and by which he enters so thoroughly into the most strange and wayward idiosyncrasies of other men.

"It must not degrade him into a poetical harlequin. He has higher work to do than that of disporting himself amongst 'mystics' and 'flowing philosophers.' He knows that 'the Poet's mind is holy ground'; he knows that the poet's portion is to be

> 'Dower'd with the hate of hate, the scorn of scorn,
> The love of love';

he has shown, in the lines from which we quote, his own just conception of the grandeur of a poet's destiny; and we look to him for its fulfilment. It is not for such men to sink into mere verse-makers for the amusement of themselves or others. They can influence the associations of unnumbered hearts; they can disseminate principles; they can give those principles power over men's imaginations; they can excite in a good cause the sustained enthusiasm that is sure to conquer; they can blast the laurels of the tyrants and hallow the memories of the martyrs of patriotism; they can act with a force, the extent of which it is difficult to estimate, upon national feelings and character, and consequently upon national happiness." If the author of this criticism had known that he was impressing upon a future laureate the dignity of his office, the warning could hardly have been more strenuous.

In *The Englishman's Magazine*, Arthur Hallam made a discriminating as well as appreciative estimate of the book. He found in it luxuriance of imagination held in control, a power of embodying self in character or moods of character, a picturesque delineation of objects, and the skill to hold them "fused in a medium of strong emotion," a variety of lyrical measures, and an elevated habit of thought; and he concluded with a very characteristic defence of Tennyson's selection of words:

"The language of the book," he wrote, "with one or two exceptions, is thorough and sterling English. A little more respect, perhaps, was due to the '*jus et norma loquendi*,' but we are inclined to consider as venial a fault arising from generous enthusiasm for the principles of sound analogy and for that Saxon element which constitutes the intrinsic freedom and nervousness of our native tongue. We see no signs in what Mr. Tennyson has written of the Quixotic spirit which has led some persons to desire the reduction of English to a single form by excluding nearly the whole of Latin and Roman derivatives. Ours is necessarily a compound language; as such alone it can flourish and increase, nor will the author of the poems we have extracted be likely to barter for a barren appearance of symmetrical structure that fertility of expression and variety of harmony which 'the speech that Shakespeare spoke' derived from the sources of southern phraseology." It was good criticism for a lad of nineteen, and in itself too good to warrant the very amusing attack from "Christopher North" in *Blackwood's*. "Fusty Christopher," as Tennyson afterwards called him, had little sympathy with expansive admiration on the part of any critic, and he delighted to declare that Hallam's article had sent *The Englishman's Magazine* to its early grave ; while his condemnation of the *Westminster* article will serve to show the present generation how little restraint was demanded of reviewers in the early years of the century :

"It [the *Westminster* article] is a perfect specimen," he wrote, "of the super-hyperbolical ultra-extravagance of outrageous Cockney eulogistic foolishness, with which not even a quantity of common-sense less than nothing has been suffered for an indivisible moment of time to mingle, the purest mere matter of moonshine ever mouthed by an idiot-lunatic slavering in the palsied dotage of the extremest super-annuation ever inflicted on a being long ago, perhaps, in some slight respects and low degrees human, but now sensibly and audibly reduced below the level of the Pongoes." This phenomenal passage is a fine example of the "shallow head and restless temper" in the "numerous host" of reviewers so much despised by Coleridge ; but "Christopher" was not so rash as to conclude his paper without disclosing his actual attitude toward the young poet :

"Perhaps in the first part of the article," he admitted, "we may have exaggerated Mr. Tennyson's not unfrequent silliness, for we are apt to be carried away by the whim of the moment, and in our humorous moods many things wear a queer look to our aged eyes which fill young pupils with tears ; but we feel assured that in the second part we have not exaggerated his strength, that we have done no more than justice to his fine faculties, and that the millions who delight in Maga will with one voice confirm our judgment that Alfred Tennyson is a poet."

When we consider that he was at this time only twenty-one, that his natural bent was toward a style demanding infinite patience and training, and that Wordsworth had risen, pure and luminous, above the level horizon of literature, a very trying star for lesser lights to shine against, we may decide that Tennyson was faring well among his friends and foes.

The greatest of these friends, as the world well knows, was Arthur Henry Hallam, a learned boy, a year and a half Tennyson's junior, already a traveller when the two met at Cambridge, much read in poetry and philosophy, and careless of mathematics. His nature, vigorous and bright, his kindliness of temper, and the generosity of his affections won him the exuberant love that seems to belong to those who die young. Physically he was delicate, but in spirit indomitable—as one would know almost in advance, so often is the mystery repeated.

In him Tennyson found the charm that others found, with something more compelling, an attraction that made their friendship singular, and equal to the great friendships of the earlier world. Curiously pertinent to it, in fact, is this—Montaigne's description of his own perfect "inviolate" intimacy with Estienne La Boëtie : "Having so short a time to endure, and having so late begun (for we were both men grown, and he by several years), it had no time to lose, nor could it be built upon the model of regular and feeble friendships, for which is needed such precaution of long and previous conversation." And we may venture even a little farther along the dangerous parallel, to quote in its fitness to Tennyson's experience one other passage from Montaigne's threnody,—so touching as one comes upon it, rising and falling like music overcome by coarser sound, through the cynicism of many pages :

"For in truth if I compare all the rest of my life, which by the grace of God I have passed pleasantly, comfortably, and, excepting the loss of such a friend, exempt from weighty affliction, full of tranquillity of mind, having taken in payment my natural and original commodities without seeking others ; if I compare all this, I say, to the four years that it was given me to enjoy the gentle companionship and society of this person, all is as smoke, as a dark and weary night. There is no action or imagination in which I do not miss him, as he would also have missed me, for just as he surpassed by infinite degrees in all other virtue and sufficiency, so would he in the exercise of friendship." Such, also, was the intimacy between Hallam and Tennyson ; and from the long lament of *In Memoriam* we learn how this personal relation deepened and made beautiful all the associations with Cambridge and with Somersby where Hallam visited the Tennysons and became the lover of Emily Tennyson, and where, in the shadowy garden, he

> " ———— shook to all the liberal air
> The dust and din and steam of town ;

and

> " ———— lay and read
> The Tuscan poets on the lawn."

CHAPTER III.

THE VOLUME OF 1832, AND *In Memoriam.*

TENNYSON, called from Cambridge by his father's illness, which resulted in death, went back to Somersby in 1831. He had not, of course, taken his degree, but a degree seems not to have been regarded as a matter of much importance by the Cambridge students of the time. The separation from his congenial friends was probably much harder to bear. We hear of the leave-taking celebrated by a dance, and of the youth driving away in the light of the street lamps, and looking back to catch a last glimpse of the handsome face of one of his comrades. Later there were frequent letters and visits from the various "Apostles" who kept him informed of their pre-occupations. The Tennyson family continued to occupy the Somersby Rectory until 1837, and there was plenty of opportunity for life in the open air, at all events, and for the study of nature.

We can imagine Tennyson, often with Hallam for a companion, taking his long walks over the wold after the wholesome fashion of athletic young Englishmen, or loafing along the brookside like Landor, " meditating native rhymes," or amusing his friends with the performance of herculean feats of strength. There were also occasional visits to London, where he and Hallam rambled about among the æsthetic sights of the great town.

Under these influences, favourable enough to poetic production of a gentle kind, he made up the volume which was published in December, 1832, and is known as the 1833 volume.   It contained very much the sort of poetry one might look for from a nature inclined toward reflection and dwelling aloof from the stir of towns.   Mr. Stedman, in his *Victorian Poets*, says of it : " All in all a more original and beautiful volume of minor poetry never was added to our literature. . . .   Even if these lyrics and idyls had expressed nothing, they were of priceless value as guides to the renaissance of beauty.   Thenceforward slovenly work was impossible, subject to instant rebuke by contrast.   The force of metrical elegance made its way and carried everything before it."   This is high praise, and might not be accepted by Mr. Swinburne, who has said of Tennyson's first period that it contains whole poems " which are no more properly to be called metrical than the more shapeless and monstrous parts of Walt Whitman, which are lineally derived as to their form—if form that can be called where form is none—from the vilest example set by Cowley, when English verse was first infected and convulsed by the detestable duncery of sham

Pindarics," adding : "At times, of course, his song was then as sweet as ever it has sounded since ; but he could never make sure of singing right for more than a few minutes or stanzas."

Nevertheless, the thirty poems, written with a natural fineness and grace that dropped easily into weakness, showed very unusual sensitiveness to pleasant sounds and visions. The flight of birds, swallow and rook, the grasses on the wold, the chalky hills, the rich sentiment of the Lincolnshire landscape, were reproduced as they could have been only in the first delight of artistic creation, with eager spontaneity. And, like any lad, he sounded all the notes he knew. "The Palace of Art" was his introduction to the problem poem, and claimed the attention of his fellow-Englishmen, who discussed it seriously. It does not seem an over-bold excursion into speculative thought ; the poet conceived the idea of building for his soul, which he endows with personality, a "lordly pleasure-house" filled with everything to please intellectual and æsthetic tastes, in which the arrogant tenant may dwell apart to con-template and to enjoy. When "four years were wholly finished" she wearied of such surroundings and turned back to humanity :

> " ' Make me a cottage in the vale,' she said,
> ' Where I may mourn and pray.' "

John Sterling, "that remarkable soul who fash-ioned himself eagerly by whatsoever of noble pre-

sented itself," found this philosophy untrustworthy :
" The writer's doctrine seems to be," he wrote,
" that the soul, while by its own energy surrounding
itself with the most beautiful and expressive images
that the history of mankind has produced, and sympathising wholly with the world's best thoughts, is
perpetrating some prodigious moral offence for which
it is bound to repent in sackcloth and ashes.   A more
rational and not less religious view would seem to
be that we should repent of the errors we commit
from the inactivity of our higher powers and feelings."
Other critics found the very obvious moral appropriate to the intellectual pride of the age, and Stopford
Brooke reflects, discriminatingly, that it is " a good
subject for an essay or a sermon, but as the subject
of a poem it must first be filled with human passion,
and secondly it must be ornamented with lovely
images," and he adds : " Passion is given to it by
Tennyson by making the soul a person who goes
through pride to dreadful pain and through pain into
repentance.   Beauty is given to it by the description
of the palace which embodies all the various arts and
wisdom of the world in imaginative symbolism.
And surely no more superb and lovely house was
ever built by the wit of man."   Attractive the house
certainly is, with its swinging bells and mosaic floors,
its courts, and fountains, and tapestries.   It is, however, a fine example of Tennyson's reluctance to
leave anything to the reader's imagination.   Bayne
very pertinently calls attention to the contrast be-

tween Poe's description of a palace and Tennyson's.[1]
Poe wrote, vaguely and with his own charm :

> " In the greenest of our valleys
> By good angels tenanted,
> Once a fair and stately palace,
> Radiant palace, reared its head.
>
> In the monarch Thought's dominion
> It stood there.
> Never seraph spread a pinion
> Over fabric half so fair.
> Banners yellow, glorious, golden,
> On the roof did float and flow."

This leaves the reader to dream almost as he will of the house in the green valley. If he admits the floating flags he may arrange the rest to suit his fancy. But Tennyson will have no one's palace but his own. He visualises every detail and makes what profanely has been called a " catalogue raisonnée " of the contents. " If you paint it, you must be careful," Bayne declares ; " if you painted it a hundred times, you would be constrained to make the great features the same."

Another significant poem in the collection of 1832 was "The Lady of Shalott," in which Tennyson found his entrance to the Arthurian legend and gave free indulgence to his fondness for pictorial words and phrases. In it the little breezes " dusk and shiver," and the lady floats among " willowy hills and fields," while Launcelot rides like " a bearded meteor, trail-

[1] Chapter on " Tennyson and his Teachers " in Bayne's *Essays in Biography and Criticism*.

ing light," a true herald of the coming of Arthur. Then we have "The Miller's Daughter," a pastoral picture of soft slopes, and sunshine on the banks of the stream, and rural life. The Reverend Stopford Brooke says of the love story involved : " This was the sort of love for which Tennyson cared, for which Byron and Shelley did not care, which was not in the world where Keats lived at all,—but which was in Wordsworth's world, and which, after all our excursions into phases of passion, is not only the deepest and highest of the affections, but the father and mother of all other loves on earth." However much or little we may concede this father- and motherhood, Tennyson certainly gave to the passion of the humble a natural dignity and beauty that made it a very fit subject for his poetry, and one in the treatment of which he continued to be singularly felicitous. Some one has said that his country girls are all English ladies transferred from the hall to the cottage ; but his gentle chivalry toward these could ill be spared from our poetry.

Among these poems of promise were interpolated certain boyish verses that strike one as does an awkward attitude in a stripling. Such are the lines on "The Little Room," which gave to caustic reviewers delicious opportunity, but which Hallam in his friendliness found "mighty pleasant."

The volume met with a moderately favourable reception. The British world was ready for its melodious placidity, after the turbulence of Byron, the remoteness of Keats and Shelley, and the exigent asceticism of Wordsworth. The new poet was not disturbing, he had no pagan views, no rebellious sentiments ; he was pre-eminently an English gentleman with the qualities that England loves. His women, if somewhat shadowy, were fair and winning ; his imagery was luxuriant and suggested a well-fed mind ; his landscape was the lovely English landscape, filled with homes and dewy pastures and full-foliaged trees. Nevertheless, he was not to be accepted without rebuff. There were charges of affectation, overquaintness, and mannerism "bleated down the ranks of the innocent 'sillie' critics as they went, one after another, to water."[1] Certain later critics who have drunk at other fountains have " bleated" on the same notes, and with a curious sound of wisdom ; but the early reviewers, to whom a young poet was fair game, had, some of them, little mercy and much rough wit. The critic of *The Quarterly Review*, presumably Lockhart, was the most virulent of all, and let his poisoned arrows fly with malicious delight. It must be confessed that they were cleverly aimed, although he was both unjust and insulting in his method of attack. His style may be seen from this treatment of a poem which he describes as "a kind of testamentary paper addressed 'To ——'

> ' Then let wise Nature work her will,
> And on my clay her darnels grow,

[1] Richard Hengist Horne in *A New Spirit of the Age*.

> Come only when the days are still,
>   And at my headstone whisper low,
>   And tell me ——'

"Now what would an ordinary bard wish to be told under such circumstances? Why, perhaps, how his sweetheart was, or his child, or his family, or how the Reform Bill worked, or whether the last edition of the poems had been sold—papæ! Our genuine poet's first wish is

> ' And tell me—*if the woodbines blow!* '

When, indeed, he shall have been thus satisfied as to the *woodbines* (of the blowing of which in their due season he may, we think, feel pretty sure) he turns a passing thought to his friend and another to his mother——

> ' If *thou art blest*, my *mother's* smile
>   Undimmed——'

But such inquiries, short as they are, seem too commonplace, and he immediately glides back into his curiosity as to the state of the weather and the forwardness of the spring.

> ' If thou art blest, my mother's smile
>   Undimmed—*if bees are on the wing?*'

No, we believe the whole circle of poetry does not furnish such another instance of enthusiasm for the sights and sounds of the vernal season!" This was criticism in the days of *The Quarterly Review*, and it is plain that a poet needed all the friendly enthusiasm of his friends to keep his spirits from sinking.

In 1833, Tennyson came full upon tragedy. His friendship with Hallam had ripened in deep sincerity and was enjoyed by both with undiminished freshness until Hallam was taken abroad in the summer of this year to recover his slight store of natural strength after a tedious illness. On the journey from Pesth to Vienna, a wet day gave rise to a threatening of intermittent fever, and with this meagre warning he was found apparently asleep upon a sofa, but in reality quite dead. His body was brought back to England and taken to the Church of Clevedon, a Somersetshire village near Bristol. There it was placed in a vault in the transept, on the west wall of which is a tablet with this touching inscription :

TO THE MEMORY OF
ARTHUR HENRY HALLAM,
OF TRINITY COLLEGE, CAMBRIDGE, B.A.,
ELDEST SON OF HENRY HALLAM, ESQUIRE,
AND OF JULIA MARIA HIS WIFE,
DAUGHTER OF SIR ABRAHAM ELTON, BART.,
OF CLEVEDON COURT,
WHO WAS SNATCHED AWAY BY SUDDEN DEATH
AT VIENNA, ON SEPT. 15TH, 1833,
IN THE 23RD YEAR OF HIS AGE.
AND NOW IN THIS OBSCURE AND SOLITARY CHURCH
REPOSE THE MORTAL REMAINS OF
ONE TOO EARLY LOST FOR PUBLIC FAME,
BUT ALREADY CONSPICUOUS AMONG HIS CONTEMPORARIES
FOR THE BRIGHTNESS OF HIS GENIUS,
THE DEPTH OF HIS UNDERSTANDING,
THE NOBLENESS OF HIS DISPOSITION,
THE FERVOUR OF HIS PIETY,
AND THE PURITY OF HIS LIFE.
VALE DULCISSIME
VALE DILECTISSIME, DESIDERATISSIME,
REQUIESCAS IN PACE,
PATER AC MATER POSTHAC REQUIESCAMUS TECUM
USQUE AD TUBAM.

This was the tablet of which Tennyson wrote :

" When on my bed the moonlight falls,
  I know that in thy place of rest
  By that broad water of the west
There comes a glory on the walls:

Thy marble bright in dark appears,
  As slowly steals a silver flame
  Along the letters of thy name
And o'er the number of thy years."

Stopford Brooke, visiting thirty years ago the little church where Hallam rests, writes of it : " It was
then a lonely, quiet place, in a furrow of the sandy
slopes, not a house standing near it ; and fifty yards
from it, but hidden from view, the broad estuary of
the Severn filled with the tide. I heard the water wash
the feet of the low cliffs as it passed by. Sorrow
and death, peace that passeth understanding, the
victory of the soul, seemed present with me ; and
the murmuring of the Severn became, as I dreamed,
the music of eternal love, into whose vast harmonies
all our discords are drawn at last."

It was Tennyson's habit of mind to feel seriously,
and it is not difficult to imagine the overwhelming
effect upon him of such a loss. Where he had been
before concerned with little else than lovely words
and chosen metres, he was now interrogating the
universe for an explanation of the inexplicable mystery. For a time he thought he could no longer
write, the sympathy upon which he had been so
richly nourished being withdrawn, but from the con-

Arthur Hallam.

From the bust by Chantrey.

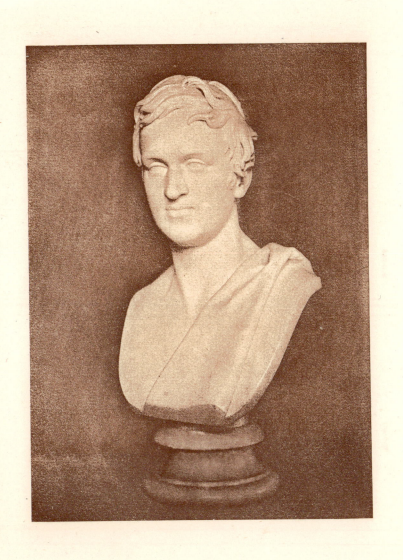

tradiction of this mood resulted *In Memoriam*. The elegy was early in his mind, and though it lay there for seventeen years, a treasure too sacred to be shown until he had spent upon it all the art he knew, it belongs essentially to this period of his life, and we may interrupt the sequence of dates to consider it here.

Although more than any other poem that Tennyson wrote it has moved hearts, it has been, perhaps, more severely attacked than any other. The word passionless has often been applied to it, and it has been said that grief which could so pour itself out was not so much grief as a calm regret. M. Taine, applying to it his severe and alien standard of criticism, finds it "cold and monotonous and too daintily arranged." The poet, he says, "goes into mourning, but like a very correct gentleman with perfectly new gloves, who dries his tears with a cambric handkerchief, and during the religious service which ends the ceremony, manifests all the grief of a respectful and well-trained layman." Mr. Stedman attributes the harshness of this criticism to M. Taine's inability to feel the spirit of such a poem through the unfamiliar medium of the English language, and Mr. Swinburne says that M. Taine gave proof "that as far as daring is concerned his motto might be Strafford's word 'Thorough,' when he struck with the sharp point of his lance 'the spotless shield' which bears inscribed the words *In Memoriam*. His impeachment of Lord Tennyson's great monumental poem

. . . may be classed for perfection of infelicity with Jeffrey's selection of the finest lines in Wordsworth's finest ode for especially contemptuous assault on the simple charge of sheer nonsense." Mr. Swinburne's own decidedly frank criticism of the Laureate of his country follows hard upon. Referring to "the pretentiously unpretentious philosophy of the book," he continues : "Lord Tennyson is so ostentatious of his modesty, so unsparing in his reserve, so incessant and obtrusive in his disclaimer of all ambition to rank as a thinker or a teacher, while returning again and yet again to the charge as an ethical apostle or a sentimental theosophist, that we are almost reminded of the philosopher whose vociferous laudation of the dumb, and ear-splitting inculcation of silence, might seem to all half-deafened hearers enough to 'crack his lungs and split his brazen pipe'—if possibly such a thing might have been possible. I trust it may be held allowable and compatible with loyalty to observe that it is hardly reasonable to touch repeatedly and with obvious earnestness on the gravest and the deepest questions of life and death, of human affection and mortal bereavement—to pour forth page upon page of passionate speculation, of love and fear and hope and doubt and belief, and then to turn round on the student to whose sympathy the book —if there be any reason whatever for its existence or publication—must surely be supposed to appeal, with the surely astonishing protest that it does not pretend to grapple with the questions on which it harps and the mysteries of which it treats. The fitfulness of a mourner's mood will hardly be held as a sufficient excuse to justify or to reconcile such incompatible incoherences of meditation and profession. To say that these effusions of natural sorrow make no pretence, and would be worthy of contempt if they pretended, to solve or satisfy men's doubts—and then to renew the appearance of an incessant or even a fitful endeavour after some such satisfaction or solution—is surely so incongruous as to sound almost insincere. But the possession of a book so wholly noble and so profoundly beautiful in itself is more precious than the most coherent essay towards the solution of any less insoluble problem."

The American critics have been less strenuous. Mr. Stedman in his *Victorian Poets* does not hesitate to find in Tennyson's poem qualities in which Milton's and Shelley's marvellous dirges are wanting. "It is the great threnody of our language by virtue of unique conception and power," he says; "*Lycidas* with its primrose beauty and varied lofty flights is but the extension of a theme set by Moschus and Bion. Shelley in *Adonais* despite his spiritual ecstasy and splendour of lament followed the same masters,—yes, and took his landscape and imagery from distant climes ; Swinburne's dirge for Baudelaire is a wonder of melody ; nor do we forget the *Thyrsis* of Arnold, and other modern ventures in a direction where the sweet and absolute solemnity of the Saxon tongue is most apparent. Still as an original and intellectual production *In Memoriam* is beyond them all, and a more important though possibly no more enduring creation of rhythmic art." This, certainly, is going very far in generosity of appreciation, and Dr. Van Dyke goes farther still in a different direction, finding in the sorrowful beauty of the liquid music the ever-desired testimony to immortality. "The heart of man which can win such victory out of its darkest defeat," he writes, "and reap such harvest from the furrows of the grave, is neither sprung from dust nor destined to return to it. A poem like *In Memoriam* more than all flowers of the returning spring, more than all shining wings that flutter above the ruins of the chrysalis, more than all sculptured tombs and monuments of the beloved dead, is the living evidence and intimation of an endless life."

Thus the pendulum of criticism has swung on the subject of *In Memoriam*, and we are much too near to it and to Tennyson to attempt to find the precise resting point of truth ; but when the favourite complaint of its adversaries is made—that it is shallow in feeling because it ripples so musically, we may remind ourselves that it is not the type of man's deepest suffering. Tennyson when Hallam died was only twenty-four years old, and although the two were united by ties of intellectual sympathy and ardent love, they had known one another but four years, and there had been but little time to build up that close and massive structure of accumulated associations the tearing down of which marks for so many the passing of joy. It was not the kind of grief which strikes into silence. There was remaining the insistent impulse of youth to act, to show reverence, to lay the sacrifice of words upon an altar. The result was a tender poem which should hardly be criticised because it does not lift the mind out of its own familiar atmosphere.

In biographical interest *In Memoriam* is singularly rich. Tennyson fixed by instinct upon the definite, the visible, to give his poem solidity. In the midst of perplexing obstructions he never forgot his narrative, the story of his friendship and of his bereavement. With the exception of the single passage in which the shepherd recalls hours spent together "upon the self-same hill," Milton's "Lycidas" might be a wail from the genius of a pine forest, so unexpressive is it of man's natural fondness for recalling scenes and incidents. *In Memoriam*, on the contrary, tells us how individual hours were spent, and the aspect of the immediate surroundings. We thus get beautiful pictures of our own world if not the wild, unearthly music of a different sphere.

We see Cambridge as it was, and as it long will be :

> " I past beside the reverend walls
>   In which of old I wore the gown ;
>   I roved at random thro' the town,
> And saw the tumult of the halls ;
>
> And heard once more in college fanes
>   The storm their high-built organs make,
>   And thunder-music, rolling, shake
> The prophets blazon'd on the panes ;

And caught once more the distant shout,
   The measured pulse of racing oars
     Among the willows ; paced the shores
And many a bridge and all about

The same grey flats again, and felt
   The same, but not the same ; and last
     Up that long walk of limes I past
To see the rooms in which he dwelt."

These rooms are on the west side of the new court, with the quadrangle on one side, and on the other looking out upon the "long walk of limes," the chief beauty of Cambridge. The trees are beginning to show signs of decay, and Professor Church says that "in another sixty years, if the ground has not been meanwhile laid out in allotments, the avenue will have given place to the successor which has been prudently provided, but which will hardly equal it in beauty."

We see also the dark house in the "long, unlovely street," where Hallam lived in London, and had his little jest about being found "always at sixes and sevens." (The house was 67 Wimpole Street.) We see the old yew that grasps at the stones in Clevedon churchyard, and we have final glimpses of the landscape in the neighbourhood of Somersby. The bells that Tennyson brought into his poems whenever he could, are characteristic of Lincolnshire and have been since Drayton wrote of its "bells and bagpipes." Tennyson refers to them in the twenty-eighth canto with his usual precision of detail :

> " The time draws near the birth of Christ :
>   The moon is hid ; the night is still ;
>   The Christmas bells from hill to hill
> Answer each other in the mist.
>
> Four voices of four hamlets round,
>   From far and near, on mead and moor,
>   Swell out and fail as if a door
> Were shut between me and the sound."

And from the same lines we learn another characteristic of the county, the nearness to each other of its villages, and the old custom of beginning to ring the bells a month or six weeks before Christmas. We catch curious glimpses also of the holidays spent at Somersby and their idyllic occupations, when Emily Tennyson brought her harp into the garden and "flung a ballad to the brightening moon," or when in the woods or by the sea they had their "picnics," ever the joy of youth, with

> "The wine flask lying couch'd in moss,
> Or cool'd within the glooming wave."

We get delicious suggestions of sounds

> " ———to rout the brood of cares,
>   The sweep of scythe in morning dew,
>   The gust that round the garden flew,
> And tumbled half the mellowing pears !"

And we feel more, perhaps, than from any other poem that Tennyson is the poet of the English home ; as Burns of the Scotchman's cottage.

We feel from it, also, that he is the poet of religious sentiment as it exists in the general English mind.

Concerning Tennyson's religion a vast amount has been written ; he has been proven and disproven gnostic and agnostic, theist and atheist and Christian ; and the chief burden of his religious message rests upon *In Memoriam.* It is not in the least necessary to go over the ground again, as the first stanza of the introduction to the poem, written in 1849, contains enough " creed " to satisfy the anxious :

> " Strong Son of God, immortal Love,
> Whom we, that have not seen thy face,
> By faith, and faith alone, embrace,
> Believing where we cannot prove."

For the rest, Tennyson is absolutely lucid in his expression of religious feeling ; and appeals to those who make it their intention to believe against all difficulties. He does not propose to doubters the relief of action, and therefore he would hardly bring comfort to those in whom the deep forces of instinctive skepticism play ; for such, Browning has written :

> " What I aspired to be,
> And was not, comforts me ;
> A brute I might have been, but would not sink i' the scale."

Nor would Tennyson in the attitude of philosopher delight the truly philosophic soul which finds it possible to contemplate the life already lived as its own sufficient reward ; which asks with Matthew Arnold :

> " Is it so small a thing
> To have enjoyed the sun,
> To have lived light in the spring,

To have loved, to have thought, to have done,
To have advanced true friends, and beat down baffling foes?"

The message of *In Memoriam*, of "Vastness," of "The Ancient Sage," of "Akbar's Dream," and of all the other many poems into which Tennyson's religion enters, is a message of reverence for the consecrated traditions of Christianity, and of faith unlimited by those or by any other traditions.

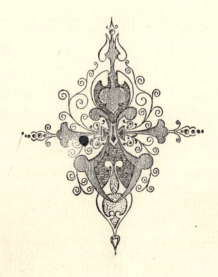

CHAPTER IV.

MATURITY.

THE ten years' space after Hallam's death was for Tennyson an important period. Until 1837 he dwelt at Somersby, where every object had its associations, but the doors had closed upon his actual youth. He made occasional trips to London that were dependent apparently on the state of his purse, and he saw there his friends, but in the main he was content to shun delights and live laborious days, if we may form any conclusion from the list of his studies. He had a study for every day in the week, and he added a language for the afternoons of five days. It was characteristic of him that on Sundays he studied theology. He was preparing the mind from which *In Memoriam* was to spring, enriching it with such ideas and knowledge of words as should, he thought, give force and colour and grace to his poetry. Science interested him in its testimony to the order and symmetry of the universe; metaphysics interested him as throwing light upon the intricate workings of the human mind; the beauty of nature, the significance of

46

solemn skies and "leaves that redden to their fall," contributed to the reverence with which he regarded the Giver of life and death. In the poem that was slowly forming in his mind he grouped knowledge and faith, fact and sentiment, with a curious harmonising of contradictory elements. His method has been condemned for its eclecticism by those who find their greatest satisfaction in a certain classic severity of diction not readily departing from the old vocabulary. Mr. Pater, on the other hand, wrote in his essay on "Style":

"English, for a quarter of a century past, has been assimilating the phraseology of pictorial art; for half a century, the phraseology of the great German metaphysical movement of eighty years ago; in part, also, the language of mystical theology: and none but pedants will regret a great consequent increase of its resources. For many years to come its enterprise may well lie in the naturalisation of the vocabulary of science, so only it be under the eye of a sensitive scholarship—a liberal naturalisation of the ideas of science too, for, after all, the chief stimulus of good style is to possess a full, rich, complex matter to grapple with."

Tennyson did precisely this, bending his nineteenth-century intellect to the task of naturalising and also of spiritualising scientific and metaphysical ideas and their phraseology, in a most unprecedented fashion. This adaptation of his art to his age constituted, perhaps, his chief claim to originality. His mind was not like Browning's, a quarry of native marble ; it was rather a mint, receiving and giving current value to the ore of a thousand mines. He anticipated, in his dreams and visions, subjects that were presently to be chief interests with the public, with much of the instinct that serves the true journalist who makes an art of his profession. He kept writing and destroying, forming and reforming his style, pursuing his ideal in silence, until he felt himself ready to face his earlier critics with the old material improved, and new poems superior to those they had found wanting. There was no tendency in him to faint and fail under adverse criticism as poor Keats was supposed to have done. He chose the honourable defence of increased striving toward unassailable performance. This was the sort of artistic control that FitzGerald admired. He wrote to Donne in the autumn of 1833 :

" Tennyson has been in town for some time. He has been making fresh poems which are finer, they say, than any he has done. But I believe he is chiefly meditating on the purging and subliming of what he has already done ; and repents that he has published at all yet. It is fine to see how in each succeeding poem the smaller ornaments and fancies drop away and leave the grand ideas simple."[1]

The field of poetry was at this time occupied by Wordsworth alone, of the greater poets. Coleridge had departed, Browning was not yet fairly recog-

[1] FitzGerald's *Letters*.

nised, Byron was dead and his exaggerated influence was waning fast, Shelley and Keats were dead, and the spirit of their poetry was passing into the poems of their successors. With such voices upon the air, Tennyson did well faithfully to develop his genius before again submitting it to the judgment of the public. He could not, however, escape the beguilements of Annuals. His poem of "St. Agnes" went into the *Keepsake* of 1837 by the persuasion of Lady Emmeline Stuart Wortley, and it sounds as though he had written it especially for the lady. Monckton Milnes found it there, "looking funny between Lord Londonderry and Lord W. Lennox," and promptly besought him to contribute to another Annual which a Marquis was getting up for charitable purposes. Tennyson mirthfully declined, declaring Annuals to be "vapid books," and assuring Milnes that he had only written for Lady Wortley because he had heard she was beautiful, adding :

"But whether the Marquis be beautiful or not, I don't much mind ; if he be, let him give God thanks and make no boast. To write for people with prefixes to their names is to milk he-goats—there is neither honour nor profit."

Milnes had a gusty temper, and this energetic playfulness so roused him that Tennyson, in the interests of peace and good-fellowship, was obliged to yield the point. He wrote another letter of charming forbearance, rallying Milnes on his irritability, and inquiring : "What has so jaundiced your good-na-

4

tured eyes as to make them mistake harmless banter
for *insolent irony?* . . . Had I spoken the same
things to you laughingly in my chair, and with my
own emphasis, you would have seen what they
really meant; but coming to read them, peradven-
ture, in a fit of indigestion, or with a slight matu-
tinal headache after your Apostolic symposium, you
subject them to such misinterpretation as, if I had
not sworn to be true friend to you till my latest
death-ruckle, would have gone far to make me indignant."[1]   The poem sent was the one beginning,

> " O that 't were possible,
>   After long grief and pain,
> To find the arms of my true love
>   'Round me once again."

This was the germ of *Maud*, conceived, like so
many of Tennyson's poems, years before its ripening.   Mr. Swinburne calls the poignant verses " a
gentler echo to the Duchess of Malfi's exceeding bitter cry,

> ' O that it were possible we might
>   But hold some two days' conference with the dead !
> From them I should learn something, I am sure,
>   I never shall learn here,' "

and finds in them a supreme example of the " heavenly beauty "-in the higher early notes of Tennyson's
then " girlish muse," declaring, " He never has written anything of more potent perfection, of more
haunting and overpowering charm."

[1] Wemyss Reid's *Life of Lord Houghton.*

In 1837, Tennyson's studies and meditations were broken in upon by cares of a domestic nature. The family were obliged at last to leave Somersby, and seek another home. Frederick Tennyson, the wonderful old man who has recently died, far along in his ninety-first year, was then a young devotee of music. He was living at Corfu, where his cousin, George d'Eyncourt, was secretary to the High Commissioner, and there are picturesque stories of his sitting in the midst of his forty fiddlers in a large hall designed by Michael Angelo. He was clearly out of the question as a guide, philosopher, and friend in the humble affair of moving. The other one of the two brothers older than Alfred had become a clergyman, and had been appointed to the curacy of Tealby. In 1836, he had married Louisa Sellwood, a younger sister of Emily Sellwood who, fourteen years later, was to become the wife of Alfred Tennyson. Emily was bridesmaid to her sister, and, if we may trust the internal evidence of Tennyson's sonnet to "The Bridesmaid," it was upon this occasion that he fell in love with her, and thought :

"O happy bridesmaid, make a happy bride ! "

The elder brothers being thus removed from the circle, Tennyson was obliged to take up the responsibilities of house-hunting, and his practical sense and readiness in the business give a nice touch to his character as a brother and son. He took thought even for the kitchen utensils, and his healthy human energy in such unpoetic occupation lends perceptibly to the large impression of absolute sincerity that is given by the total of his records. Unworldliness is said to have been a family trait, and indolence "the besetting sin of the race," but upon occasion they could work, and work well. One of Miss Mitford's "sweet young friends" brings her a gleeful story of making Alfred dig up the whole garden at her father's country-living near Sevenoaks, "and he did it capitally."

The family seem not to have left any very strong impression of their characteristics with the country-people among whom they had dwelt for so many years.

Mr. Roberts relates an interview with the old parish clerk at Bag Enderby in which he asked him if he could remember anything about Tennyson.[1]

"'Tennyson?' said he. 'D'ya meän the owd doctor?' Said I, 'Not the doctor particularly, but any of the Tennyson family?' He replied, 'Tha doctor was a fine owd gentleman. I remember on 'im dying. It's a strange long time agoä, an' he's in a fine big tomb ageän the church.' I asked, 'Do you remember any of the family—any of the sons—Charles or Alfred?' He began to think, stared vacantly, and, as the past dimly rose before him, slowly said, 'Ye-e-s, I do remember Master Alfred, sewerly; he was alus walkin' about the lanes and closins wi' a book in 'is 'and; but when he grew up he wornt at

---

[1] Nicoll and Wise's *Literary Anecdotes.*

'oäme much ; assiver he went up to Lunnun or some big place, and when he yeust ta cum 'oäme fur a bit one o' the sarvants teld me he yeust ta goä upstairs in a top room, an' 'ing a mat ower 'is doär. I doant kna' what fur, but they sed he did n't want ta 'ear noä noise.'" Mr. Roberts tried many of the villagers, but could not find that they remembered much beyond Dr. Tennyson's fine stature and "big beard," and Alfred's habit of always "dawdlin' about wi' a book." An old housekeeper gave him, however, a vivid description of the "owd doctor glowering" in his study, the walls of which were covered "wi' 'eathen gods and goddesses wi'out cloäs," and of his habit of lying in bed until late in the afternoon.

After leaving Somersby, the family moved first to High Beach, in Epping Forest, where there were "no sounds of nature and no society," Tennyson complained ; "equally, a want of birds and men." In 1840, they went to Tunbridge Wells, and the next year to Boxley, near Maidstone. These changes brought Tennyson nearer to London and to his friends, who were, most of them, servants of literature. A gentle trait of character shines in his unreadiness to leave home at night when his mother was suffering from nervousness—only one of many indications of his loyalty to her upon whose "sweet lips" perpetually did reign "the summer calm of golden charity."

The Cock Tavern, where Tennyson was in the habit of dining when in town, is depicted in "Will

Waterproof's Lyrical Monologue." ; it is there that he pledges the Muse in a pint of port, and in fancy sees himself grow

> " ―――― in worth, and wit, and sense,
>   Imboding critic-pen
> Or that eternal want of pence,
>   Which vexes public men,
> Who hold their hands to all, and cry
>   For that which all deny them―
> Who sweep the crossings, wet or dry,
>   And all the world go by them."

Spedding, dining with him at The Cock, sends their bill-of-fare to Milnes. "We had two chops," he writes, "one pickle, two cheeses, one pint of stout, one pint of port, and three cigars." The port could be of any grade for Tennyson, so long as it was "sweet, and black, and strong," although "Will Waterproof" demands a special kind :

> " ―――― not such as that
>   You set before chance-comers,
> But such whose father-grape grew fat
>   On Lusitanian summers."

Concerning this ancient tavern Mr. Arthur Waugh writes :

"The old 'Cock' is swept away now, with a bank on its site ; and the enthusiast who is anxious to get a notion of its appearance must content himself with the pictures of its staircase and dining-room, which hang in a room in a new tavern under the old name, opposite the Fleet Street end of Chancery Lane. The 'old grill-room,' as it is called, is refitted with the boxes 'larded with the steam of thirty thousand dinners,' with their brass rods and rusty curtains. The fine old oak fireplace has been moved there bodily ; the floor is still sanded, and the crockery is of the willow pattern.   And ever bustling and hustling his two boy assistants, Paul, himself a waiter at the former house, strives with a genial contempt for conventionality to keep the old spirit astir in the new surroundings.   'Chump-chop—opposight the fireplace ! Two kippers in order.   Hurry up that rabbit for the chair-table, please.   Good evening, gentlemen, and thank you.'   And Paul rattles you out as hurriedly as he welcomed you in."[1]

Upon the occasions when Tennyson visited his friends in their homes, he clung to the habit of his college days, sitting up late and reading his poetry aloud in his chanting voice, which has been variously described as deep, sonorous, bell-like, organ-like, flexible, monotonous, musical, indistinct, and metallic. Blakesly did not wonder that he complained of nervousness.   "How should he do otherwise, seeing that he smokes the strongest and most stinking tobacco out of a small blackened clay pipe on an average nine hours every day ?"   The aroma of tobacco hangs about all the early years, and is hardly less perceptible in the later accounts of the poet, who probably thought with his friend Carlyle that "sedative, gently soothing, gently clarifying tobacco smoke, with the obligation to a minimum of speech," gives human intellect and in-

[1] Waugh's *Alfred, Lord Tennyson.*

sight their best chance. In the spring of 1835, we find Tennyson and FitzGerald with the Speddings in the Lake country. Spedding's father, a practical old man with the shrewder temper of the earlier generation, grumbled amusingly at the amount of time given up to poetry during the visit. FitzGerald pacified the elders with checkers while smoke and poetry were going on upstairs, and old Mr. Spedding would inquire sarcastically : "Well, Mr. Fitz-Gerald, and what is it ? Mr. Tennyson reads and Jim criticises ? Is that it ?" And that was it. But the enthusiasm had good stuff to feed upon. Tennyson's friends took him seriously because they understood him, not because they were foolish hero-worshippers. At that time FitzGerald himself, who was later to be the most dissatisfied of critics, found every promise in the young, noble poetry of his companion: "When he has felt life," was his confident comment, "you will see him acquire all that at present you miss : he will not die fruitless of instruction as he is."

In 1842, Moxon, of Dover Street, got out two volumes of *Poems by Alfred Tennyson*, containing the cream of the earlier volumes, and much new material that showed steady and consistent progress toward an exigent ideal. The tremulous boyish tone had changed to one much graver and more certain. The toys of fancy were for the most part laid aside ; in their place were inquiry and reflection, a reaching out toward life, and a realisation of the ultimate mystery. The poem "Ulysses" is, perhaps, the most

James Spedding.

By G. F. Watts, R.A.

profoundly intelligent poem to be found in the now complete works, and "The Gardener's Daughter" and the "Idyl of Dora" show the influence of Wordsworth's point of view, if not of his method, and are the better for it. The elder poet, always chary of his praise and difficult to please, was beginning to distinguish the genuine note of Tennyson's verse. After seeing him in London he wrote to Professor Reed : " He is decidedly the first of our living poets, and I hope will live to give the world still better things. You will be pleased to hear that he expressed in the strongest terms his gratitude to my writings. To this I was far from indifferent, though persuaded that he is not much in sympathy with what I should myself value in my attempts, viz., the spirituality with which I have endeavoured to invest the material universe, and the moral relations under which I have wished to exhibit its most ordinary appearances."

Mr. Wace quotes from the life of Thomas Cooper an interesting passage showing Wordsworth's attitude towards his subsequent successor. The conversation recorded took place in 1846 : " Cooper asked Wordsworth's opinion of the poetry of the day. 'There is little that can be called high poetry,' he said ; ' Mr. Tennyson affords the richest promise. He will do great things yet, and ought to have done greater things by this time.' ' His sense of music ' observed Cooper, ' seems more perfect than that of any of the new race of poets.' ' Yes,' he replied ;

' the perception of harmony lies in the very essence of the poet's nature, and Mr. Tennyson gives magnificent proofs that he is endowed with it.' Cooper instanced Tennyson's rich association of musical words as proofs of his possessing as fine a sense of music in syllables as Keats and even Milton, and the patriarchal poet, with an approving smile, assented." [1]

A year or two before Carlyle had written to Emerson : " Singing, in our curt English speech, contrived expressly and almost exclusively for ' despatch of business,' is terribly difficult. Alfred Tennyson, alone of our time, has proved it to be possible in some measure."

The demonstrative Carlyle, flinging his challenges right and left, delighting in brave words and rough virtues and angry remonstrance, also delighted in Tennyson both as man and poet. He sketched him in words so vividly that we should have to go far afield to get a better picture of him as he was in the bloom of his manhood. In 1844 he wrote : " Moxon informs me that Tennyson is now in Town and means to come and see me. Of this result I shall be very glad. Alfred is one of the few British or foreign figures (a not increasing number, I think) who are and remain beautiful to me, a true human soul or some authentic approximation thereto, to whom your own soul can say ' Brother ! '—However, I doubt he will not come ; he often skips me in these brief visits to Town ; skips everybody, indeed, being

a man solitary and sad, as certain men are, dwelling in an element of gloom, carrying a bit of Chaos
about him, in short, which he is manufacturing
into Cosmos."

And again :

"Alfred is the son of a Lincolnshire Gentleman
Farmer. I think, indeed, you see in his verses that
he is native of 'moated granges' and green fat pastures, not of mountains and their torrents and storms.
He had his breeding at Cambridge as if for the Law
or Church ; being master of a small annuity on his
Father's decease, he preferred clubbing with his
Mother and some Sisters, to live unpromoted and
write Poems. In this way he lives still, now here,
now there, the family always within reach of London,
never in it ; he himself making rare and brief visits,
lodging in some old Comrade's rooms. I think he
must be under forty, and not much under it. One
of the finest-looking men in the world. A great
shock of rough, dusty-dark hair ; bright-laughing
hazel eyes, massive aquiline face, most massive yet
most delicate ; of sallow-brown complexion, almost
Indian-looking. Clothes cynically loose, free and
easy ;—smokes infinite tobacco. His voice is musical
metallic,—fit for loud laughter and piercing wail ; and
all that may lie between ; speech and speculation
tree and plenteous. I do not meet in these late
decades, such company over a pipe. We shall
see what he will grow to. He is often unwell, very
chaotic—his way is through Chaos and the Bottom-

less and Pathless ; not handy for making out many miles upon."

To a mind less dramatic than Carlyle's, Tennyson's "Chaos" was of the surface rather than of the depths. His spirit moved with orderly development. His new poems showed his various inclinations toward nature and romance, toward themes of the past, and visions of the future. He was interested rather than passionate, little of a partisan, and occupied with ultimate beauty and good more than with immediate revenges or reforms. In spite of grave spiritual questionings, there was no tumult of inquiry into the buried life such as might be found in *Paracelsus*, published in the same decade. Nor was there any violence of political passion, such as Wordsworth and Coleridge and Shelley had felt. The deep and quiet philosophy of the Laureate-to-be was expressed by "Will Waterproof" when he soliloquised :

> "Ah yet, tho' all the world forsake,
>   Tho' fortune clip my wings,
> I will not cramp my heart, nor take
>   Half-views of men and things.
> Let Whig and Tory stir their blood ;
>   There must be stormy weather ;
> But for some true result of good
>   All parties work together."

The riots in England, the Chartist and Socialist agitations, were painful to him but did not excite him beyond reason. His attitude toward social questions is examined at some length by Stopford

Brooke, who manifestly disapproves the calm and reverential temperament :

"One would have thought that a poet," he says, "touched by the reality of misery and its exceeding bitter cry, would have held the balance equally poised at least, and not yielded too far to the reaction ; that he would have had indignation at the state of society, and been inwardly urged to give, in the manner of a prophet, some prediction of a hope near at hand for the woes and weakness of the oppressed. But though there are many passages where Tennyson does try to hold an equal balance, and to excuse or even to advocate the impassioned rising of the oppressed in speech or act against their fate, these passages are short, are tentative ; he is, as it were, forced into them ; and the main line he takes is the line of careful protection of the old against the onset of the new, of steady but very prudent advance through obedience to existing law, of protest against that which he calls 'raw haste,' of discouraging of indignant speech and act on the part of the people, of distrust, even of contempt for what seemed to him the mob and for their 'lawless din' ; and in consequence of all this, he puts off the regeneration of society to a period so far away that it may be counted by thousands and thousands of years. It is with almost a scientific analysis of the whole question of the future society, and with arguments drawn from geology (as if humanity were in close analogy to Nature), that he predicts the enormous time in which the betterment or the perfection of society will be wrought. He had really little or no faith in man as man, but he had faith in man as conducted, in reasonable obedience, to the final restitution by an entity which he called law, and which was in reality his own conception of the Constitution of England built up into power, not by the people, but by a few great men and by the bulk of the educated and landed classes, who alone were fit to direct the blind forces of the people."[1]

This position was not, perhaps, adapted to the poetic pose, but Tennyson, so far as he maintained it in his poetry, invested it with much dignity and charm ; and he did not hesitate to relinquish it where the question seemed to him one of liberty for those qualified to use it intelligently. Dr. Van Dyke has compared his patriotism to Milton's, finding both poets " Englishmen to the heart's core. They do not say, ' My Country, right or wrong!' They protest in noble scorn against all kinds of tyrannies and hypocrisies. They are not bound in conscienceless servility to any mere political party. They are the partisans of England, and England to them means freedom, justice, righteousness, Christianity." He points out Tennyson's sympathy with the American spirit, quoting from the poem called " England and America in 1782 " :

" What wonder, if in noble heat
Those men thine arms withstood,

[1] Stopford Brooke's *Tennyson : His Art and Relation to Modern Life.*

Retaught the lesson thou hadst taught,
And in thy spirit with thee fought—
  Who sprang from English blood !

Whatever harmonies of law
  The growing world assume,
Thy work is thine—the single note
From that deep chord which Hampden smote
  Will vibrate to the doom."

And he adds : " Here is the Miltonic spirit of patriotism, not now disturbed and roughened by the harshness of opposition, the bitterness of disappointment, the sadness of despair, but rounded in the calm fulness of triumph." [1]

To a plain mind acquiescing in the impossibility of ever getting at the precise truth of anything, Tennyson's point of view is refreshing. It is high and it has a wide scope. There is no valid reason for rejecting it as unpoetic. A belief founded in strong national common-sense, scornful alike of causeless rebellion and of tyranny, calm with the placidity of the long view, may be quite as artistic a choice, compared to the storm and stress of a more zealous creed, as the choice of a painter who goes for his subject to flat marshes and wide horizons, preferring them to mountain peaks and waterfalls. Wordsworth, who had had his hour of sympathising with the " red fool fury of the Seine," or at least with the emotions that led up to it, could none the less appreciate the poem beginning,

[1] Van Dyke's *The Poetry of Tennyson*.

" Love thou thy land with love far brought
From out the storied past,"

and feel the " solidity and nobility " of the thought,
and the " stateliness of the diction."

As Tennyson's mind gradually filled with the
affairs of humanity, his power of depicting nature did
not diminish. His 1842 work is rich with lovely,
intimate studies of landscape, and he felt the genius
of places, of country places at all events, as an English poet should. But by his own confession he grew
less inclined to enjoy nature alone. In spite of occasional craving for the solemn isolation of the sea,
he grew more and more to consider the world of
nature as the habitation of man. Stopford Brooke
finds him chilling in this as in his political and social
views, and complains that his attitude toward nature
is that of a scientist with an eye for beauty. " The
descriptions," he writes, " are vivid, accurate, lovely
on the outside, but cold. They have no voice of love
or comfort for the heart of man. When I say this, I
apply it only to his descriptions of Nature apart from
humanity, of Nature by herself. When he mingles up
human life with Nature, then his descriptions of her
seem warm. But it is the human sentiment transferred to Nature which warms her. By herself in the
poetry of Tennyson, she remains without any sympathy of her own for us." Ruskin found the same
fault. He accused Tennyson of employing " the
pathetic fallacy," and endowing Nature with his own
feelings in place of describing her with classical direct-

ness as Homer would, or giving her a sentiment of her own. Scott, he said, would never have altered Nature to make her larkspurs listen for his lady's foot. He would be much more inclined to say: "What am I that I should trouble this sincere Nature with my thought? I happen to be feverish and depressed, and I could see a great many sad and strange things in those waves and flowers; but I have no business to see such things."[1]

It happens, however, that most people like their nature to reflect the human, and Tennyson's landscapes appeal to the majority of readers by virtue of the quality that irritates Ruskin and wearies Stopford Brooke. The poet arranges such pleasant scenes, and points out such charming, interesting truths that one can verify with careful observation, he places man in such idyllic surroundings and so artfully brings them into harmony with his mood, that it seems discourteous, almost churlish, not to admire and be grateful. Even the caustic Swinburne fell captive and ceased to search for the inevitable flaw, when he came under the charm of the outward and visible world seen through Tennyson's eyes. He recounted this yielding in the most genial passage he ever accorded the elder poet until he came to sing his threnody.

"Many years ago," he wrote, "as I have always remembered, on the appearance of the first four *Idylls of the King*, one of the greatest painters now living

---

[1] Ruskin's *Modern Painters.*

pointed out to me, with a brief word of rapturous admiration, the wonderful breadth of beauty and the perfect force of truth in a single verse of 'Elaine':

'And white sails flying on the yellow sea.'

I could not but feel conscious at once of its charm and of the equally certain fact that I, though cradled and reared beside the sea, had never seen anything like that. But on the first bright day I ever spent on the eastern coast of England I saw the truth of this touch at once, and recognised once more with admiring delight the subtle and sure fidelity of that happy and studious hand. There on the dull yellow foamless floor of dense discoloured sea, so thick with clotted sand that the water looked massive and solid as the shore, the white sails flashed whiter against it and along it as they fled: and I knew once more the truth of what I never had doubted—that the eye and the hand of Tennyson may always be trusted, at once and alike, to see and to express the truth."[1]

The fact of the distinction remains, however. Tennyson's pictures of nature are usually presented as backgrounds to the human figure, and are as personal as Shelley's are impersonal. He tried always to represent a seeming significance in the aspect of field or sky. His landscapes do not ever let one alone to dream at will—they impose the dream; it must be a chosen vision, and the poet himself must be the one to choose it. It is like the painting of

[1] Swinburne's *Miscellanies*.

Turner, who transfers his mood to the mountains or waves that he paints for you, in contrast with the method of Whistler, who merely sets before you the prodigious strangeness of the truth and lets you think as you like about it. Or, to use a more obvious illustration, Tennyson's poetry is throughout like a certain kind of hospitality where the day is planned for the guest—with the utmost care, with the utmost skill, but there is no escape.

It is curious that a poet, in whom the classic spirit, if it dwelt at all, underwent some amazing transformations, should nevertheless have made his best poems upon subjects drawn from the far past. Had he let the first and great "Ulysses," the revised "Œnone," and the "Morte d'Arthur" stand for what he could do in the way of reviving an ancient story and fitting it to a modern taste, there would probably have been very little adverse criticism of his efforts in this direction. Gleams of light played for him over the long-dead world of myths and epics, and showed him beautiful ghosts who warmed to a strange familiar life at his touch. The "Morte d'Arthur" was read to Landor as early as 1837, and he says of it: "It is more Homeric than any poem of our time, and rivals some of the noblest parts of the *Odyssea*." He cannot refrain from adding a comparison between Tennyson's simplicity and Wordsworth's, with a delicious parody of the latter's least engaging manner.

Miss Barrett, who was soon to be chided for affecting Tennyson's style, wrote, upon receiving the new volumes from her cousin, John Kenyon :

"I ought to be thanking you for your great kindness about this divine Tennyson. Beautiful! beautiful! After all it is a noble thing to be a poet. But notwithstanding the poetry of the novelties, nothing appears to me quite equal to 'Œnone,' and perhaps a few besides of my ancient favourites. That is not said in disparagement of the last, but in admiration of the first. There is, in fact, more thought—more bare, brave working of the intellect—in the latter poems, even if we miss something of the high ideality, and the music that goes with it, of the older ones. Only I am always inclined to believe that philosophic thinking, like music, is involved, however occultly, in high ideality, of any kind."[1]

In spite of this enthusiasm, Miss Barrett was far from conceding every virtue to the "divine Tennyson," and a letter to Mr. Westwood in 1843 is interesting, not only in its criticism, but in the note of loneliness and the preoccupation with moral sentiment. At this time Miss Barrett was lying "all day and day after day" on her sofa, and her windows did not even look into the street. The ivy, striking its leaves on the pane when the wind blew somewhat briskly, was all she had to bring the sound of forests and groves into her life. The Prince had not yet penetrated the Wood.

"You are probably right in respect to Tennyson,"

[1] Frederick G. Kenyon's *The Letters of Elizabeth Barrett Browning.*

she wrote, "for whom, with all my admiration of him, I would willingly secure more exaltation and a broader clasping of the truth. Still it is not possible to have so much beauty without a certain portion of truth, the position of the Utilitarians being true in the inverse. But I think as I did of 'uses' and 'responsibilities,' and do hold that the poet is a preacher and must look to his doctrine.

"Perhaps Mr. Tennyson will grow more solemn, like the sun, as his day goes on. In the meantime we have the noble 'Two Voices,' and, among other grand intimations of a touching power, certain stanzas to J. K. (I think the initials are)[1] on the death of his brother, which very deeply affected me.

" Take away the last stanzas, which should be applied more definitely to the *body* or cut away altogether as a lie against eternal verity, and the poem stands as one of the finest of monodies. The nature of human grief never, surely, was more tenderly intimated or touched—it brought tears to my eyes. Do read it. He is not a Christian poet, up to this time, but let us listen and hear his next songs. He is one of God's singers whether he knows it or does not know it."

The same year she was trying to formulate her opinion of the "rising" poet for publication in Mr. Horne's curious and daring book called *The New Spirit of the Age*, a collection of criticisms upon contemporaries, including a paper on Tennyson. Miss

[1] The lines " To J. S."

Barrett's name does not appear; but her contributions to the article are separated from it, and published in Nicoll and Wise's *Literary Anecdotes*. She begins prophetically, in her expansive way:

"The name of Alfred Tennyson is pressing slowly, calmly, but surely,—with certain recognition but no loud shouts of greeting,—from the lips of the discerners of poets, of whom there remain a few even in the cast-iron ages, along the lips of the less informed public ' to its own place ' in the starry house of names. That it is the name of a true poet, the drowsy public exerts itself to acknowledge; testifying with a heavy lifting of the eyelid to its consciousness of a new light in one of the nearer sconces. This poet's public is certainly awake to him,—although you would not think so."

There could hardly be a worse example of the parenthetical style; but the thought was sound enough. The public was awake, not only in England but in America.

Lowell greeted his contemporary with the decisive declaration that it might be centuries before another such thinker and speaker as Tennyson appeared. Edgar Allan Poe, who had a natural sympathy with lyric metres, was inclined to rank him "the greatest of poets," and wrote: "By the enjoyment or non-enjoyment of the 'Morte d'Arthur' or 'Œnone' I would test anyone's ideal sense." He felt, however, the same deficiency in rhythm that Coleridge had found at the very first: "Tennyson's shorter pieces abound in minute rhythmical lapses sufficient to assure me that, in common with all poets living or dead, he has neglected to make precise investigation of the principles of metre. But, on the other hand, so perfect is his rhythmical instinct in general that he seems to see with his ear."

In 1842, Charles Sumner wrote to Milnes : " T.'s poems have been reprinted in Boston, and the reprint is a precise copy of the English edition in size, type, and paper, so that it is difficult to distinguish the two editions. It is reprinted for the benefit of the author, to whom the publisher hopes to remit some honorarium. Emerson and his followers are ardent admirers of Tennyson, and it is their enthusiastic, unhesitating praise that induced a bookseller to undertake the reprint. There are some things in the 2nd volume which I admire very much. 'Locksley Hall' has some significant verses and others hardly intelligible. 'Godiva' is unequalled as a narrative in verse, and the little stories of 'Lady Clare' and the 'Lord of Burleigh' are told in beautiful measure. I am struck with the melody of his verse, its silver ring, and its high poetic fancy ; but does it not want elevated thought and manliness ? Yet in its way what can be more exquisite than Œnone making Mount Ida echo with her complaints ? Was her story ever told in a sweeter strain in any language ? I understand that Emerson is afraid that Tennyson since he published his first volume has become 'a fine gentleman,' by which I suppose he means that his free thought and voluntary numbers will be constrained by the conventions of the world."

Thomas Aird, the Scotch poet, gave a judgment of mingled praise and blame : "I have been sauntering for some time, reading Alfred Tennyson's poems and other light matters. Alfred's brother lent me his poems. Beautiful they are certainly, strong and manly often, but oftener capricious, silly, and affected. 'Godiva' was a difficult affair, certainly, yet treated with what perfect grace and beauty !"

In the *Edinburgh* and the *Quarterly*, James Spedding and John Sterling had appreciative and discriminating reviews. Sterling naturally took a different tone from that which Lockhart had used with reference to the earlier volume. "The blank-verse poems," he wrote, "have a quiet completeness and depth, a sweetness arising from the happy balance of thought, feeling, and expression, that ranks them among the richest of our recent literature." He adds, however, a keen criticism of Tennyson's notable failing : "His feelings are always strictly watched by his meditative conscience, too strictly not for wisdom but for rapture. The poetry would have streamed out in a freer gush and flushed the heart with ampler joy had the moral been less obtruded as its constant aim."

Thus, on the eve of Wordsworth's appointment to the Laureateship, while Browning was having *Bells and Pomegranates* printed as pamphlets with cheap type, to be sold at sixpence, and Landor was playing

Robert Browning.

From life.

with the little dog '' Pomero'' among his daphnes and hyacinths, and writing poems for Lady Blessington, Tennyson stepped into his permanent place among the greater British poets.

CHAPTER V.

"THE PRINCESS," AND PARALLEL PASSAGES.

AFTER the publication of the 1842 volumes, Tennyson was much in London among the literary men of the time. Carlyle, Wordsworth, Thackeray, the aged Rogers, Dickens, Leigh Hunt, Aubrey de Vere,—these are names taken at random from the lists of his acquaintances, and in such company he must have found sufficient enjoyment. Emerson, visiting London in that fifth decade, found English society very rich, though, to his oxygenated mind, not entirely satisfying.

"There is nowhere so much wealth of talent and character and social accomplishment," he writes to a friend; "every star outshone by one more dazzling, and you cannot move without coming into the light and fame of new ones. I have seen, I suppose, some good specimens, chiefly of the literary fashionable, and not of the fashionable, sort. . . . They have all carried the art of agreeable sensations to a wonderful pitch; they know everything, have everything; they are rich, plain, polite, proud, and admirable. But, though good for them, it ends in the using. I shall or should soon have enough of this play for my occasion."[1]

During this visit, Emerson met Tennyson at the house of Coventry Patmore. One can imagine the inspired rustic face to face with the writer of "Godiva" and "The Lady of Shalott"; and the description he gives of the meeting is very suggestive. "I was contented with him at once," he writes in his journal; "he is tall and scholastic-looking, no dandy, but a great deal of plain strength about him, and though cultivated, quite unaffected. Quiet sluggish sense and thought; refined as all English are, and good-humoured. There is in him an air of general superiority that is very satisfactory. He lives with his college set, . . . and has the air of one who is accustomed to be petted and indulged by those he lives with. Take away Hawthorne's bashfulness and let him talk easily and fast and you would have a pretty good Tennyson. I told him that his friends and I were persuaded that it was important to his health an instant visit to Paris, and that I was to go on Monday if he was ready. He was very good-humoured, and affected to think that I should never come back alive from France; it was death to go. But he had been looking for two years for somebody to go to Italy with, and was ready to set out at once, if I would go there. . . . He gave me a cordial invitation to his lodgings (in Buckingham Place), where I promised to visit him before I went away."

[1] Cabot's *Memoir of Ralph Waldo Emerson*.

There is ample testimony that Tennyson was not at this time or ever the unsocial man he has been called. In Thoreau's phrase, he was glad of all the society he could get to go up with, but he would have nothing to do with society that kept or pulled him down. He felt no temptation to fritter away his time in the " little arts of happiness." Even as a child, great thoughts had taken quaint precedence in his mind ; witness his advice to his brother to over-come a boyish diffidence by thinking of Herschel's great star-patches. He was a much-loved member of the Sterling Club, and very likely he was "petted" and "indulged" by the old "Apostles," who were pardonably proud of him, but there is no evidence that he was spoiled—in the common acceptance of the term. Emerson, however, coming straight from the society he found in the passengers of the lumbering Concord coach, from companionship with Thoreau, who was "with difficulty sweet," from the little knot of plain livers and high thinkers who drifted to the wooded town, was inevitably struck with a sense of mighty contrast.

Tennyson had every reason for clinging to his habits of industry and declining self-indulgence. Aside from his ambition as a poet, he had the young man's not unusual impulse toward success ; he was engaged to Miss Sellwood, without money enough as yet to marry. With the hope, no doubt, of hastening things, he put his little inheritance into a wood-carving scheme, which promptly collapsed and carried with it his money and much of his courage. He became positively ill, and hypochondria threatened. Very likely it was sympathy with this misfortune that stirred up his friends to act for him in the matter of a pension. The story of the episode runs as follows: Without Tennyson's knowledge or consent, Milnes was appealed to as having influence with Sir Robert Peel, to urge the poet's claim to an annuity sufficient to provide his daily bread and give the freedom of mind coveted, if not actually needed, by the writer of verse. Some of the many books about Tennyson have represented Milnes as very eager and valiant in this service, but the truth seems to be that at first he did not particularly enjoy the part he had to play. Most men who do not like to ask money for themselves like only a little less to ask it for others. "It was not until Milnes had played the part of devil's advocate," remarks his biographer, "that he ever heartily espoused any cause." Carlyle prodded him after his own fashion.

"'Richard Milnes,' said Carlyle one day, withdrawing his pipe from his mouth, as they were seated together in the little house in Cheyne Row, 'when are you going to get that pension for Alfred Tennyson?'

"'My dear Carlyle,' responded Milnes, 'the thing is not so easy as you seem to suppose. What will my constituents say if I do get the pension for Tennyson? They know nothing about him or his poetry, and they will probably think he is some poor relation of my own, and that the whole affair is a job.'

"Solemn and emphatic was Carlyle's response. 'Richard Milnes, on the Day of Judgment, when the Lord asks you why you did n't get that pension for Alfred Tennyson, it will not do to lay the blame on your constituents; it is *you* that will be damned.'"[1]

Milnes finally consented to do what he could, and being in he bore himself bravely. There were two applications for a pension of two hundred pounds made to Peel, Tennyson's, and one for Sheridan Knowles, who was old, infirm, and poor. Peel was at that moment head over ears in Irish questions and knew nothing of either man. Milnes told him that if the pension were to be bestowed as charity, Knowles should have it ; but if it were to be bestowed in the interests of English literature and the nation at large, it should go to Tennyson beyond all question. Then he sent the 1842 volumes to the Prime Minister, "Locksley Hall" and "Ulysses" marked. Mr. Browning afterwards said that he thought the latter poem must have "come home to Peel, then at the height of his power and prosperity, as an image of his own spirited, active, contentious life." At all events, Peel's choice fell upon Tennyson, but it is a pleasing relief to know that subsequently Knowles also received a pension of the same amount,—two hundred pounds.

[1] Wemyss Reid's *Life of Lord Houghton.*

Thomas Carlyle.

From life.

Tennyson, himself, only half liked his good fortune, and expressed himself as feeling "the least bit possible Miss Martineau-ish" about it, Miss Martineau having refused a pension on the ground that she should be robbing the people who did not make laws for themselves. This particular argument, however, Tennyson considered nonsense, remarking that her non-acceptance of the pension "did not save the people a stiver," and that if the people *did* make laws for themselves no literary man would ever get a lift.[1]

It is, perhaps, hard for an American to understand that this was not an unnatural attitude, though so unfamiliar to American poets. One can hardly imagine Lowell advocating an unearned "lift" for literary men, although he seemed to feel quite at liberty to marry on an income that could not have amounted to much more than a thousand dollars a year, and gayly confessed his inability to live on it. He had, however, sufficient knowledge of our human nature to admit that "few of us would hold an umbrella, at any rate right side up, against a golden shower." The difference is probably more in the point of view than in the essential nature of the men, for Tennyson, we learn from his son, "never could or would write a line for money offered," while Lowell accepted, though much against his will, a salary for his Anti-Slavery articles, and wrote for a number of years under a feeling of restriction.

[1] Hallam Tennyson's *Alfred, Lord Tennyson.*

Edward Lytton Bulwer was very ungracious about the golden shower which had fallen upon a young man without a family to support, and wrote a poem containing the following sharp lines :

> " Let schoolmiss Alfred vent her chaste delight
> In darling little rooms so warm and bright,
> Chant 'I'm a-weary' in infectious strain,
> And catch 'the blue fly singing i' the pane.'
>
> Tho' praised by critics and admired by Blues,
> Tho' Peel with pudding plump the puling Muse,
> Tho' Theban taste the Saxon purse controls
> And pensions Tennyson while starves a Knowles."

Unfortunately, Tennyson could not suffer the attack in silence, not being of those who can " dismiss what insults the soul" without a protest. He replied with "The New Timon and the Poets," a mere doggerel ending with this edifying stanza :

> " What profits how to understand
> The merits of a spotless shirt—
> A dapper boot—a little hand—
> If half the little soul is dirt?"

His admirers will get comfort from the assurance in the *Memoir* that his friend—" Save us from our friends!"—John Forster, and not he himself, sent the lines to *Punch*. Immediately after, he sent another poem conceived in dignity. It commenced :

> " Ah God! the petty fools of rhyme
> That shriek and sweat in pigmy wars
> Before the stony face of Time,
> And look'd at by the silent stars ; "

and ended with the candid admission :

"And I, too, talk, and lose the touch
  I talk of.   Surely, after all,
The noblest answer unto such
  Is perfect stillness when they brawl."

The episode was humiliating, but Tennyson was too large in spirit to cherish petty animosities, and he and Lytton were afterwards friends.

In 1847, Tennyson added "The Golden Year" to the fourth edition of the *Poems* and the same year published his first long poem, which he called *The Princess, A Medley.*   His friends were somewhat imprudently demanding a long poem, and he naturally wished to find an original and suitable theme.   The "Woman Question" provided one ; it was already in the air, but there had been no general infection. Two years later Alexander Scott declared that "female education" was a perfectly untried experiment, and therefore peculiarly interesting ; and Clara Balfour, lecturing on the subject, took the very modest and extremely conservative ground that "really good and solid education does but enable a woman to perform the most trifling duties of domestic life more thoroughly well, and why should it make her more vain and pedantic than an equally educated man ?"   England in the main was taken up with Irish problems, and Tennyson's poem was decidedly in advance of its hour.   The precise suggestion from which it sprang has been variously traced.   Mr. Wace and others think they have hunted it to this passage from Dr. Johnson's *Rasselas :*

6

"The Princess thought that of all sublunary things, knowledge was the best. She desired first to learn of sciences, and then proposed to found a college to teach women, in which she would preside."

In the *Memoir* there is mention of an old college joke commemorated in a few gleeful stanzas ; and the converse of the idea may be found in *Love's Labour's Lost*, where the King affirms :

> "Our Court shall be a little Academe,
>   Still and contemplative in living art.
>   You three, Birone, Dumaine, and Longaville,
>   Have sworn for three years' term to live with me,
>   My fellow-scholars, and to keep those statutes
>   That are recorded in this schedule here :"

the statutes reading, "Not to see ladies, study, fast, not sleep." It was not within Shakespeare's province to turn the thing around, but had it been, what a comedy we might have owned to put beside *The Taming of the Shrew!*

Whatever its source, *The Princess* was a gay mingling of theory and fancy, luxuriant description, teasing analyses of improbable states of mind, romance, and humour. It was not remarkably well received by the English critics. FitzGerald hated it, as Tennyson had foreseen he would, and wrote to Frederick Tennyson in 1848 : "I am considered a great heretic for abusing it, but it seems to me a wretched waste of power at a time of life when a man ought to be doing his best, and I almost feel hopeless about Alfred now.   I mean about his doing what he was born to do."

The verdict of Mrs. Browning also was unflatter-ing.   Writing to Miss Mitford about housekeeping in the Guidi Palace, and shopping for chairs and tables with the author of *Strafford* and *Sordello*, she winds up with : "At last we have caught sight of Tenny-son's 'Princess,' and I may or must profess to be a good deal disappointed.   What woman will tell the great poet that Mary Wollstonecraft herself never dreamt of setting up collegiate states, proctordoms, and the rest, which is a worn-out plaything in the hands of one sex already, and need not be *transferred* in order to be proved ridiculous ?   As for the poetry, beautiful in some parts, he never seems to me to come up to his own highest mark in the rhythm especially. The old blank verse of Tennyson was a divine thing; but this—new-mounted for certain critics—may please them better than it pleases me.   Still the man is Ten-nyson, take him for all in all, and I never shall forgive whatever princesses of my sex may have ill-treated him."

Miss Mitford, never too enthusiastic over Tenny-son, found the story "very unskilfully told, with an en-tire want of dramatic power, and full of the strangest words brought in after the strangest fashion"; but she adds, "there are fine things in it."   She reports the poet as vexed by small applause, and Mrs. Browning responds : "Why did Mr. Harness and others who 'never could understand' his former divine works, praise this in manuscript until the poet's hope grew to the height of his ambition ? Strangely unfortunate ! "

By 1850, however, three large editions of the poem had been sold, and Mrs. Browning, experienced in the business uncertainties of literature, declined longer to sympathise. "If he is n't satisfied, after all," she writes, "I think he is wrong. Divine poet as he is, and no laurel being too leafy for him, yet he must be an unreasonable man, and not understanding of the growth of the laurel-trees and the nature of a reading public."

A very interesting review appeared in 1848 in the *Massachusetts Quarterly*. It was unsigned ; but from Lowell's *Letters* we learn that he was the author. The praise is very high, but discriminating, and the tiresome expedient of " explaining " the poem, which explains itself, is altogether ignored. After a preliminary tussle with " Timms," who is supposed to represent the American " Jeffrey," and who has pronounced *The Princess* an entire failure, the critic proceeds :

" In the first place, we must look at the poem not as the work of a beginner, but of an acknowledged poet, and of one who has gained his rank and maintained it by the unerring certainty with which he has produced his effects, and his conscientious adherence to the truths of Art. We know of few poets in whose writings we have found that entire consistency which characterises those of Tennyson. His conception is always clear, his means exactly ade-

quate, and his finish perfect.   So entirely free is he
from any appearance of effort, that many have been
led to underrate him, and to praise his delicacy at
the expense of his strength.   It is true that he never
wastes an atom of force.   He never calls all his muscles
into play for the plucking of a flower.   Yet he is
never found wanting to the demand of the occasion.
Milo, with his fingers in the oak-cleft, made, after all,
rather a sorry display of sinew.   Though one chief
characteristic of Tennyson's mind be a flowing grace,
and a feminine sensitiveness to every finest suggestion of beauty ; though thought in him seems to be
rather a luxury of sensation than an activity of intellect ; though his metres adapt themselves to every
subtle winding of expression with the yielding freedom of water, yet his outlines are always sharp-cut
and severe.   Perfection of form seems to be with
him a natural instinct, not an attainment.   We must
therefore regard *The Princess* as the work of a master,
and it must argue a poverty in ourselves if we cannot see it as a harmonious whole.   For so perfect
is Tennyson's appreciation of his own strength, that he
has never in a single instance fallen below himself.
His self-command is not the least wonderful quality
in him.

"The growth of the poem is as natural as its plan
is original.   The gradual absorption of the author in
his subject, till what was begun as a song 'turns out
a sermon,' the growing predominance of the poet
over the mere story-teller, as the higher relations of

his subject appeal to him, and the creative faculty feels itself more and more taxed, are exquisitely true to the intellect and the heart.   We know of no other man who could have mingled the purely poetical with the humorous in such entire sympathy as nowhere to suggest even a suspicion of incongruity. But Tennyson's humour is peculiar to himself.   It is as refined as all the other parts of his mental constitution.   We were about to compare it with Chaucer's. It is as genial and simple, but not so robust.   It has more of the polish of society.   It is like Addison's, etherealised and sublimated by the poetic sense.   It has none of that boisterousness which generally goes with it when it is the predominant quality of the mind.   It is not a laugh, but a quiet smile and a light in the eyes.   It is a delicate flower which we can perceive and enjoy, but which escapes definition.   In short, it is Tennyson's.   If we take by itself any one of the little touches of humour scattered through *The Princess*, it will seem nothing extraordinary, and we shall wonder whither its charm has flown, so perfectly and artistically dependent on each other are all parts of this delicious poem.   For Art is like the invention of the arch.   Each piece, taken singly, has no especial fitness.   The material is no rarer than that of the Cyclopean doorway, two upright blocks with a third laid across the top.   Nor is the idea less simple after we have once found it out.   We feel this book to be so true an expression of the man, its humour is so thoroughly a part of him, and leads up to or falls

off from the higher and graver passages with so graceful an undulation, that the whole poem would suffer
vitally by losing the least shade of it.   It subsides
out of the story as unobtrusively as it had entered,
at the moment when the interest, becoming concentrated in the deeper moral to which the poem is naturally drawn, necessarily excludes it.   The progress
of the poem is carried forward, and its movement
modulated with the truest feeling and tact.   It is as
if some composer, in a laughing mood, had seated
himself at the organ to *fantasy* for the entertainment
of a few friends.   At first he is conscious of their
presence, and his fingers run lightly over the keys,
bringing out combinations of notes swayed quaintly
hither and thither by the magnetism of the moment.
But gradually he becomes absorbed in his own power
and that of his instrument.   The original theme re-
curs less and less often, till at last he soars quite
away from it on the uplifting wings of his art.

"One striking excellence of Tennyson's poetry,
as noticeable in *The Princess* as elsewhere, is its
repose and equilibrium.   There is nowhere the least
exaggeration.   We are never distracted by the noise
of the machinery.   No one beauty is so prominent as
to divide the effect, and to prevent our receiving the
full pleasure arising from our perception of completeness.   The leading idea keeps all the rest in perfect
subjection.   He never gives us too much.   With
admirable instinct he always stops short where the
reader's imagination may be safely trusted to suggest

all the minor accessories of a thought or a situation. He gives all that is essential, not all that he can. He never indulges his invention with two images where one is enough. And this self-denial, this entire subordination of the author to his work, has been remarkable in him from the first. It marks the sincere artist, and is worthy of all praise. If some of his earlier poems were chargeable with slight excesses of mannerism, it was only the mannerism natural to a mind which felt itself to be peculiar, and was too hasty in asserting its peculiarity before it had learned to discriminate clearly between the absolute and the accidental. But he has long since worked himself clear of this defect and is now only a mannerist because he is a Tennyson.

"The profound and delicate conception of female character for which Tennyson is distinguished, and which, from the nice structure of his mind, we should expect to find in him, is even more perfectly developed in *The Princess* than hitherto. It marks the wisdom of the man no less than the insight of the poet. Whatever any woman may think of the conclusions he arrives at, she cannot help being grateful to the man who has drawn the Lady Psyche and Ida.

"The design of *The Princess* is novel. The movement of the poem is epic, yet it is redolent, not of Homer and Milton, but of the busy nineteenth century. There are glimpses of contemporary manners and modes of thought, and a metaphysical question is argued, though without infringing upon the freedom of the story. Indeed, it is the story itself which argues. On the whole we consider this to be the freest and fullest expression of Tennyson which we have had. The reader will find in it all the qualities for which he is admirable, so blended and interfused as to produce a greater breadth of effect than he has elsewhere achieved.

"The familiarity of some passages, while it is in strict keeping with the character he assumes at the outset, indicates the singer at last sure of his audience, and reposing on the readiness of their sympathies."

This criticism contains substantially all that has been said in favour of *The Princess*. The poem seems on the whole to have gained with time, and those who do not take it too seriously, and do not hunt too persistently for its precise pedagogic intention, may comfortably enjoy its oddity, its freakish, irresponsible strain, so unlike anything else permitted by the intellectual conscience of its author. Perhaps to a world that reads without "reviewing," its chief recommendation is the pervading humour which attracted Lowell, and which seems to separate this one poem from the mass of Tennyson's work. Mr. Traill, indeed, finds Tennyson satisfactorily humorous throughout. Without a deep sense of humour, he argues, the poet would never have been able to keep the balance in his work and avoid the extravagant and the ridiculous. While he recognises the absence of the light touch corresponding in literature

to the ready repartee in talk, he finds abundance of
what he calls the " sympathetic humour " with which
Dickens and Thackeray were endowed. Not only
does the " Northern Farmer " delight him, as well it
may, with its large comedy ; but " Will Waterproof's
Monologue " is deliciously amusing to him. All of
which in the present case serves to demonstrate the
old truth : You may lead a reader to a joke, but
you cannot make him laugh. To a less buoyant intelligence than that of Mr. Traill, Tennyson's best fun,
compared, for example, with Thackeray's " White
Squall," which ends as suddenly as the squall, in
tears, shows plainly the contrast between the somewhat elaborate and self-conscious wit of an essentially unhumorous mind, and humour that is of the
essence.

FitzGerald said, apropos of the absurd little poem
" The Skipping Rope," " Alfred, whatever he may
think, cannot trifle ; his smile is rather a grim one."
Grim is not the most fitting adjective for " The Skipping Rope " ; but in spite of Mr. Traill's delightful
argument, it is difficult not to side with FitzGerald and
deny Tennyson's claim to the real thing in humour.
A certain detachment of spirit, the power to see oneself small and far off, seems to go with that perception of congruities and incongruities which makes
for humour of the more subtle sort, and of such detachment Tennyson was innocent. To use Pater's
phrase, there is in his lighter poetry a " misconception
of the perfect manner," a missing of " the delicate

shade of unconcern" that marks the "perfect manner." He took his poetry rather solemnly, if not, as
Froissart says his countrymen take their pleasures,
sadly. He could not let it slip joyously from him as
Lowell did ; a reason, perhaps, why he, more than
Lowell, needed a pension. He felt the responsibility
of being a poet, and he tilled his field so assiduously
that there were few spontaneous growths of weedy
fun. When he tried for sheer levity the result was
amazing. His gambolling in such poems as "The
Amphion" and "The Golden Goose," is about as
airy as Wordsworth's jaunty couplet :

> "I've measured it from side to side,
> 'T is three feet long, and two feet wide."

But it was characteristic of him absolutely to contradict himself from time to time, and show himself
capable of success precisely where one had grown
accustomed to failure. The possibilities for badinage
and high spirits in the treatment of *The Princess*
irresistibly appealed to him. Lovely as the Princess
is, stately and charming, Tennyson has succeeded in
making her father's mental attitude sufficiently con-
vincing when he proclaims that

> "———awful odes she wrote,
> Too awful, sure, for what they treated of,
> But all she is and does is awful."

And it is quite easy to give an affirmative answer
when Mr. Traill inquires persuasively if you do not
feel, as you listen to the placid murmur of the

stream of humour rippling through the poem, "that already, well-nigh fifty years ago, this poet had penetrated to the heart of that great Woman Question which is agitating so many humourless minds at the present day, and that he has reached it by the aid of the only guide that knows the way to it—by the power of humorous sympathy?"[1]

Stopford Brooke, more emancipated, perhaps, than Mr. Traill, does not reach perfect contentment with Tennyson's attitude toward the "Question." Ida surrendered too much, he thinks, when that

"——something wild within her breast,
A greater than all knowledge, beat her down,"

and the prince accepted "too much of masterhood." Nor did the poet make allowance for the women who have no homes and "are hungry to become themselves, to realise themselves in the life and movement of the whole." Emphatically true. The attitude of the waning last decade of the century was not attained in Tennyson's poem of 1847; but the reader who remembers that poets are human, and that Tennyson was nearing his own ideal of a home and marriage with the woman he had loved for more than a dozen years, will hardly wonder at his over-looking the unmarrying element in society.

In 1850, the "Songs" were added to *The Princess.* Charles Kingsley describes them as follows :

"At the end of the first canto, fresh from the

[1] "Tennyson as a Humourist," *Nineteenth Century*, May, 1894.

description of the female college with its profes-
soresses, and hostleresses, and other Utopian mon-
sters, we turn the page, and—

'As thro' the land at eve we went,

O there above the little grave,
    We kiss'd again with tears.'

"Between the next two cantos intervenes the
well-known cradle-song, perhaps the best of all ; and
at the next interval is the equally well-known bugle-
song, the idea of which is that of twin-labour and
twin-fame in a pair of lovers.   In the next, the sight
of the fallen hero's child opens the sluices of his
widow's tears ; and in the last the poet has succeeded in the new edition in superadding a new form
of emotion to a canto in which he seemed to have
exhausted every resource of pathos which his
subject allowed."[1]

In these songs we are reminded that for Tennyson
poetry was music.   To read them carefully is to mar-
vel at the flawless expression of exquisite sentiment.
Nothing could be more tenderly developed than their
simplicity, and if anything is wanting in them it is
the avenue of escape into the peccable world.   Their
workmanship is full of fine detail, like some fragment
of choicest cloisonné.   Among other things to be
observed is the poet's fondness for the lingual, *l*, and
its influence upon his verse.

[1] *Fraser's Magazine*, September, 1850.

For

> " Low, low, breathe and blow,
>> Wind of the western sea !
> Over the rolling waters go,"

try reading,

> " Go, go, breathe and go,
>> Wind of the western sea !
> Over the rocking waters go ";

or read

> " The sunbeam shakes across the lakes,"

for

> " The long light shakes across the lakes,"

to find how subtly the melodious charm of the syllables is gained.   Whoever reads Tennyson in German may multiply such comparisons.   Take for example the passage in "The Marriage of Geraint," where Enid's singing is likened to the sweet voice of a bird that

> "Heard by the lander in a lonely isle,
> Moves him to think what kind of bird it is
> That sings so delicately clear,"

and try to recognise the liquid music of the first and third lines in these sibilants and gutturals :

> " Auf fernem Inselstrand ein Schiffer hört,
> Und lauscht und sinnt wess' Art der Vogelsei
> Der so bezaubernd singt."

Sometimes the insistence on the liquid note is too monotonous, as where the Prince sings, "maidenlike,"

> " O Swallow, Swallow, flying, flying South,
> Fly to her and fall upon her gilded eaves
> And tell her, tell her, what I tell to thee ";

but for the most part it is used with infinite skill and charm to the end not merely of *The Princess* but of the whole long melody down to

> " The mellow lin-lan-lone of evening bells."

If Tennyson delighted in the letter *l*, he abhorred the sibilant *s*, and in the *Memoir* his son quotes him as declaring that he " never put two ' ss ' together in any verse." " My line is not," he said, " as often quoted,

> ' And freedom broadens slowly down,'

but

> ' And freedom slowly broadens down.' "

It is not surprising to find this rather extravagant statement contradicted here and there in *The Princess*, as well as in the later poems. We find, for example,

> " Who shines so in the corner,"

and

> " The blood
> Was sprinkled on your kirtle,"

and

> " Are castles shadows ?   Three of them ?   Is she
> The sweet proprietress a shadow ? "

and

> " As strangely as it came,"

as random exceptions to the professed rule of " kicking the geese out of the boat."   A writer in *Scribner's Magazine* has cited further examples of " Homer nodding," and has also pointed out that Shakespeare, who was tolerably well acquainted with the art of blank verse, had no such hostile feeling toward sibilation. "He did not 'kick the geese out of the boat,' he only taught them when and where to hiss."

In Mr. Dawson's *Study of "The Princess"* attention is called to the essential correspondence of certain passages in the poem with passages in the poems of Shelley and Wordsworth.

This passage,

> " A wind arose and rush'd upon the South,
> And shook the songs, the whispers, and the shrieks
> Of the wild woods together ; and a Voice
> Went with it, 'Follow, follow, thou shalt win'";

is compared with this from Shelley's *Prometheus Unbound :*

> " A wind arose among the pines ; it shook
> The clinging music from their boughs, and then
> Low, sweet, faint sounds, like the farewell of ghosts,
> Were heard : 'Oh follow, follow, follow me !'"

Again this passage,

> " He has a solid base of temperament ;
> But as the water-lily starts and slides
> Upon the level in little puffs of wind,
> Tho' anchor'd to the bottom, such is he,"

has certainly the look of deriving from this in Wordsworth's *Excursion :*

> " And, like the water-lily, lives and thrives,
> Whose root is fixed in stable earth, whose head
> Floats on the tossing waves."

This drew from Tennyson a very interesting letter. "Your explanatory notes are very much to the pur-

pose," he wrote, " and I do not object to your finding parallelisms. They must always occur. A man
(a Chinese scholar) some time ago wrote to me saying that in an unknown, untranslated Chinese poem
there were two whole lines of mine almost word for
word !¹ Why not ? Are not human eyes all over
the world looking at the same objects, and must there
not consequently be coincidences of thought and impressions and expressions ? It is scarcely possible
for anyone to say or write anything in this late time
of the world to which, in the rest of the literature of
the world, a parallel could not somewhere be found.
But when you say that this passage or that was suggested by Wordsworth or Shelley, or another, I de-
mur ; and more, I wholly disagree. There was a
period in my life when, as an artist, Turner for instance, takes rough sketches of landskip, etc., in
order to work them eventually into some great picture, so I was in the habit of chronicling, in four or
five words or more, whatever might strike me as
picturesque in Nature. I never put these down, and

¹ The *Memoir* states that the two lines referred to were from " The Voice and
the Peak " :

" The Peak is high and the stars are high,
And the thought of a man is higher."

May it not be possible that the Chinese verse was the one written by Yang
Ta-nien and recently translated by Mr. Herbert A. Giles, which runs as follows, in the
English version :

" Upon this tall pagoda's peak
My hands can nigh the stars enclose ;
I dare not raise my voice to speak
For fear of startling God's repose " ?

The idea is certainly similar, and had the Chinese lines been literally followed they
might have corresponded more closely with Tennyson's.

7

many and many a line has gone away on the north wind, but some remain ; *e.g. :*

> ' A full sea glazed with muffled moonlight.'

Suggestion.

"The sea one night at Torquay, when Torquay was the most lovely sea-village in England, tho' now a smoky town. The sky was covered with thin vapour, and the moon behind it.

> ' As the water-lily starts and slides.'

Suggestion.

"Water-lilies on my own pond, seen on a gusty day with my own eyes. They did start and slide in the sudden puffs of wind till caught and stayed by the tether of their own stalks, quite as true as Wordsworth's simile and more in detail.

> ' A wild wind shook,——
> Follow, follow, thou shalt win.'

Suggestion.

"I was walking in the New Forest. A wind did arise and

> ' Shake the songs, the whispers and the shrieks
> Of the wild wood together.'

"The wind I believe was a west wind, but because I wished the Prince to go south, I turned the wind to the south, and naturally the wind said ' follow.'

I believe the resemblance which you note is just a chance one. Shelley's lines are not familiar to me, tho' of course if they occur in the *Prometheus* I must have read them. I could multiply instances, but I will not bore you, and far indeed am I from asserting that books as well as Nature are not, and ought not to be, suggestive to the poet. I am sure that I myself, and many others, find a peculiar charm in those passages of such great masters as Virgil or Milton where they adopt the creation of a bygone poet and re-clothe it, more or less, according to their own fancy. But there is, I fear, a prosaic set growing up among us, editors of booklets, bookworms, index-hunters, or men of great memories and no imagination, who *impute themselves* to the poet, and so believe that *he*, too, has no imagination, but is for ever poking his nose between the pages of some old volume in order to see what he can appropriate. They will not allow one to say 'Ring the bell,' without finding that we have taken it from P. Sidney, or even to use such a simple expression as the ocean 'roars,' without finding out the precise verse in Homer or Horace from which we have plagiarised it (fact !)."

This letter, though addressed to Mr. Dawson, is an all-sufficient response to a very different class of commentators ; those who, wishing Tennyson less and lower than he is in the judgment of his admirers, have fastened the charge of plagiarism upon him at the merest hint of parallelism. Some of the suggestions made in this connexion are extremely amusing and not a little aggravating.

It is discovered, for example, that "Crossing the Bar" closely resembles the death-scene in *Dombey and Son ;* and the charming simile in "Locksley Hall,"

" On her pallid cheek and forehead came a colour and a light
As I have seen the rosy red flushing in the northern night,

is found with a few unimportant elemental changes in Uhland's "Minstrel's Curse":

" Der König furchtbar prächtig, wie blut'ger Nordlichtschein."

There are cases, however, in which the resemblance is very striking, and these have an interest of their own which has nothing at all to do with the revolting question of plagiarism. Lowell's comment upon the subject in his essay on *Milton* is a fine example of precisely the right spirit in which to treat them :

" If there is one thing more striking than another in this poet," he says, " it is that his great and original imagination was almost wholly nourished by books, perhaps I should rather say set in motion by them. It is wonderful how, from the most withered and juiceless hint gathered in his reading, his grand images rise like an exhalation ; how from the most battered old lamp caught in that huge drag-net with which he swept the waters of learning, he could conjure a tall genius to build his palaces. Whatever he

touches swells and towers.   That wonderful passage
in *Comus* of the airy tongues, perhaps the most imaginative in suggestion he ever wrote, was conjured
out of a dry sentence in Purchas's abstract of Marco
Polo.   Such examples help us to understand the poet.
When I find that Sir Thomas Browne had said before
Milton that Adam ' was *the wisest of all men since,*' I
am glad to find this link between the most profound
and the most stately imagination of that age.   Such
parallels sometimes give a hint also of the historical
development of our poetry, of its apostolical succession, so to speak.   Everyone has noticed Milton's
fondness for sonorous proper names, which have not
only an acquired imaginative value by association,
and so serve to awaken our poetic sensibilities, but
have likewise a merely musical significance.   This
he probably caught from Marlowe, traces of whom
are frequent in him.   There is certainly something of
what afterwards came to be called Miltonic in more
than one passage of *Tamburlaine*, a play in which
gigantic force seems struggling from the block, as in
Michel Angelo's *Dawn.*"

If, then, we entirely dismiss the question of plagiarism, we shall find a perfectly legitimate pleasure
either in tracing the influence of other minds upon
Tennyson's or in observing how the same ideas are
apt to clothe themselves in very similar words under
the direction of totally different intelligences.   It is
interesting, for example, to find how closely the sentiment of the lovely lyric in *The Princess,*

" Home they brought her warrior dead:
     She nor swoon'd nor utter'd cry :
 All her maidens, watching, said,
     ' She must weep or she will die.'

         .   .   .   .   .

" Rose a nurse of ninety years,
     Set his child upon her knee—
 Like summer tempest came her tears—
     ' Sweet my child, I live for thee,' "

resembles the sentiment of this passage in Scott's
Lay of the Last Minstrel :

" O'er her warrior's bloody bier
 The Ladye dropp'd nor flower nor tear!

         .   .   .   .   .

 Until, amid his sorrowing clan,
 Her son lisped from the nurse's knee,—
 ' And if I live to be a man
 My Father's death revenged shall be !'
 Then fast the mother's tears did seek
 To dew the infant's kindling cheek."

Not only is Tennyson's version much more beautiful metrically, but the little warlike touch in the baby's words did not occur to him, or if it occurred did not commend itself.   The tears are there, but no revenge, no martial infant.

In Scott's *Woodstock* is also a passage that runs fairly parallel with a part of the " Ode on the Death of the Duke of Wellington."   If either pass into immortality it will probably be the latter, by virtue of the fervently religious inspiration of the closing lines, an exquisite expression of the joy over and above the victory of holiness :

" But Duty guides not that way—see her stand
  With wand entwined with amaranth, near yon cliffs.
  Oft where she leads thy blood must mark thy footsteps,
  Oft where she leads thy head must bear the storm,
  And thy shrunk form endure heat, cold, and hunger ;
  But she will guide thee up to noble heights
  Which he who gains seems native of the sky."

SCOTT, Woodstock.

" Not once or twice in our fair island story
    The path of duty was the way to glory ;
    He that ever following her commands,
    On with toil of heart and knees and hands,
    Thro' the long gorge to the far light has won
    His path upward, and prevail'd,
    Shall find the toppling crags of Duty scaled
    Are close upon the shining table-lands
    To which our God Himself is moon and sun."
      "Ode on the Death of the Duke of Wellington."

A metrical correspondence is found between the famous song in *Maud* and this by Dryden :

" Shall I marry the man I love ?
      And shall I conclude my pains ?
    Now bless'd be the Powers above,
      I feel the blood bound in my veins ;
    With a lively leap it began to bound
      And the vapours leave my brains."

A metaphor in the " Morte d'Arthur,"

" For so the whole round world is every way
    Bound by gold chains about the feet of God,"

occurs also in Archdeacon Hare's sermon on *The Law of Self-Sacrifice* : " This is the golden chain of love whereby the whole creation is bound to the throne

of the Creator "; and in the Epilogue to " Morte
d'Arthur " is this expression :

> " On to dawn, when dreams
>   Begin to feel the truth and stir of day ";

which certainly sufficiently resembles the line in
Shelley's " Hellas,"

> " The truth of day lightens on my dreams,"

to suggest a derivation.

Some of these parallel passages [1] are very plausibly
accounted for on the theory of recurrent ideas, or
" cycles of thought," as Dr. Holmes puts it. Most
of us remember his story of meeting Mrs. Sigourney
and replying to her pleasant reference to his many
wanderings with the remark : " Yes, I am like the
Huma, the bird that never lights, being always in the
cars as he is always on the wing." Years passed,
the same place was visited. Another meeting with
Mrs. Sigourney. "You are constantly going from
place to place," she said. " Yes," he answered, " I am
like the Huma," and finished the sentence as before.

In the same way a mind steeped in poetry may
retain lines once read and reproduce them in their
general form after all remembrance of the reading has
passed away. Such forgetfulness is no more astonishing than that of some of Tennyson's critics, two of
whom record having been challenged by him with

---

[1] I cannot claim them as the reward of my own " undiscourageable search " ;
most of them, in fact all that I have quoted, I think, and many more, were discovered by contributors to *Notes and Queries.*—AUTHOR.

writing certain passages which they could not in the least recall.

Alfred Austin, the present Laureate, is one of these, and writes of the incident in his article on "Tennyson's Literary Sensitiveness [1]":

"'I never could see I am so like Keats,' he [Tennyson] once said to me, as we were walking alone in his garden.

"'Who said you are like Keats?'

"'You did, and you said I had taken a line from Keats and spoiled it. But it does n't matter now.'

"I had completely forgotten the circumstance."

Certain parallelisms, too, are almost sure to occur where men of the same nationality look out upon the same scenes and are moved by them. When Butler writes:

> "Where'er you tread, your foot shall set
> The primrose and the violet,"

and Tennyson follows with this in *Maud*:

> "From the meadow your walks have left so sweet
> That whenever a March wind sighs
> He sets the jewel-print of your feet
> In violets blue as your eyes,"

it is not so much testimony in favour of conscious or unconscious imitation as a revelation of a certain aspect of the English meadows. In the same way Tennyson's line,

> "You scarce could see the grass for flowers,"

[1] *National Review*, 1892.

and Peele's, which is almost identical with it,

> "Ye may no see for peeping flowers the grasse,"

might have occurred to any English poet who had once set eyes upon Chaucer's "ground so proud" in its Spring robe

> "Of gras and floures, wide and pers,
> And many hewes ful dyvers."

If we pass from single lines and passages to the subjects of the poems we find that Tennyson apparently cared very little whence came his suggestions, so long as they were suited to his poetic quality. He would take his inspiration with equal cheerfulness from a classic fable, a contemporary newspaper, or a personal experience; and the excellence of the result did not depend at all upon the character of the source. It was Sir Henry Taylor who said of him: "He wants a story to treat, being full of poetry with nothing to put it in."

CHAPTER VI.

MARRIAGE AND LAUREATESHIP.

B Y the time *The Princess* was published Tennyson had drawn his public about him, and his
large popularity was well begun. He had
been already translated into German, and in America,
as we have seen, he was early known. Those " followers of Emerson " had devoted the ardent spirit of
their youth to spreading the new light among the
new generation. One of the most enthusiastic and
efficient of them was, we learn from Mr. Norton, a Mr. Charles S. Wheeler, " a handsome blond
youth, full of vigour, a lover of Nature,—introducing
Thoreau even to some of her intimacies to which he
had not then attained : a lover of books as well, and
an excellent scholar for the time. From 1838 to 1842
he was Instructor in History at Harvard, and Tutor in
Greek. He edited the first American edition of Herodo-
tus, and his editing showed both scholarship unusual
for his age, and taste perhaps equally unusual. His
soul was open to all the spiritual influences of the
time, and he was one of Emerson's nearest friends

and followers. I suppose that he might have been classed among the Transcendentalists, but he had a saving grace of common-sense which protected him from some of the follies, which in that period of spiritual ferment a good many of our best youth displayed." He died in the June of 1843, before he was twenty-seven years old. In the fall of 1842 he wrote to Lowell from Heidelberg :

" I must tell you that Tennyson has addressed me a very kind note since I took up my abode in Heidelberg. I am going to copy out some paragraphs therefrom, even at the risk of a vanity-tax. He says : ' I am very glad to hear that you are in the old world, and indeed half inclined to be envious of those sensations which belong to you as an American first setting foot among the ruins of ancient empires. Would that I could be with you and sympathise with your pleasure. I am only afraid that after the sunshine and colour and antiquities of Southern Europe our milder beauties and worse climate will disappoint any expectations you may have raised ; not the less I ought not to forget that your bond with England is nearer and dearer than with Greece or Italy, and I do not fear that you will bring among us the spirit of Fenimore Cooper. I have full faith that you have made as good a bargain for me as was possible under the circumstances, and that your friend will manage as well as may be for my interests : these things will all be remedied with the progress of years, though perhaps the grass will wave over our graves before the

coming of the better day. . . . When do you intend to visit England ? I suppose you can hardly tell at present. You must give me a little notice beforehand, or I may be out of the way, and I should be sorry to miss the pleasure of seeing you.' Very nice, is it not ? Tennyson mentions that he has not received a copy of the reprint, and that he would like to see one. Will you ask Ticknor whether one has been despatched, and see to it, if there has not ? "

Altogether the keenest American estimate of Tennyson's poetry at this period was made by Emerson in those curiously plain-spoken, familiar letters to the American public, which he called *English Traits.*

"Tennyson is endowed precisely in points where Wordsworth wanted," he says. "There is no finer ear, nor more command of the keys of language. Colour, like the dawn, flows over the horizon from his pencil, in waves so rich that we do not miss the central form. Through all his refinements, too, he has reached the public,—a certificate of good sense and general power, since he who aspires to be the English poet must be as large as London, not in the same kind as London, but in his own kind. But he wants a subject, and climbs no mount of vision to bring its secrets to the people. He contents himself with describing the Englishman as he is and proposes no better. There are all degrees in poetry, and we must be thankful for every beautiful talent. But it is only a first success when the ear is gained. The best office of the best poets has been to show how low and uninspired was their general style, and that only once or twice they have struck the high chord."

During the later forties Tennyson travelled in Wales, Scotland, and Ireland. In 1848 he was among the coves and quarries of Cornwall, with the subject of Arthur reviving in his mind. Miss Fox, in her journal, speaks of meeting Henry Hallam, who reported the poet's rapture over the Cornish scenery: "At one little place, Looe, where he arrived in the evening, he cried: 'Where is the sea? Show me the sea!' So after the sea he went stumbling in the dark, and fell down and hurt his leg so much that he had to be nursed for six weeks by a surgeon there, who introduced some of his friends to him, and thus he got into a class of society entirely new to him, and when he left they gave him a series of introductions, so that instead of going to hotels, he was passed on from town to town, and abode with little grocers and shop-keepers along his line of travel. He says that he cannot have better got a true impression of the class and thinks the Cornish very superior to the generality. They all know about Tennyson, and had read his poems, and one miner hid behind a wall that he might see him. Tennyson hates being lionised, and even assumes bad health to avoid it." This story and the one in the *Memoir* about Samuel Bamford, the weaver, rather contradict a favourite impression that Tennyson is a poet for the cultivated only. He certainly did not stoop to the taste of the uncultivated, and many of his phrases must be unintelligible to readers with a limited vocabulary; but his poetry comes within the range of the many. A writer for the *Spectator* who said, after his death, that "he bridged the gulf so often unnecessarily widened between the uneducated mind and the educated," had the true conception of his gift, and very happily compared the effect upon an imperfectly furnished mind of the rich, ornate verse, to the pleasure given a poor man by "a kind word or a visit from Royalty." It was this principle that led Mrs. Wiggin to put on her finest gown to read before an audience of charity children. And Mr. Stevenson followed it to its logical conclusion, when, in his paper on *Popular Authors*, he explained that the poor man does not, "in his rare hours of rumination" consider his own life as he lives it, "but that other life, which was all lit up for him by the humble talent of a Hayward—that other life which, God knows, perhaps he still believes that he is leading— the life of Tom Holt." Tennyson's talent was not "the humble talent of a Hayward," but his own very splendid endowment; nevertheless he performed this gentle office for the poor : he glorified their miserable lives, and made them Miller's Daughters, and Enoch Ardens, and Beggar Maids, to whom "in robe and crown the King stept down."

In 1850, Tennyson published *In Memoriam*, at first anonymously. This poem, the manuscript of which was once lost in a London lodging-house, and rescued by Mr. Coventry Patmore, marked a very important turning-point in Tennyson's life. He had been inflexible in his loyalty to his vocation, and its pecuniary rewards had not been swift to come. Now Moxon was willing to offer a satisfactory arrangement, and he at last felt justified in making Emily Sellwood his wife. On June 13, 1850, the wedding took place in Shiplake Church, of which Mr. James T. Fields got so charming an impression when he drove with Miss Mitford through laurel hedges to reach the " superb pile, rich in painted glass windows and carved oak ornaments." Pictures of the church as it is now, do not, it is said, bear a very close resemblance to the place as it must have looked to Tennyson and his bride. The ivy-covered tower is built of flint with " large, roughly dressed blocks of chalk," and, with the north aisle, constitutes the oldest portion of the structure. For the rest, it was restored in 1870, and according to the ideas of restoration then prevalent, much was swept away which, would probably now be retained.[1]

The wedding, Tennyson said, was " the nicest " he had ever been at, and apparently was of the simplest kind. The account of it in the *Memoir* contains all the essential elements of delightful, wholesome romance, with a very modest and genuine tribute from Hallam Tennyson to her whom he " loved as perfect mother and ' very woman of very woman.' " Concerning her very little has been written. She has

---

[1] Church's *The Laureate's Country.*

had no special halo cast about her, but the impression gained from fragmentary descriptions is one of singular charm. Mrs. Fields recalls her as she was in the prime of life, standing in her hospitable doorway "in her habitual and simple costume of a long grey dress and lace kerchief over her head. . . . Something in her bearing and trailing dress, perhaps, gave her a mediæval aspect which suited with the house." She lay on the couch, a "slender, fair-haired lady," and sat at dinner "in her soft white muslin dress tied with blue, at that time hardly whiter than her face or bluer than her eyes." Her boys, Hallam and Lionel, were born in 1852 and 1854, and in their black velvet dresses they looked to Mrs. Fields like Millais's picture of the princes in the Tower.

At the Manchester exhibition of 1857, Hawthorne and his family ran across the Tennysons, to the unspeakable delight of the former, who were nevertheless too shy or too delicate to approach the poet. Hawthorne's description of him in the *Note Books* is well known, and Mrs. Hawthorne wrote home a full and jubilant account of the occasion. Tennyson was satisfactorily picturesque, "very handsome and careless looking, with a wide-awake hat, a black beard, round shoulders, and slouching gait; most romantic, poetic, and interesting." His voice was deep and musical, and his hair was wild and stormy: "He is clearly the 'love of love and hate of hate,' and 'in a golden clime was born.' He is the Morte d'Arthur, In Memoriam, and Maud. He is Mariana

8

in the moated grange, he is the Lady Clara Vere de Vere, and rare, pale Margaret."

Very likely he was all that to the outward view, but at that time he was leading a particularly straight-forward, unaffected life as an English gentleman, hap-pily married, with two fine boys. He had recently bought Farringford, whither he had come from Twickenham, where his first two years of married life were spent ; and the *Memoir* gives bright, delight-ful glimpses of father and sons playing battledore and shuttlecock in the fine grounds, going flower-hunting through the fields, blowing bubbles, brushing up leaves from the beautiful lawns, and making new glades through the shrubs. Unlike Browning, Ten-nyson had all the Paternal qualities.

Mrs. Hawthorne's rapturous experience had a pretty sequel. She continues :

"Again Mr. Hawthorne, Una, and I were at the Palace all day. We went up into the gallery of en-graving to listen to the music, and suddenly Una exclaimed, 'Mamma! there is Tennyson!' He was sitting by the organ, listening to the orchestra. He had a child with him, a little boy in whose emotions and impressions he evidently had great interest, and I presumed it was his son. I was soon convinced that I saw also his wife and another little son, and all this proved true. It was charming to watch the group. Mrs. Tennyson had a sweet face, and the very sweetest smile I ever saw, and when she spoke to her husband or listened to him, her face showered a tender happy rain of light. She was graceful too, and gentle, but at the same time had a slightly peasant air. . . . The children were very pretty and picturesque, and Tennyson seemed to love them immensely. He devoted himself to them and was absorbed in their interest. Allingham, another English poet, told Mr. Hawthorne that his wife was an admirable one for him,—wise, tender, and of perfect temper, and she looks all this, and there is a kind of adoration in her expression when she addresses him. If he is moody and ill, I am sure she must be a blessed solace to him." On the way out of the place, the younger son dallied behind with a nurse, while Tennyson and the others went on. Mrs. Hawthorne seized the opportunity and the child, whom she kissed motherly, and " he smiled and seemed well pleased." She also was well pleased to have had in her arms Tennyson's child.

It is rather amusing to find that Mrs. Browning doubted the perfect fitness of Mrs. Tennyson to her husband's needs. She would have had her more a critic, and less an acquiescent admirer; in other words, more as Mrs. Browning herself was to her own remarkably self-reliant poet. The criticism need hardly be taken seriously since all that we know of Tennyson's home-life is shining testimony to its perfect harmony with his character as shown in his writings. His own words concerning his wife are these: " The peace of God came into my life when I married her,"[1] and they seem the exact expression

[1] Hallam Tennyson's *Alfred, Lord Tennyson*.

ot the atmosphere in which he worked with un-
wearied patience and unfailing skill for more than
forty years after his union with the " Dear, near, and
true," of whom he rightly prophesied

> "———— No truer Time himselt
> Can prove you, though he make you evermore
> Dearer and nearer."

On April 23, 1850, Wordsworth died at Rydal
Mount, and in November of the same year the
laurel passed to Tennyson, "greener," he said, "from
the brows of him who uttered nothing base." The
line of Laureates had hitherto not been crowded by
distinguished poets. "Rare Ben Jonson" had dignified the office which properly began with him,
Dryden was intellectually great, and Southey certainly
gave to literature a few stanzas as lovely as the mass
of his poetry was commonplace. But of the rest
Colley Cibber is the only one remembered of the
people, and his peculiar distinction rests upon his
singular name and exhaustive vanity. Wordsworth
himself had celebrated his brief term of office in an
almost absolute silence. After his death the honour
was proffered to Samuel Rogers who possessed two
distinctions : he was the oldest poet then living, and
in his youth he had run away from Dr. Johnson's
door without knocking. Nothing in his career as a
poet so became him as his declination of the offer on
the ground of his great age and wealth. Leigh Hunt,
also, was suggested, and it is said that he wanted the
office. It probably did not occur to him that his

appointment would have been a singular example of royal impartiality, after his imprisonment some forty years before on account of a newspaper criticism made on the then prince-regent. Mrs. Browning was urged by the *Athenæum* as a suitable Laureate for the household of a female sovereign, and as a poet, furthermore, whose claim was higher than that of any other living poet of either sex. Mrs. Browning's biographer, Mr. Kenyon, remarks that "the fact that in Robert Browning there was a poet of equal calibre with Tennyson though of so different a type, seems to have occurred to no one."

It is easy now to recognise that Tennyson was Wordsworth's natural successor. Browning alone rivalled him in the scope and excellence of his poetry, and Browning's genius was of a sort to prevent his being chosen as in any sense representative. His thoughts and emotions were not those that the majority of the English people recognise as belonging to themselves and like to have expressed. Tennyson, on the other hand, was supremely if not comprehensively national. There is a peculiar zest in the way his countrymen speak of "Tennyson as an Englishman." Neither Wordsworth nor Keats, Shelley nor Byron nor Coleridge, could have inspired quite that tone. Save Wordsworth any one of them might have belonged to some other land, and sung in some other language, and Wordsworth was too much aloof, too clear and simple and plain, as well as too majestic, to be identified with the desires and ideals of a multitude who never can be depended upon to worship the beauty of severity. But Tennyson had beautifully draped the sturdy form of the average and typical English thought. He had reproduced the familiar English landscape and the sacred English home, and already in *The Princess* had indicated his ability to make a "picture-story." *In Memoriam* had drawn deeper, and had given perfectly comprehensible expression to the great undercurrent of national faith above which played the waves of fluctuating doubt. There was nothing in all this to puzzle or to repel. If a curious word or simile caused a momentary interruption of the thought, the reader went at the task of interpretation with a good heart, knowing the fundamental idea to be well within his range. If there were excursions beyond the boundaries of the usual and the conventional, there was always the safe return to the path the English mind has kept from generation to generation. In fact, though Tennyson was always noble in sentiment and frequently uplifting, he was never out of reach "upon a peak in Darien," and if this prevents our placing him with the great masters, it also accounts for his hold upon his own generation in his own country.

As Laureate he produced no large amount of what may be called national verse; but his official and patriotic poems are extremely characteristic, not so much of his literary style, which they often contradict, but of his quality "as an Englishman." Sir Henry Taylor thought him "too simple and childlike" to see political questions on all sides; but to the side of caution he was usually awake, with deep conviction and sympathy. It is interesting to find that the early poem beginning, "You ask me why, tho' ill at ease," was little more than a poetical version of a speech of James Spedding on political "Unions" in the Cambridge Debating Club; but whether Spedding or another gave the suggestion, the view taken in the poem precisely fitted Tennyson's mind. When he was called a Conservative, he replied that he would "conserve progress," which was an admirable definition of his mental attitude; and he declined to be a candidate of either the Conservative or the Liberal party, when at different times each party wished to nominate him for the Rectorship of Glasgow University. Wherever in his poetry he gives adequate expression to the true dignity of his large view, he is, as we have said, sufficiently refreshing and inspiring. In some of his poems, however, he emphasises the conservation until the idea of progress is minimised, and he seems preoccupied with the conservative method in place of the progressive principle. This frequently gives to his patriotic poetry a temporal sound of politics and expediency which lays him open to Stopford Brooke's charge of unpoetical prudence. His poetical lapse seems, however, to be not in the side he takes, but in the difficulty with which he breathes the ample ether of abstract thought; and in his reluctance to rise above the atmosphere of England, of Royalty and

Parliaments and temporary legislation, to the region of eternally governing law.

The year of his appointment to the Laureateship was far from being one of literary dearth. Rossetti was contributing to the *Germ;* Thackeray had just published *Vanity Fair* and *Pendennis*, and had *Esmond* in train ; Carlyle was writing his brilliant *Life of John Sterling;* Landor, who had written, the year before, his exquisite quatrain, " I warmed both hands against the fire of life," was weeping over *David Copperfield;* Macaulay was in the midst of his greatest and final task, and Browning printed *Christmas Eve* and *Easter Day.* In America, Emerson had published *Representative Men*, in which he had said, most appropriately to Tennyson : " A poet is no rattlebrain, saying what comes uppermost, and, because he says everything, saying at last something good ; but a heart in unison with his time and country." Lowell was writing the *Nooning*, feeling " very young for a man of thirty," and making up his mind to " try more wholly after Beauty " in his poetry ; Longfellow was writing slowly on the *Golden Legend;* Hawthorne's *Scarlet Letter* appeared, and Whittier's *Songs of Labour*, with their humble and beautiful dedication. In France, Alfred de Musset, whom Taine and Swinburne were so intimately to associate with Tennyson, was writing *Carmoisine*, the final flicker of his adolescent genius ; Gautier was contributing art criticisms to *La Presse;* Hugo, in exile, was preparing his *Napoléon le petit*, and George

The Very Reverend Dr. Jowett.

(Master of Balliol, Oxford.)
From life.

Sand was translating and prefacing revolutionary works. Ibsen, in Norway, was publishing his first tragedy. Some of these were greater than Tennyson, some were certainly less; but none was more representative of the bland fusion of old thought with new thought, of ancient style with modern style, in one pellucid stream of genius. Besides the stimulus of so much activity among his fellow-writers, Tennyson had opportunity to cull stirring and sufficiently poetic themes from the political events of the 'fifties. In 1851, he prefaced the seventh edition of his poems with an address to the Queen containing one stanza that has since been removed:

> " She brought a vast design to pass
>   When Europe and the scattered ends
>   Of our fierce world did meet as friends
> And brethren in her halls to class."

This referred to the first Manchester Exhibition; but in spite of that international effort, the friendly feeling among the various nations of the fierce world was not specially obvious just then. "A military spirit was exhibiting itself everywhere not unlike that told of in Shakespeare's *Henry the Fourth*. The England of 1852 seems to threaten that 'ere this year expires we bear our civil swords and native fire as far as France.' At least the civil swords were sharpened in order that the country might be ready for a possible and even an anticipated invasion from France."[1]

The " meddle and muddle policy " of the Liberal

[1] McCarthy's *History of the Nineteenth Century*.

administration had justified the jibes of foreigners, the
anti-Papal excitement following the Papal Bull ap-
pointing Roman Catholic bishops throughout England had filled the newspapers with fervid articles.
The people of England were hardly less agitated than
the people of France over the *coup d'état*, and the
Duke of Wellington, who in English eyes was England's Washington, was dead. Disraeli and Gladstone were facing one another over the meaty bone
of the foreign policy. The country needed exhortation and counsel, as any country always does, and
Tennyson had the great examples of Milton and
Wordsworth to inspire him. The fact that he could
not rise to their height in his national poems merely
shows what all his poetry shows, that he was not
born to be a leader, much less a reformer. The poems
"Hands All Round," "Britons, Guard Your Own,"
and the "Third of February, 1852," have fire enough ;
but it is not the great still flame that burns in Wordsworth's sonnet, "September, 1802," or in his "London, 1802." A single stanza from "Britons, Guard
Your Own" will serve to show the attitude toward
Louis Napoleon :

> " Peace-lovers we, sweet Peace we all desire,
> Peace-lovers we, but who can trust a liar ?
> Peace-lovers, haters
> Of shameless traitors ;
> We hate not France, but this man's heart of stone :
> Britons, guard your own."

The appeal to America in "Hands All Round" is char-

acteristic of the feeling of its author, who wrote in
1867 to Longfellow : " We English and Americans
should all be brothers as none other among the nations can be ; and some of us, come what may, will
always be so, I trust."

" Riflemen, Form," or, as it was first called, " The
War," was published in the *Times* of Monday, May 9,
1859, bearing the signature of " T.," and therefore by
some astutely credited to Mr. Tupper, and by others to
Archbishop Trench.   Twelve days before it appeared
the Austrians had crossed the Ticino and six days after its publication the French marched into Genoa.
A writer in the *Athenæum* says : " The fourth line of
the second stanza as then printed,

> ' How should a despot set men free ? '

had a meaning, and a prophetic meaning, which is lost
in the new version,

> ' How can a despot feel with the Free ? ' "

And he contrasts with Tennyson's lines :

> " Let your reforms for a moment go !
>   Look to your butts, and take good aims !
> Better a rotten borough or so
>   Than a rotten fleet and a city in flames ! "

the following sentences from a contemporary letter
of John Bright to the Rev. Newman Hall :

" Surely," writes the Tribune of the People, " after
spending twenty-eight millions a year in military
services our population might be expected to be left

at home in peace. The Volunteer movement is the most foolish of our time ; it is a hoax on the nation."

Writing of the Volunteer movement of the early 'fifties, Mr. McCarthy refers to this poem as follows :

"The meaning of all this movement was explained some years after by Mr. Tennyson, in a string of verses which did more honour perhaps to his patriotic feeling than to his poetic genius. The verses are absurdly unworthy of Tennyson as a poet ; but they express with unmistakable clearness the popular sentiment of the hour ; the condition of uncertainty, vague alarm, and very general determination to be ready at all events for whatever might come. ' Form, form, riflemen, form,'—wrote the Laureate ; ' better a rotten borough or two than a rotten fleet and a town in flames.' 'True that we have a faithful ally, but only the devil knows what he means.' This was the alarm and the explanation. We had a faithful ally, no doubt, but we certainly did not know what he meant."[1]

The best-known patriotic poem of the first years of Tennyson's Laureateship is undoubtedly "The Charge of the Light Brigade," which was printed in the *Examiner* of December 9, 1854, with the note, "Written after reading the first report of the *Times* correspondent where only 607 sabres are mentioned as having taken part in the charge." It was reprinted later with another note :

"Having heard that the brave soldiers at Sebasto-

[1] McCarthy's *History of the Nineteenth Century*.

pol, whom I am proud to call my countrymen, have a liking for my ballad on the charge of the Light Brigade at Balaclava, I have ordered a thousand copies of it to be printed for them. No writing of mine can add to the glory they have acquired in the Crimea ; but if what I heard be true, they will not be displeased to receive these copies of the ballad from me, and to know that those who sit at home love and honour them.

"ALFRED TENNYSON.

"8th August, 1855."

Milnes said of this poem : "A real gallop in verse and only good as such." It has, however, stirred some stout hearts. A writer in the *Athenæum* at the time of Tennyson's death referred to it with reminiscent enthusiasm : "Only the oldsters among us," he said, "can pretend to remember the first appearance of 'The Charge of the Light Brigade' (in the *Examiner*, December 9, 1854), and the commotion it made. At this distance we read quite calmly :

' "Forward the Light Brigade !"
Was there a man dismay'd ?
Not tho' the soldier knew
Someone had blunder'd,—'

but in that winter of 1854 the *Times* correspondence from the Crimea made the air electrical and Tennyson's charge drew sparks." He adds that the following lines, which in the *Examiner* preceded those quoted, and which have never been reprinted, reflect

even more vividly the local colour of the letters from
the camp :

> " Into the valley of Death
>   Rode the six hundred,
> For up came an order which
>   Someone had blunder'd.
> 'Forward the Light Brigade !
> Take the guns !' Nolan said.
> Into the valley of Death
>   Rode the six hundred."

The " Ode on the Death of the Duke of Wellington " is pretty generally recognised by English critics
as the finest of Tennyson's Laureate poems. The
German critics, for some inconceivable reason, have
found it pompous and prosaic. It was this ode that
made the tears stream from Jowett's eyes when Tennyson read it in his presence ; and discounting the
natural emotion that the subject would cause, there
is reason enough for that sort of tears in the mournful power of the long poem that ends in a strain so
lofty as to seem almost unimpeachable in mood and
music :

> " He is gone who seem'd so great.—
> Gone ; but nothing can bereave him
> Of the force he made his own
> Being here, and we believe him
> Something far advanced in State,
> And that he wears a truer crown
> Than any wreath that man can weave him.
> Speak no more of his renown,
> Lay your earthly fancies down,
> And in the vast cathedral leave him,
> God accept him, Christ receive him."

Poems of this order, elegiac and sympathetic, were much better suited to Tennyson's feeling and philosophy than poems of more violent occasion. In cases where rebuke seemed to him necessary he was particularly unfortunate, the "Third ot February, 1852," being the only successful example. Much of the verse he produced under stress of circumstance showed a discomposure so marked as almost to suggest *déshabille* and touch the ludicrous. Mr. Swinburne declares : "With all due admiration for the genuine patriotism of his ' Ballad of the Fleet ' and ' Defence of Lucknow,' I must be permitted to observe that his general tone of thought and utterance on large questions of contemporary national history is such as might with admirable propriety find such expression as it finds at the close of *The Princess* from the lips not even of ' the Tory member ' but of the Tory member's undergraduate son—supposing that young gentleman to be other for the nonce than a socialist. There is a strain, so to speak, as of beardless bluster about it, which could by no possible ingenuity have been so rendered as to suggest a more appropriate mouthpiece. It has the shrill unmistakable accent, not of a provincial deputy, but of a provincial schoolboy."[1] One does not expect moderation from Mr. Swinburne, and it may certainly be said that he has overstated the case. In the passage from which the above quotation is taken he excepts from his condemnation the sonnets on Poland

[1] Swinburne's *Miscellanies*.

and Montenegro, " Hands All Round," and " Britons, Guard Your Own." If we add to these the " Defence of Lucknow " and the " Ballad of the Fleet," we have so large a proportion of Tennyson's political utterance as to make a judgment of his quality based upon the remainder quite one-sided. Mr. Swinburne's real quarrel with him seems to be on the subject of his attitude toward France.

" In a sonnet addressed to Victor Hugo," he says, " Lord Tennyson, with rather singular and rather more than questionable taste, informed the master poet of his age that he was said not to love England. No doubt, as I have elsewhere found occasion to remark, he did not love England as he loved his mother France, and his foster-mother Spain ; and against certain phases of modern English policy as against certain shades of modern English character, Hugo did undoubtedly think fit once and again to utter a frank and friendly word of protest. But such a tone as Lord Tennyson's almost invariable tone towards France is simply inconceivable as coming from Victor Hugo with reference to any great nation in the world. Now this sort of strident anti-Gallican cackle was all very well, if even then it was not very wise, in the days of Nelson. But in our piping times of peace it is purely ludicrous to hear a martial shepherd of idyllic habits thus chirping defiance and fluting disparagement of the world beyond his sheep-cote."

Yet the sonnet on Victor Hugo ends suavely enough :

1 Burlington St.
Brighton
Jany. 25th.

Mr Alfred Tennyson begs
to present his compliments
to Messrs Chapman and
Hall and to thank them
for their kind gift of the
Westminster Review
Containing one of the very
few favourable publications
of his Ode

LETTER FROM TENNYSON TO THE PUBLISHERS OF
• "THE WESTMINSTER REVIEW"

> " ——England, France, all man to be
> Will make one people ere man's race be run :
> And I, desiring that diviner day,
> Yield thee full thanks for thy full courtesy
> To younger England in the boy my son."

But the impeachment is not to be evaded, however much its form is to be deprecated. There is undoubtedly a note of insularity in Tennyson's work. He held rightly enough that "that man's the best Cosmopolite who loves his native country best," but as a matter of fact he was no Cosmopolite at all. What he disliked he dubbed "foreign"; war, of which Britain had certainly known her share, was "this French God, the Child of Hell," and art "with poisonous honey" was "stol'n from France." In the fine "Third of February, 1852," which Herr Engels has called a "bold achievement" (eine kühne Tat) for a Poet Laureate, the German critic is obliged to place the exclamatory mark against the line,

> "No little German state are we,"

and naturally finds the verse arrogant and purely English, although at the time of its writing some of the German states were certainly little enough to justify the phrase.

On the other hand Tennyson was warmly in sympathy with the cause of freedom in Italy, and "England and America in 1782" showed the breadth of his sympathies when it was a question of Englishman versus Englishman.

> " O thou, that sendest out the man
>   To rule by land and sea,
> Strong mother of a Lion-line,
> Be proud of those strong sons of thine
>   Who wrench'd their rights from thee ! "

If we examine his dedications and odes and addresses on national occasions we find their strongest characteristic an almost touching admiration of England and Englishmen.   He is never so happy as when he is praising national worth, his infelicity is never so apparent as when he is arraigning England for her failings.   He is on the side of the patriotism that de-demands justice and liberty " in the name of the Queen."   As Dr. Van Dyke has suggested, we cannot imagine him on the Stuart side in 1642, and his good fortune lay in the essential integrity and wisdom of the class toward which his taste directed him.   He was seldom moved by the impulse that moved Wordsworth in the sonnet beginning,

> " England! the time is come when thou should'st wean
>   Thy heart from its emasculating food,"

although instances of specific weakness and injustice roused his indignation, no matter in what class he found them.   He saw that in the main the progress of his country was toward wider freedom and fuller light, and he was very well content to look far ahead for perfection or the nearest human approach to it, without insisting upon sudden and revolutionary moves.   His appreciation of an honest, if imperfect, obedience to motives on the whole excellent and just, endeared him to the people of England who were trying for the right with conservative methods. One fears they could not so much have loved a soul that was "like a Star and dwelt apart" and discerned and rebuked all selfishness and error. They certainly did not so much love Milton. No one has better expressed the limitation in Tennyson's patriotism than Professor Dowden in a single passage of his comparison of Tennyson with Browning :

"Without reverence for duty, of which freedom is the essential condition, there is no true love of freedom. That is Mr. Tennyson's part of the truth. But passion for a righteous cause may create new forms of duty, and give the adequate power to fulfil them ; and if it does not, the failure is itself a success which God, who can give the morning star, will approve. That is Mr. Browning's part."

CHAPTER VII.

FARRINGFORD.

TENNYSON'S home at Farringford was of those that lend themselves readily to enthusiastic description. In spite of all that has been said of its seclusion, we know it through a hundred pens, and none has depicted it more happily than Mrs. Ritchie's. She takes us back to the life of the place "when the houses were few and the present generation very young," and shows us "a green and sunshiny little republic," with Tennyson presiding, and everyone going his own way and following his own bent.[1] "I can hardly imagine Eden itself," she says, "a sweeter garden, more sunny and serene than Farringford. From Eden, as we know, there was no sight of the sea, but from Farringford, all day long and by moonlit nights, you may watch the distant waters, beating time to the natural life in the green glades round the Poet's house." She goes on to quote from Henry Cameron's reminiscences of "the garden, 'careless ordered,' and its beds of tur-

[1] *Lord Tennyson and His Friends.*

Farringford House, Freshwater.

quoise forget-me-not ; of the wood-pigeons, and the blackbirds and their notes ; of the great ilex tree and the solemn cedar in the front of the house.

" Beyond the house lies the kitchen-garden, sunning itself in fragrance, with its straight beds full of lavender and bright flowers, and the big rosemary bush at the far end, and the old walls standing bravely under their load of green. Tennyson's old shepherd used to say that of early summer mornings, about four o'clock, when he went out to look after his flock, 'the birds all round the house would be singing like a charm.' How often have we listened to them ! Yellow-hammers, tom-tits, blackbirds in chorus, with the thrushes and the cuckoo's notes striking into the sweet babel. Of an evening the rooks would join in with priestly whirls and flights in the high sunsets. Besides all this there were the people living in the cottages all round about ; even the dependents and the humbler dwellers in this little island promontory caught something of the light from the mountain, and used to seem more interesting than other people in other places. Lord Tennyson's old shepherd was like some character out of the Bible—simple, pious, assiduous, living among his flocks and tending them to the last. There was the good old fisherman down by the beach, there were the children who used to come down from the fort with flowers and who planted Mrs. Cameron's banks with primrose roots."

From the same source comes an endearing picture

of the Tennyson family as they appeared among
these fair surroundings :

"The beloved Lady Tennyson in her long chair
carriage, pushed gently across the lawn by her boys,
and the Poet moving on with his peculiar, slow step,
perhaps with a spade in his hand, and a young tree
which he was about to transplant.   How can his
splendid personality be described ?"

The house itself is faintly sketched in Mrs.
Ritchie's *Records ;* it seemed to her "like a charmed
palace with green walls without and speaking walls
within.   There hung Dante with his solemn nose and
wreath ; Italy gleamed over the doorways ; friends'
faces lined the passages, books filled the shelves,
and a glow of crimson was everywhere ; the oriel
drawing-room window was full of green and golden
leaves, of the sound of birds, and of the distant sea."
Phillips Brooks, who visited a Farringford, speaks
of a pleasant habit in the family of leaving the table
at dinner just before the coffee and fruit, and having
that part of the meal served on a fresh table by the
windows, where they could watch the lovely view.

The vision evoked by these fragments of description differs very much from the pictures we keep in
mind of the American homes of American poets: from
the Craigie House at Cambridge, standing back from
Brattle Street among the lilac bushes ; from Elm-
wood, looking out upon the fields and the "long
curve of the Charles" and the marshes beyond; and
from the plain Concord house with the little garden in

which the corn was "sure to come up tulips"; and the difference is much the same as that between the American poetry and Tennyson's, the first a little bare and plain and stiff, and yet with its own crisp charm, the second so draped and furnished and flexible and rambling.

Bayard Taylor was at Farringford in 1857 and wrote with enthusiasm:

"The drive across the heart of the island, from Newport to Freshwater, was alone worth the journey from London. The softly undulating hills, the deep green valleys, the blue waters of the Solent, and the purple glimpses of the New Forest beyond formed a fit vestibule of landscape through which to approach a poet's home.

"As we drew near Freshwater my coachman pointed out Farringford—a cheerful grey country mansion, with a small, thick-grassed park before it, a grove behind, and, beyond all, the steep shoulder of the chalk downs, a gap in which, at Freshwater, showed the dark-blue horizon of the Channel. Leaving my luggage at one of the two little inns, I walked to the house, with the lines from *Maud* chiming in my mind. 'The dry-tongued laurel' shone glossily in the sun, the cedar 'sighed for Lebanon' on the lawn, and 'the liquid azure bloom of a crescent of sea,' glimmered afar.

"I had not been two minutes in the drawing-room before Tennyson walked in. So unlike are the published portraits of him that I was almost in doubt as to his identity.[1]   The engraved head suggests a moderate stature, but he is tall and broad-shouldered as a son of Anak, with hair, beard, and eyes of southern darkness.   Something in the lofty brow and aquiline nose suggests Dante, but such a deep, mellow chest voice never could have come from Italian lungs.

" He proposed a walk as the day was wonderfully clear and beautiful.   We climbed the steep comb of the chalk cliff, and slowly wandered westward until we reached the Needles, at the extremity of the island and some three or four miles distant from his residence.   During the conversation with which we beguiled the way, I was struck with the variety of his knowledge.   Not a little flower on the downs which the sheep had spared, escaped his notice, and the geology of the coast, both terrestrial and submarine, was perfectly familiar to him.   I thought of a remark which I had once heard from the lips of a distinguished English author, that Tennyson was the wisest man he ever knew, and could well believe that he was sincere in making it.   I shall respect the sanctity of the delightful family circle to which I was admitted and from which I parted the next afternoon with true regret.   Suffice it to say that the poet is not only fortunate and happy in his family relations ; but that with his large and liberal nature, his sympathies with what is true and noble in humanity, and his depth and tenderness of feeling, he deserves to be so."

[1] This refers to 1857, when only Laurence's portrait and Woolner's medallion had appeared.

Professor Church, in *The Laureate's Country*, has given a very careful account of the history and situation of Farringford, a portion of which may be of service to American travellers.

"Freshwater, to use the name without qualification," he says, "is an extensive parish occupying the south-western corner of the Isle of Wight. It is divided into the five hamlets of Easton, Weston, Norton, Totland Bay, and School Green, extends over more than five thousand acres, and contains between two and three thousand inhabitants. Freshwater Gate is, properly speaking, a natural cave in the cliff, but the name is sometimes used of the opening in the line of downs that form the south-western coast of the island, an opening that may be otherwise described as Freshwater Bay. The 'fresh water' from which it gets its name, probably given by seafarers eastward bound who found here their first opportunity of replenishing their empty barrels, is to be found not many yards from the beach, in the springs of the Yar, a little stream which soon opens out into a wide estuary, and so flows into the channel of the Solent at the ancient little town of Yarmouth.

"The Gate or Bay is a picturesque little stretch of beach not more than a few hundred yards in length. At its eastern point are some curious detached masses of chalk cliff, which stand out in the sea, some five hundred yards from the shore at high water, one of them hollowed by the action of the water into the shape of an arch. Beyond these, as the traveller pushes his way eastward, the down continues to ascend, though not without interruption, till it reaches, in St. Catherine's Hill, the highest point of the island, an altitude of more than eight hundred feet above the sea-level. Westward of the Bay there is a somewhat steep ascent, which leads to one of the many forts which guard the approaches to the Channel." Mrs. Browning regarded the building of this fort, which Tennyson much disliked, as "a piece of pure poetical justice" toward him for having written "Riflemen, Form!"

Professor Church continues: "Beyond the fort the traveller comes upon a fine stretch of open down, now called Tennyson's Down. Its seaward boundary is a range of lofty cliffs, sometimes showing a sheer fall into the water, sometimes sufficiently inclined to allow of a somewhat perilous descent into one of the little shingly bays which have been hollowed out by the waves. At the western extremity of the island they have been broken by the storms of centuries into those strangely shaped rocks which are known as The Needles, a name associated with many a tragic story of shipwreck. Above The Needles is the lighthouse, standing on the highest point of the downs, and not less than six hundred feet above the sea. The Needles passed, our faces being now turned from northward to eastward, we come first to Alum Bay, with its sand cliffs so picturesquely diversified in colour, then to Totland Bay, and so to the cliffs' end, when nearly opposite the formidable bastions of Hurst Castle on the mainland. The domain of Farringford can be seen on the traveller's right hand as he makes his way westward from Freshwater Bay, lying at the foot of the inland slope of the down. The house itself is not visible from any point of this route, but a glimpse of the roof may be caught from the ascent on the eastern side of the bay. The estate extends to between four and five hundred acres, part of them downland, and contains what is known as King's Manor. The royal ownership indicated by this name is recorded by Domesday Book, where we find the following entry : ' Ye King holds Frescewatre in demesne. It was held by Tosti [Earl Tostig, brother of King Harold—this, of course, refers to ' the time of King Edward,' a standard of comparison used throughout the Survey], and was then assessed at 15 hides. It is now assessed at 6 hides. There are fifteen ploughlands, two ploughlands are in demesne, and 18 villagers and 10 borderers employ 8 ploughs. There are seven servants and six acres of meadow. It was worth in King Edward's time sixteen pounds, and afterwards twenty pounds, but it is let at thirty pounds.' At this time, therefore, all Freshwater was what we should call Crown land. But it would appear that part of it was afterwards bestowed on some ecclesiastical body. This body seems to have been the Abbey of Quarr or Quarrera [so called from the stone quarries in the neighbourhood]. Quarr was near the town of Ryde, and was one of the first Cistercian monasteries established in England. Its first foundation was due to Baldwin, Earl of Devon, who endowed it in the thirty-second year of Henry I. Subsequent benefactors added to its revenues, and at the dissolution, its income was estimated at a net sum of £134 3s. 11d. Some of the local names recall this ecclesiastical ownership. Among them are 'Maiden's Croft' ['Virgin Mary's Field'], 'Abraham's Mead,' and 'The Clerk's Hill.'"

Tennyson has himself described the Farringford surroundings in various passages of his later poems, and most specifically in the invitation to Maurice, who had stood godfather to Hallam. Maurice, it will be remembered, was deprived of his professorships at King's College on account of his *Theological Essays*, in which his inherent breadth of belief manifested itself too boldly for the time and place. He had dedicated the second edition of his book to Tennyson in this touching letter, which reveals, among other things, the character of Tennyson's influence upon students of religion, and the confidence this particular student felt in his sympathy with broad human interpretations of theological doctrines :

"To ALFRED TENNYSON, ESQ., Poet Laureate.
"*My dear Sir :*
"I have mentioned in these Essays that a theology which does not correspond to the deepest thoughts and feelings of human beings cannot be a true theology. Your writings have taught me to

enter into many of those thoughts and feelings. Will you forgive me the presumption of offering you a book which at least acknowledges them and does them homage?

"As the hopes which I have expressed in this volume are more likely to be fulfilled to our children than to ourselves, I might perhaps ask you to accept it as a present to one of your name, in whom you have given me a very sacred interest. Many years, I trust, will elapse before he knows that there are any controversies in the world into which he has entered. Would to God that in a few more he may find that they have ceased! At all events, if he should ever look into these Essays they may tell him what meaning some of the former generation attached to words which will be familiar and dear to his generation, and to those that follow his,—how there were some who longed that the bells of our churches might indeed

> 'Ring out the darkness of the land,
> Ring in the Christ that is to be!'

"Believe me, my dear sir,
"Yours very truly and gratefully,
"F. D. MAURICE."

Tennyson spoke at once with no uncertain sound:

> "Should all our churchmen foam in spite
> At you, so careful of the right,
> Yet one lay-hearth would give you welcome
> (Take it and come) to the Isle of Wight;
> .   .   .   .   .

" Where, far from noise and smoke of town,
  I watch the twilight falling brown
    All round a careless-order'd garden,
  Close to the ridge ot a noble down.

" You 'll have no scandal while you dine,
  But honest talk and wholesome wine,
    And only hear the magpie gossip
  Garrulous under a roof of pine ;

" For groves of pine on either hand,
  To break the blast of winter stand ;
    And further on, the hoary Channel
  Tumbles a billow on chalk and sand."

In his life at Farringford, Tennyson seems to have been uniformly simple and generous. Many people visited him there,—men of science, painters, writers, and statesmen : Professor Tyndall, Professor Jebb, Jowett, Woolner, Millais, Longfellow, Sir John Simeon, Dean Bradley, and Garibaldi to plant the famous little tree. There is a story of the Prince of Wales calling upon him and finding him absent, and over-awing the maid with the simple remark, " Say the Prince of Wales called " ; and there are other stories involving high personages and clever talkers, so that one gains a general impression of " good company " at Farringford ; but the more charming and revealing anecdotes are those that show the childlike nature of the great, rugged " Son of Anak," who went about, as a little boy said of him, " making poets for the Queen under the stars." He seems not always to have been amiable, and somewhat to have cherished the picturesque gloom so fascinating to his younger admirers. Sir Henry Taylor wrote that he came to call one morning "in an agreeable mood though it *was* in the morning. His agreeable moods are generally in the evening." And he added a comment on his independence of wind and weather : "Mrs. Cameron says that in one of the great storms of this year he walked all along the coast to The Needles, which is six miles off. With all his shattered nerves and uneasy gloom, he seems to have some sorts of strength and hardihood. There is a great deal in him that is like ——. But his tenderness is more genuine, as well as his simplicity ; and he has no hostilities, and is never active as against people. He only grumbles."

Mrs. Taylor wrote of going to see the Tennysons, and of being invited up to the poet's attic rooms :

"When I had said all I had to say about the beauty of his views (not quite enough to satisfy him, though, for I liked one view—*his own*—much the best, and he growled out, 'How very odd you are! One view is just as fine as the other.'), he took me all over his place, which is really very lovely, and he was very kind and cordial, though full of complaints of the wickedness of the islanders, who look at him and pick his cowslips ; cordial to the girls, too, though he heard me encourage them to fill their basket from his woods."

A pleasanter glimpse of him is gained from an account in the *Spectator* of his visit to an old lady living near Grasmere, where he seems to have been an ideal guest : "At the old-fashioned family dinner he was interested by the four generations about the long table, noticing especially one little boy of three : 'There is a *glory* about that child'; and the homely fare seemed to please him greatly, his face quite lighting up at the sight of a dish of beans and bacon, the like of which he had not seen of late, and wished he saw oftener. On taking leave he said, 'I've had a very jolly day,' and altogether the union of enthusiasm and simplicity struck us as another instance of what we had long known in Wordsworth."

Edith Nicholl, in *St. Nicholas*, gives an attractive sketch of him as he appeared to a little girl who was "thwee" the day that he was forty-five, and who was celebrating her birthday on top of a haystack when he came to call. In the *Memoir* are anecdotes in any number, amusing and tender, illustrating his genuineness and want of elaboration, qualities that seem not to belong to the author of the poems, but that certainly belonged to the man. People have grown to think of him as holding himself aloof and surrounding himself with visions of the Round Table ; but, in reality, he was very eager over the present day and the living person. It is one of the paradoxes of truth that he should have been so fond of the luxury of cultivated existence, and so natural and plain and almost Bohemian, it would seem, in himself. It delights one's fancy, for balance, to find him rejoicing in a diet of corned beef and potatoes, and teasing Mrs. Cameron by meddling with

Tennyson's Lane, Farringford.

her poisonous toys. In his personal appearance he was noticeably careless—"no dandy," as Emerson truly said. When the University of Oxford, in 1855, conferred upon him the degree of D.C.L., and he came in sight in his robes with his customary air of negligence, the gallery testified its appreciation of his somewhat dishevelled look by the tender inquiry: "*Did* your mother wake and call you early, Alfred dear ?" But ridicule was not the only emotion called forth by the tall figure, so obviously out of place in the ceremonious atmosphere :

"We ourselves," wrote Mr. Gladstone, editorially, "with some thousands of other spectators, saw him receive, in that noble structure of Wren, the theatre of Oxford, the decoration of D.C.L., which we perceive he always wears on his title-page. Among his colleagues in the honour were Sir De Lacy Evans and Sir John Burgoyne, fresh from the stirring exploits of the Crimea ; but even patriotism, at the fever heat of war, could not command a more fervent enthusiasm for the old and gallant soldiers than was evoked by the presence of Mr. Tennyson."[1]

One of the most interesting features of the Freshwater neighbourhood appears to have been the Cameron home, which stood half-way between Farringford and the sea. Mr. Cameron was "a Benthamite jurist and philosopher of great learning and ability." His wife was the daughter of an Indian civil servant high in office. When they came from India to the

[1] Gladstone's *Gleanings of Past Years.*

10

Isle of Wight they established there a carnival of
harmless eccentricity, beside which Tennyson's mild
vagaries must have seemed the stiffest conventionality.   Zeal was the key-note of Mrs. Cameron's character and her ardour in friendship was sometimes
rather appalling.   " Does Alice ever tell you," wrote
Sir Henry Taylor, " or do I, of how we go on with
Mrs. Cameron, whom you saw the beginning of at
Tunbridge Wells ? how she keeps showering upon
us her ' barbaric pearls and gold '—India shawls,
turquoise bracelets, inlaid portfolios, ivory elephants,
etc.,—and how she writes us letters of six sheets long
all about ourselves, thinking that we can never be
sufficiently sensible of the magnitude and enormity
of our virtue ?   And, for our part, I think that we do
not find flattery, at least this kind (for hers is sincere), to be so disagreeable as people say it is ; and
we like her and grow fond of her."   In pursuing this
particular affection the lady employed unique methods :   " The transference of her personal effects is
going on day after day," continued Sir Henry, " and
I think that shortly Cameron will find himself left
with nothing but his real property."   One of the
gifts was an Indian shawl of much value which was
accepted at the point of the sword by Mrs. Taylor,
and afterwards returned.   After a time Mrs. Taylor
had occasion to visit a hospital at Putney, and found
there " a very expensive piece of mechanism in the
form of a sofa " inscribed with her own name.   Mrs.
Cameron had sold the shawl and had thus used the

proceeds. The result of all this startling fervour was at last satisfactory, and in 1850 Sir Henry described the final yielding :

" The Camerons have grown to be a great deal to us in our daily life—more than one would have thought possible in the course of a year's intercourse arising out of an accidental meeting. Mrs. Cameron has driven herself home to us by a power of loving which I have never seen exceeded, and an equal determination to be beloved. On meeting with some difficulty last winter she told Alice that before the year was over she would love her like a sister. She pursued her object through many trials, wholly regardless of the world's ways, putting pride out of the question ; and what she said has come to pass, and more ; we all love her, Alice, I, Aubrey de Vere, Lady Monteagle—and even Lord Monteagle, who likes eccentricity in no other form, likes her."

The house at Freshwater had been bought on a sudden impulse from an old sailor who sold two houses to his impetuous customers ; and the place was called *Dimbola*, after a Ceylon estate belonging to the Camerons. Here Mrs. Cameron began her famous photographing, turning her coal-house into her dark room, and her fowl-house into her studio, the society of hens and chickens being " soon changed into that of prophets, painters, and lovely maidens." She is reported as saying of the persons she invited to sit for her that she only took " the young, the fair, and the famous," and she seems very nearly if not

entirely to have made her words good. Remarkable
men and women, the notables of the century, lent
themselves to her bewitchery, and she succeeded in
working them up to a state approaching her own enthusiasm. Mrs. Ritchie remembers a procession of
young men, carrying foot-pans full of photographs
by moonlight across the garden : " They were strange
young men from Oxford who had only called by
chance, and for the first time ; they are now grave
and reverend signors, making speeches in Parliament,
directing fleets, armies, and elections ; also never
were pans of photographs more carefully carried by
moonlight."

The entire family were original and unconventional
in their ways : Mrs. Cameron and her sisters designed
their own gowns, for one thing, and to see one of
them " float into a room with sweeping robes and
falling folds was almost an event in itself, and not to
be forgotten." Whatever their hands found to do
they did it with their might, and the Laodicean offence was unknown to them. Mrs. Ritchie tells the
story of one of Sir Henry Taylor's visits to Dimbola
after an illness. An eastern room was ready for him,
and of course it missed the afternoon sunlight. Mrs.
Cameron went into it the day before he arrived, decided that another window was necessary to his
comfort, and when the hour of arrival came the window was ready, with the afternoon sun glinting
through the white muslin curtain which had been
hung just as the carriage drove up. It is not surpris-

ing that Sir Henry felt himself at home in so hospitable an atmosphere, and described the manner of life among the Camerons with zest. The house, he said, was one to which " everybody resorted at pleasure, and in which no man, woman, or child was ever known to be unwelcome.

" Conventionalities had no place in it ; and though Cameron was more of a scholar and philosopher than a country gentleman, the house might easily have been mistaken for that of the old English squire who is said to have received his guests with the announcement, kind though imperious, ' This is Liberty Hall, and if everybody does not do as he likes here, by God I 'll make him ! '

"One day, I remember, a lady and gentleman and their daughter came to luncheon, and Mrs. Cameron, wishing to introduce them to me, took the liberty of asking them what were their names. She had met them in the steamboat when crossing from Lymington to Yarmouth the day before, and had invited them without knowing anything about them. Another day she met a tourist on the cliffs without a hat ; and being asked what had become of it, he said it had been blown into the sea. Whereupon she told him he must not go about with no hat to his head, and he must call at her house and she would find him one. The attractions of the house, as well as the easy access to it, soon became known far and wide, and it swarmed with guests. Cameron himself, agreeable as he was in society and much more than agreeable, was not particularly fond of it. Nevertheless, he seemed quite content that the house should be always full, and when he preferred seclusion he went to bed."

Mr. O'Connor, in his *Century* article, speaks of the friendship between Mr. Cameron and Tennyson, and also of the bright daring of Mrs. Cameron's intercourse with the poet. He tells the story of her bringing some strangers who had been denied admission to the Tennyson house, boldly into his presence with the remark, "Alfred, these are strangers from overseas come to see a lion, and behold! a bear."

Many of the illustrations for this book are reproductions of Mrs. Cameron's photographs, and Tennyson's portraits are not the least successful. After Mr. Fields, the publisher, had visited Farringford she sent him some prints with this characteristic message :

"Mr. and Mrs. Tennyson have spoken with pleasure of your visit, and I can entirely understand the eternal delight it is to you to have dwelt with them in their dear home. Only in this way can one fully estimate either his or her most beautiful and endearing qualities. His immortal powers, of course, are conveyed in his books, but very few come to a perfect and real appreciation of him, who have not seen him in the intimacy of private life. . . . You will see how perfect and valuable these impressions are, and I delight in making a gift of them to those whom I know to be so worthy of the gift as you are."

CHAPTER VIII.

"MAUD" AND THE PRE-RAPHAELITE ILLUS-
TRATIONS.

AS a mere matter of chance, it is odd that a study of insanity should have been the first fruit of calm Farringford. *Maud* was conceived in the lovely garden when the outer world was full of war, and the spirit of the garden and the spirit of the outer world each entered into the poem. It is another story in verse, violent and morbid, where *The Princess* is joyous and wholesome. Madness has a certain stimulating attraction for poets, and Tennyson, though of balanced mind and sane, was not exempt. He chose to speak in the person of his hero, who, like Shelley's maniac, seems hurt

"Even as a man with his peculiar wrong
To hear but of the oppression of the strong."

A young man, with the taint in his blood, the hero lives alone in a little village, brooding over the suspected villainy that drove his father to ruin and suicide. Already he is "a nerve o'er which do creep the else-unfelt oppressions of this earth,"[1] and asks with impatience :

> "Why do they prate of the blessings of Peace? we have made
>   them a curse,
>   Pickpockets, each hand lusting for all that is not its own ;
> And lust of gain, in the spirit of Cain, is it better or worse
>   Than the heart of the citizen hissing in war on his own
>   hearthstone?"

Maud then dawns like a cool May morning on the scene, and although most of all he would "flee from the cruel madness of love," he first endures and then embraces the charming vision, and his ecstasy of pessimism changes to an ecstasy of adoration. His love is returned, and the lovers meet in the street, by the church, in the garden, and among the shining fields. Unfortunately Maud has a brother, whom the hero felicitously describes as "that dandy-despot,"

> "That jewell'd mass of millinery,
>   That oil'd and curl'd Assyrian Bull
>   Smelling of musk and of insolence,"

who,

> "Leisurely tapping a glossy boot
>   And curving a contumelious lip,"

gorgonises the lover from head to foot

> "With a stony British stare."

The situation is complicated by the fact that Maud's father is the man whom the hero suspects of bad faith toward his own father ; and in the brother he sees the old man's qualities repeated, while

[1] Shelley's *Julian and Maddalo*.

" Maud to him is nothing akin :
  Some peculiar mystic grace
  Made her only the child of her mother,
  And heap'd the whole inherited sin
  On that huge scapegoat of the race,
  All, all upon the brother."

A quarrel arises between the " huge scapegoat "
and the hero, then a duel, and the brother falls. Then,
pure grovelling madness, incarceration, and finally
the singular cruelty of recovery after Maud is dead,
an awakening to higher aims and the better mind.

Looking at the plot alone, the impression of melodrama is decided, but so might it be with *Hamlet*,
and Tennyson has called his *Maud* " a little *Hamlet*." The real test of the poem is the power it has
to penetrate the mind, and its effect upon the imagination. As a psychological study of insanity, we
learn from the *Memoir*[1] that one of the best-known
doctors for the insane has considered a part of it the
most faithful representation since Shakespeare. The
fluctuating moods, the self-absorption and continual
suspicion, are carefully rendered. The passion of
love comes in the form of rapture, overwhelming and
exuberant ; the song in the garden has grown to be
the very symbol of amorous ardour ; and is inge-
niously placed immediately before the quarrel gen-
erated while the brain is still hot.

There are elements for a psychological drama as
great as that of which Hamlet was the hero ; why,
then, is it that no reader could fancy himself Hamlet

[1] Hallam Tennyson's *Alfred, Lord Tennyson*.

without a sense of mental aggrandisement, or fancy himself Maud's lover without a sense of belittlement and silliness ?   It is merely that Tennyson could not, or did not, conceive a noble intelligence outside the bounds of order and law.   Hamlet in his madness utters philosophy so vast and so unfamiliar that he seems beside himself indeed, contemplating himself and life with an absolute and critical vision.   His malady lifts him to another sphere, his unearthly insight and ironical reflection seem products of a mind raised to the nth power.   His comprehension of all the various parts of thought is at the root of his indecision.   The hero of *Maud*, on the contrary, discovers a rather low intelligence.   There is very little fine frenzy in his complaint ; he is neurotic, irritable, and whimpering.   It is easy to pity him, but the sense of illimitable tragedy is wanting, since there is no indication that in the best of health he would have been other than an ineffectual, gelatinous sort of person.   And in his calamity he justly describes himself as

> " —— splenetic, personal, base,
> A wounded thing with a rancorous cry."

Could we for a moment imagine him uttering, in whatever pride of sanity or eloquence of delirium, words so magnificently contemptuous of human littleness as these :

> " Forgive me this my virtue ;
> For in the fatness of these pursy times
> Virtue itself of vice must pardon beg,
> Yea, curb and woo for leave to do him good ? "

To prove that *Maud* is not *Hamlet* is a tolerably simple task, but it can hardly be a dismissal. The poem contains many great and obvious beauties and many technical charms not so readily discoverable by the lay reader. What Ruskin called "the pathetic fallacy" is particularly in evidence, and not even a Ruskinian should object to it as the outcome of sleepless mania. It is one of the unenviable privileges of madness to read its own intoxication into nature and man, so the reader may as well seize the opportunity to enjoy with a clear conscience the whispering lily and listening larkspur, the rose "awake all night for your sake," and the

> "Innumerable, pitiless, passionless eyes"

of the stars in "iron skies." And if in meekness we accept this attitude toward Nature, we shall be rewarded by very delightful glimpses of her multitudinous phenomena. The pink-lined English daisy bends to show the path that Maud has followed,

> "For her feet have touch'd the meadows and left the daisies rosy";

the "madden'd beach dragg'd down by the wave" screams as the water grates on its pebbles, and in the bland and bountiful season

> "A million emeralds break from the ruby-budded lime";

the "dry-tongued laurels" imitate a light step with their "pattering talk," and the dark cedar sighs for Lebanon. For the exact mind there is also much of

the charm of accuracy in these allusions.   Once in
Notes and Queries the line,

"The May-fly is torn by the swallow, the sparrow spear'd by
    the shrike,"

was called into question by a correspondent who
thought the butcher-bird flew at nothing larger than
beetles and flies.   A cloud of witnesses at once arose
to prove Tennyson right, giving instances of small
birds having been attacked by the shrike.   The cap-
tious correspondent declined to be convinced by anything less than the precise case of a sparrow victimised
by a shrike, and such an instance was finally produced.   Undoubtedly, Tennyson had himself seen
just such a tragedy as he described.   This precision
of statement occasionally gives way when terms of
music are involved, for in spite of the musical quality
of Tennyson's verse, he seems to have had no technical knowledge of the art.   Mr. Krehbiel demands the
explanation of an orchestra consisting of a "flute,
violin, and bassoon," and inquires with mild special-
istic scorn what the poet means when he says,

" All night has the casement jessamine stirr'd
    To the dancers dancing in tune ? "

"Unless the dancers who wearied Maud were provided with even a more extraordinary instrumental
outfit than the Old Lady of Banbury Cross, how
could they have danced 'in tune'?" he asks.[1]

The delicate traits of Tennyson's poetry are neces-

[1] Krehbiel's *How to Listen to Music.*

sarily puzzling to a translator into a foreign tongue.
M. Henri Fauvel has put *Maud* into French, and
the London *Spectator*, though regarding the result as
a "masterpiece" of translation, quotes some passages
in which the sympathetic Frenchman was clearly
baffled.

Where the English reads,

" And lust of gain, in the spirit of Cain, is it better or worse
Than the heart of the citizen hissing in war on his own hearth-
stone ? "

the French gives,

"Et ceux qui, dans l'esprit de Caïn ont le désir du gain,
valent-ils mieux ou moins que le cœur du citoyen qui gerroie
en sifflant sur son propre foyer."

Where the hero trusts that if an enemy's fleet

"——came yonder round by the hill,"

the "smooth-faced, snub-nosed rogue" would

"——strike if he could, were it but with his cheating yard
wand, home,"

M. Fauvel, who may have had some haunting
memory of "Strike for your altars and your fires,"
puts it,

"Et frapperait s'il le pouvait, fût ce même avec son aune fri-
ponne pour défendre son toit."

This, the *Spectator*, in the spirit of one who hopes
himself to be forgiven, considers "a pardonable mistake." The rendering

" Le spectre de l'être que je connais bien,"

for

> " The ghastly Wraith of one that I know."

is also pardonable, and almost as infelicitous as Scherer's " quand Lucy a terminé son existence " for Wordsworth's " when Lucy ceased to be."

In spite, however, of these and other less important lapses, the *Spectator* assures its readers that " for all students who have any of the poetic element in them, this work will have a special fascination, so beautiful is the wording, so choice and so elegant are M. Fauvel's expressions, so light and delicate his hand in dealing with those rare beauties that abound in *Maud* and which are unsullied by his rendering."

When *Maud* first appeared it was decidedly without honour in its own country. The hero's predilection for war made him numerous enemies, and the public insisted upon regarding the poem as the expression of Tennyson's own sentiments in obedience to what we may call the biographical fallacy in the mind of the average critic. Even Mr. Gladstone dwelt upon the ethical and social significance of the hero's rage against the existing order of evil, quite overlooking the " purple patches " of poetic beauty. Quoting the passage,

> " When a Mammonite mother kills her babe for a burial fee,
>   And Timour-Mammon grins on a pile of children's bones,
>   Is it peace or war? better, war! loud war by land and by sea,
>   War with a thousand battles and shaking a hundred thrones,"

he comments upon it in a tone that will be used by a
certain class of thinkers so long as wars are made.

" War, indeed," he says, " has the property of
exciting much generous and noble feeling on a large
scale ; but with this special recommendation, it has,
in its modern forms especially, peculiar and unequalled
evils.   As it has a wider sweep of desolating power
than the rest, so it has the peculiar quality that it is
more susceptible of being decked in gaudy trappings,
and of fascinating the imagination of those whose
proud and angry passions it inflames.   But it is on
this very account a perilous delusion to teach that
war is a cure for moral evil in any other sense than
as the sister tribulations are.   The eulogies of the
frantic hero in *Maud*, however, deviate into grosser
folly.. It is natural that such vagaries should over-
look the fixed laws of Providence.   Under these
laws the mass of mankind is composed of men, women, and children who can but just ward off hunger,
cold, and nakedness ; whose whole ideas of Mammon-
worship are comprised in the search for their daily
food, clothing, shelter, fuel ; whom any casualty
reduces to positive want ; and whose already low estate is yet lowered and ground down, when ' the
blood-red blossom of war flames with its heart of
fire.'   But what is a little strange is, that war should
be recommended as a specific for the particular evil
of Mammon-worship. . . .   There is no incentive
to Mammon-worship so remarkable as that which it
affords.   The political economy of war is now one of

its most commanding aspects. Every farthing, with the smallest exceptions conceivable, of the scores or hundreds of millions which a war may cost, goes directly, and very violently, to stimulate production, though it is intended ultimately for waste or for destruction. Even apart from the fact that war suspends, *ipso facto*, every rule of public thrift, and tends to sap honesty itself in the use of the public treasure for which it makes such unbounded calls, it therefore is the greatest feeder of that lust of gold which we are told is the essence of commerce, though we had hoped it was only its occasional besetting sin. It is, however, more than this ; for the regular commerce of peace is tameness itself compared with the gambling spirit which war, through the rapid shiftings and high prices which it brings, always introduces into trade. In its moral operation it more resembles, perhaps, the finding of a new gold-field than anything else." [1] And considerably more to much the same effect.

Reading this suggests Symond's description of the two men, Gladstone and Tennyson, as he saw them together at Woolner's house : Gladstone more or less a man of the world, Tennyson " a child," and " Gladstone treated him as a child." But Gladstone certainly misread the intention of *Maud*, and long afterward published a note to the criticism as it appeared in the *Gleanings*, confessing that his frame of mind at the time was dislocated by the war spirit

[1] Gladstone's *Gleanings from Past Years.*

abroad, and concluding what Tennyson himself considered the recantation of "a noble-minded man"
with the words, "Even as regards the passages devoted to war-frenzy, equity should have reminded me
of the fine lines in the latter portion of X. 3 (Part I.),
and of the emphatic words, V. 11 (Part II.),

> 'I swear to you lawful and lawless war
> Are scarcely even akin.'"

The recantation was made after hearing Tennyson read Maud aloud, and no one who has put
that experience upon record seems to have escaped
its peculiar fascination. In one of her letters, Mrs.
Browning gives a very characteristic account of it.

"One of the pleasantest things which has happened to us here," she says, "is the coming down on
us of the Laureate, who, being in London for three or
four days from the Isle of Wight, spent two of them
with us, dined with us, smoked with us, opened his
heart to us (and the second bottle of port), and ended
by reading Maud through from end to end, and going
away at half past two in the morning. If I had had
a heart to spare, certainly he would have won mine.
He is captivating with his frankness, confidingness,
and unexampled naïveté! Think of his stopping in
Maud every now and then—'There's a wonderful
touch! That's very tender. How beautiful that is!'
Yes, and it was wonderful, tender, beautiful, and he
read exquisitely in a voice like an organ, rather music
than speech." One little detail with a certain inter-

est is contributed by a writer in *Notes and Queries*, who remembers that Tennyson, in reading the line,

    " And thunder'd up into Heaven the Christless code,"

made the *i* in " Christless " short.

Mrs. Browning's estimate of *Maud* was more favourable than one might have expected.

" The winding up," she writes to Mrs. Jameson, " is magnificent, full of power, and there are beautiful thrilling bits before you get so far. Still there is an appearance of labour in the early part ; the language is rather encrusted by skill than spontaneously blossoming, and the rhythm is not always happy. The poet seems to aim at more breadth and freedom, which he attains, but at the expense of his characteristic delicious music. People in general appear very unfavourably impressed by this poem, *very unjustly*, Robert and I think. On some points it is even an advance. The sale is great, *nearly five thousand copies already*." This was in August, 1855.

Tennyson himself was very fond of his *Maud*, continually choosing it to read aloud to his favoured visitors ; and, as prejudices fled before the reading as chaff before the wind, there must have been a species of magic in his sympathetic rendering of his own work. His favourite among the published criticisms was Dr. Mann's little book called " *Maud* " *Vindicated*, in which the intention of the poem is discerned, and the position of the unfriendly critics assailed.

It was while Tennyson was reading *Maud* to
the Brownings that Rossetti made the well-known
thumbnail sketch of him, as he sat curled up on the
sofa, chin pushed forward, hair in disorder, one hand
gripping his foot, and the other holding open the
recently published volume.   The sketch has wonderful freedom and vigour, and brings to mind the event
of 1857 which to some few people seems as important as the appearance of *Maud :* the publication of
Moxon's illustrated quarto edition of the *Poems*, with
Rossetti, Millais, and Holman Hunt on the staff of
illustrators.   To get an idea of the reception of this
inexpressibly charming volume by the conventional
art critic of the time, we need only glance at this
naïve notice in the *Art Journal* for 1857 :

"The peculiarity of Tennyson's style of writing,
imaginative and highly coloured, but frequently open
to the charge of affectation, was perhaps, in some degree, a justifiable reason for enlisting the services of
the Pre-Raffaellite school of artists in the work of
illustration, yet we are much inclined to doubt
whether their aid will be generally considered to
have given much additional value to the volume.
The quaintness of thought and expression that is
found in the verse needed not necessarily to be followed by quaintness of pictorial design.   The artist
may work harmoniously with the poet without any
participation in the peculiarities of the latter ; when
these peculiarities have a constrained or affected
tendency ; he must work from, as well as up to, his

model ; but then we look for his own ideas of the subject before him, expressed in the true language of pictorial art, and not in that of any particular school or creed.   Tennyson's heroes and heroines are not all men and women of the mediæval ages : but even when they belong to it, we would not have them drawn strictly after the fashion of the art of that period."   After briefly noticing Mulready, Maclise, Stanfield, Creswick, and Horsley, the reviewer continues with bland condescension and kind expostulation :

"We now come to the Pre-Raffaellite school of artists, of which Millais claims the first notice as the largest contributor, eighteen being the number of designs to which his name is affixed : the majority of these show far less of the peculiarities of the artist than might be expected from his constancy to his adopted style ; and among them are a few to which no one, we imagine, would take objection, and which are fine in conception and feeling, and by no means deficient in pictorial beauty : [Praise !] such qualities will generally be acknowledged in the second illustration of the poem 'A Dream of Fair Women,' representing Queen Eleanor,

> ' Who kneeling, with one arm about her king,
>   Drew forth the poison with her balmy breath,
>   Sweet as new buds in Spring,'

in the frontispiece to 'The Talking Oak,' and in that to 'Lord of Burleigh.'   Holman Hunt has furnished seven subjects for the volume: most graceful and poetical is the Mussulman sailing down the Tigris, one of two designs illustrating the 'Recollections of the Arabian Nights'; the frontispiece to 'The Lady of Shalott" is a strange fancy that none but an artist of genius could have invented, but the lady is not drawn after the Pre-Raffaellite fashion. Five subjects are from the pencil of Rossetti: with the exception of *Sir Galahad,* a vigorous and effective study, but, so far as we can make it out, without the slightest reference to any descriptive line in the poem it professes to illustrate, these designs are beyond the pale of criticism ; if Millais and Hunt have shown something like an inclination to abjure their artistic creed, Rossetti seems to revel in its wildest extravagances : can he suppose that such art as he here exhibits can be admired ? Is it not more calculated to provoke ridicule, or, if not ridicule, pity, for one who can so misapply his talents ?

" It is fortunate for the engravers, Messrs. Dalziel, T. Williams, W. J. Linton, Green, and Thompson, that they are not responsible for anything but what has been placed in their hands to engrave ; that they have had to do they have done with their accustomed skill ; we could only wish that subjects more worthy of their time and labour than some we could point out had been entrusted to them. However, the Pre-Raffaelite school has many admirers, and Tennyson has more, so there need be little apprehension of this volume not finding a home in many households."

There is a certain comforting sense of justice in

reproducing this delectable criticism at a moment when so few households acquainted with what is most to be prized in art would fail to give welcome to this volume, burdened by designs " beyond the pale of criticism " !

An admirable statement of the way in which competent critics now regard the volume and the illustrators is found in Mr. Layard's interesting and suggestive book, *Tennyson and his Pre-Raphaelite Illustrators.*

" Millais' illustrations," he says, " are as immediately and directly inspired by the poet as Rossetti's are not. Except in one amusing instance, where the former has tried to emulate his brother ' P. R.'s,' Millais and Tennyson have gone hand in hand. Hunt and Rossetti have sometimes sprung ahead ; sometimes, it is true, they have fallen behind. So that, judged by the ethics of book-illustrating, Millais most undoubtedly bears the palm. To put it broadly, Millais has realised, Holman Hunt has idealised, and Rossetti has sublimated, or transcendentalised, the subjects which they have respectively illustrated. The two latter have, in greater or less degree, introduced subtleties which Tennyson never dreamed of. Rossetti, indeed, has done more. He has not hesitated to *contradict* the text. Trollope, writing upon the illustrations to his novels, has said : ' An artist will frequently dislike to subordinate his ideas to those of an author.' And I think it will be evident to the student of these illustrations that Rossetti's main object has not been to

' promote the views of ' the poet, but that he has un-
hesitatingly attempted to overpower the text, and in
some cases successfully, by the brilliancy of his own
imagination. This will not be surprising to those
who were acquainted with the artist's temperament,
and, after all, it is easy to forgive him in view of the
splendid, albeit unorthodox achievement. Nor can
it be doubted that the picture-lover pure and simple
will be thrilled to the finest fibre of his nature by
Rossetti's divergences, rather than by the rhythmic
harmonies of Millais ; but, in the opinion of the well-
balanced mind, that looks for the lawful wedding of
pen and pencil, the latter unquestionably surpasses
his rivals.

"There is, however, one general characteristic
common to the work of this great brotherhood upon
which I should like to dwell for a moment, and which
cannot be, in these days of scamped and hurried
work, running riot under the garb of ' impressionism,'
too often and too strongly insisted upon. I mean
the finish, the wealth of detail, the conscientious
completeness which, although one of them at least
was working for his immediate bread-and-butter, and
one at least was eaten up with the impatience of
genius, distinguish their work."

The excellence of this criticism will be sufficiently
apparent to those so fortunate as to own the illustrated edition. The picture that has roused the most
widely different opinions is, perhaps, the *St. Cecily*,
built upon the four lines :

> " In a clear-wall'd city on the sea,
>   Near gilded organ-pipes, her hair
> Wound with white roses, slept St. Cecily ;
>   An angel look'd at her."

" Who but an artist of the utmost originality," Mr.
Layard demands, " could have begotten a design of
such apparently alien significance ? " Cecily is on
her knees before an organ, her hands limply resting
on the keys. Her head is bent back, and her hair,
the wonderful, crinkling hair of Rossetti's women,
streams about her. The angel who embraces her
is wrapped in a starry mantle. His hair is like that
of an Italian model, tumbling in a shock about his
head. Folded wings, or, according to Mr. Layard
and Mr. Hunt, " winglike somethings," are at his
back, with no indication of where they belong or
whether they belong at all. On the background are
little towers and cannon and little men busily toiling.
A miniature tree grows in a round court ; there are
ships and water beyond the city walls. A dial is
back of the organ, and down in a corner of the fore-
ground a soldier with a spear is munching an apple.
A white dove is flying out of the darkness of what
apparently is a tomb. No one could imagine more
intricacy or less conventionality. To anyone familiar
with Rossetti's painting the whole flashes at once into
colour ; the mantle is blue, with golden stars, red
gleaming hair pours over it, unexpected patches of
green and yellow come out against the grey walls.
Mr. Layard finds the whole conception highly incon-

ST. CECILY

From a drawing by Dante Gabriel Rossetti

gruous with the spirit of the poem ; especially does
he consider the angel " a great voluptuous human
being, not merely kissing (a sufficient incongruity in
itself) but seemingly munching the fair face of the
lovely martyr," something very like a grim joke on
the part of Rossetti, with the possible explanation
that the artist's intention was to draw, not an angel,
but a man masquerading as an angel.

He says that Mr. Fairfax Murray, on the other
hand, regards the picture as a serious attempt at illustration, and " believes that the hands of the angel
are wrapped in the cloak by way of emphasising his
reverence for the saintly lady." Both critics assume
that the angel's mouth is " wide open," Mr. Layard
with the idea in his mind of " munching " kisses, and
Mr. Murray ascribing it to a mistake on the part of
the engraver.

But the angel's mouth, if one looks a little closely,
is not open at all ; the face from the nose down seems
to be hidden by Cecily's head, " wound with white
roses," and one of the white roses makes a queer
accent on the angel's cheek which, by a lively imagination, may be distorted into a wide-stretched under
lip. If it were an under lip, as Mr. Layard evidently
thinks it is, the lovely outline of Cecily's brow would
be actually bitten off instead of curving back under
the roses to be lost in the heavy hair. This it is impossible to suppose when one remembers Rossetti's
passion for that particular exquisite line. Surely not
even the desire for a grim joke would have led him

to sacrifice it to pure ugliness. The fact that it is not emphasised, but interrupted by the spotty whiteness of the rose, is probably due to careless engraving, as Mr. Murray suggested.

For the rest, Mr. Layard seems somewhat to have lost sight of the idea of tapestry in finding the illustration so wide of Tennyson's mark. When we consider that the palace was full of rooms,

> "——fit for every mood
> And change of my still soul,"

and that the design Rossetti undertook was supposed to be on an arras—some old-fashioned bit of tapestry, wrought in silk—we may see it a little differently. The curious background crowded with objects all out of perspective, the mediæval figures, the lack of anything like atmospheric truth—who has not observed something like it on the tapestries conserved by museums? The angel and Cecily, however, are not to be ascribed to any influence but that of Rossetti's own mind, and none could be more incomprehensible.

In Millais's famous drawing of little St. Agnes in her night-robe, holding a candle that shines more dimly than the light sky and moonlit snow, there is no such complication. The young, exalted face, and slim form in the straight-hanging gown among the bare surroundings, are perfectly expressive of Tennyson's poem. Even the white robes are dark

> "To yonder shining ground,"

as the "taper's earthly spark" is pale to the brightness shed by

"——yonder argent round."

Mr. Layard reproduces an unpublished water-colour drawing of the same subject by Mrs. Rossetti, in which we see a little what the treatment might have been under the inspiration of Rossetti's mysticism. There is slight difference in the detail ; the girl in white is almost equally severe, but Millais's is the German and Mrs. Rossetti's the Italian rendering. A single stanza of a German translation of "St. Agnes' Eve"[1] will show the kinship of Tennyson's thought to the German thought on such a theme as this, as well as the difference in the two styles of expression :

II.

" Wie schmutzig grau mein weiss Gewand
Zu jenem hellen Grund ;
Wie dieser Kerze ird'scher Brand,
Zu jenem Silberrund ;
So tritt zum Lamm die Seele hin,
Und so zu Dir mein Geist ;
So auch im ird'schen Haus ich bin,
Zu dem, was Du verheisst.
Thu' auf den Himmel, Herr ! und fern
Durch alles Sternlicht heiss
Mich, Deine Braut, gehn wie ein Stern
In Kleidern rein und weiss."

This might easily be a German original, the meta-

[1] Made by Professor Delius, of Bonn, in *Notes and Queries*.

phors lend themselves so readily to a simple and childlike translation ; for example :

" In Kleidern rein und weiss "—

could anything be more representative of the German idea of purity and fitness than those clean, white clothes ? And could any other than Millais have made so pure and neat a maiden to match the sentiment of the poem ?

The drawing by Holman Hunt of *The Lady of Shalott* is a fair example of the third member of the interesting trio. It would be hard to describe the effect of gloom and fatality given by the droop of the Lady's figure tangled in the loosened web, and the down-sinking of the beautiful, noble head against the strong curve of the shoulder. It would be impossible to convey in words the way in which the subtle drapery is filled and modelled by the firm, sweet figure. Everyone owning the picture who deserves to own it knows that he has a possession not to be duplicated or challenged by this generation of illustrators, although the dawn of Mr. Alexander promises a new joy.

Concerning the picture of *The Lady of Shalott*, Mr. Layard quotes a pertinent story :

" ' My dear Hunt,' said Tennyson, when he first saw this illustration, ' I never said that the young woman's hair was flying all over the shop.'

" ' No,' said Hunt ; ' but you never said it wasn't,' and after a little the poet came to be wholly

From W. Holman Hunt to his good Wife Edith Marion. 1881

THE LADY OF SHALOTT

From the drawing by W. Holman Hunt, as it appeared on
the wood-block before cutting.

reconciled to it. Not so easily did he allow himself to be pacified, however, when he saw the long flight of steps which King Cophetua descends to meet and greet the Beggar Maid, on p. 359.

" ' I never said,' he complained, ' that there were a lot of steps; I only meant one or two.'

" ' But,' said Hunt, ' the old ballad says there was a flight of them.'

" ' I dare say it does,' remonstrated Tennyson; ' but I never said I got it from the old ballad.'

" ' Well, but,' retorted Hunt, ' the flight of steps does n't contradict your account; you merely say : '' In robe and crown the King stept down." '

" But Tennyson would not be appeased, and kept on declaring that he never meant more than two steps at the outside."

There could hardly have been a more appropriate union of poet with illustrator than that of Tennyson with the Pre-Raphaelites. In his attention to symbolic and significant detail, in his determination to slur nothing over, in his inability to leave vague spaces and delicately suggestive borderlands of imagination, in his modernity and liking for archaic subjects, in his sincerity and mannerism, he was himself a Pre-Raphaelite of the Pre-Raphaelites; and the student of the illustrated edition of 1857 has a fine opportunity to trace the various effects of picture upon text and text upon picture, inter-illustrating and inter-illuminating as they are.

On the practical side of the question, it is rather

interesting to learn from Mr. William Rossetti the
methods of at least one of the three artists.   To Rossetti wood-cut designs were "afflictive."   The Pre-
Raphaelites were in the habit of drawing directly on
the block, and Mr. William Rossetti writes that on
August 2, 1856, Rossetti was " at the last gasp of time
with the designs which he had undertaken to produce " for the Tennyson volume.   " He foresaw that,
with a view to working upon the blocks which yet
remained to be done, he would have to fly London
and Moxon, as he could not endure the publisher's
pestering.   I judge that he received £30 per design :
as I find in one of his letters the phrase ' Moxon owes
me £30, as I have done the King Arthur block.'
He preferred Linton as a wood-engraver to the Dal-
ziels ; and was particularly pleased with his second
proof of the Mariana subject.   Another letter—addressed this time to Mr. Moxon—sets forth that the
design of *The Lady of Shalott*, though delayed for
a week, would be soon ready : ' I have drawn it
twice over, for the sake of an alteration, so you see
I do not spare trouble.'   He speaks also of the block
for *Sir Galahad*, and of a second Sir Galahad which
he intended to do without delay ; this intention,
it appears, must have miscarried, for there is not
in the Tennyson volume any second illustration to
the poem in question."[1]

Mr. Layard thinks that Tennyson was quite indifferent about the pictures, in striking contrast to the

[1] W. M. Rossetti's *Memoir of Dante Gabriel Rossetti.*

attitude of many writers toward illustrations of their work. In the *Memoir*, however, Hallam Tennyson says that his father took a great interest, calling on most of the artists "so as to give them his views of what the illustrations ought to be."

Many writers about Tennyson seem to have the idea that he cared little for pictorial art, anyway, but a contributor to *Notes and Queries* speaks of having several pen-and-ink sketches by Tennyson, copies made in his boyhood of Maclise's portraits in *Fraser's Magazine*. "They are very clever and spirited indeed," he says, " and show more than ordinary artistic ability." And Caroline Fox speaks of Holman Hunt's surprise at the "spirited, suggestive little paintings of strange beasts" which Tennyson had "painted on the windows of his summer-house to shut out an ugly view."

CHAPTER IX.

THE "IDYLLS OF THE KING."

WHEN, in 1885, Tennyson introduced "Balin and Balan" into the volume called *Tiresias and Other Poems*, he doubtless felt that he had completed his masterpiece. The scheme that, in 1833, had been heralded by the sweet piping note of "The Lady of Shalott" was now closed, and the material for the final edition of the *Idylls of the King* was all in hand. For more than half a century the "Romance of the Round Table" had been at its work of suggestion in the poet's mind, and he had responded as only an artist of exceptional patience and persistence of purpose could have responded. From the *Memoir* we find that he had in the early years two schemes, between which he was undecided, for his treatment of the Arthurian legends : the epic form, and a "musical masque" in five acts. After 1840 he clung to the epical idea, and called his Arthurian poems "Idylls," possibly with some reference to the Greek εἶδος, shape, or image, for the conventional definition of the word fits them not at all. When, in 1859, the first edition of *Idylls of the*

King was published, Mr. Gladstone, in his review of it, said :

"The Arthurian Romance has every recommendation that should win its way to the homage of a great poet. It is national ; it is Christian. It is also human in the largest and deepest sense ; and, therefore, though highly national, it is universal ; for it rests upon those depths and breadths of our nature, to which all its truly great developments, in all nations, are alike essentially and closely related. The distance is enough for atmosphere, not too much for detail ; enough for romance, not too much for sympathy. A poet of the nineteenth century, the Laureate has in the main appropriated and adopted characters, incidents, and even language, instead of attempting to project them, on a basis of his own, in the region of illimitable fancy. But he has done much more than this. Evidently by reading and by deep meditation, as well as by sheer force of genius, he has penetrated himself, down to the very core of his being, in the representation with which he deals ; and as others, using old materials, have been free to alter them in the sense of vulgarity or licence, so he has claimed and used the right to sever and recombine, to enlarge, retrench, and modify for the purposes at once of a more powerful and elaborate art than his original presents, and of a yet more elevated, or at least of a far more sustained, ethical and Christian strain."[1]

[1] Gladstone's *Gleanings of Past Years.*

Among the later critics, some have endorsed this opinion ; others have complained of the "more elaborate art" and of the attempt to bring the elements of the old fables into relation with new conditions of thought and language ; others still have held that the introduction of a moral or ethical purpose weakened the author's hold upon his characters. One other has thought that "the moral tone of the Arthurian story has been on the whole lowered and degraded by Mr. Tennyson's mode of treatment."[1]

One claim for the *Idylls* must, however, remain always true ; they have awakened in the old story a popular interest which the more classic and duller versions of it by other modern poets failed to arouse, and which might have slept indefinitely had Tennyson not chosen this subject made to his hand. And, as usual, popular interest has been very well satisfied to accept the modern conception without much effort at comparison with the sources. The exigent critics have felt and expressed a vague dissatisfaction with Tennyson's readiness to entrust the precious chief work of fifty years to the hired service of old legends, and perhaps it is this, more than any quarrel with the lovely workmanship, that has led them to assume a somewhat disheartened tone in discussing the merits of the *Idylls*. They have asked themselves whether, if Tennyson had chosen to originate a drama, or a fable, or a long romance, to typify the struggle between good and evil, and the eternal

[1] Swinburne's *Under the Microscope.*

character of the former, he would not have made a
deeper appeal to the real heart of the world.   They
have argued that some pulse would have throbbed,
as in *Maud*, with an actual emotion stronger than is
conveyed by the joys and sorrows of uncontempo-
rary people decked out with the ornaments of contemporary diction ; even though the result had
seemed for a moment a failure, instead of a success
measured by a sale of ten thousand copies the first
week of publication.   Tennyson risked failure of the
obvious sort no more than a skilful painter who
should take an old series of Crucifixions by the great
simple masters, and copy on his own canvas a
group here and a group there, and redraw the muti-
lated human figure of the Christ until it was aca-
demically beautiful, and refine the colour and correct
the lines of the whole.   It would not be a very difficult task for an accomplished painter ; but the new
picture would probably lack that inexpressible beauty
of verity, that air of inherent likeness between the
mind conceiving and the thing conceived, which in
the actual world marks the relation between parents
and children, and makes the bond of adoption seem
fragile and pitiable.   Such art could have neither
youth nor age, nor any immortal vitality.

But the multitude who know very little or nothing
at all of the hero of "Geoffrey's book, or him of Mal-
leor's," or of *Mabinogion*, get a different idea of the
Idylls, which to them are new ground abloom with
the bright flowers of modernity.   And even if Thomas

Malory's splendid old chronicles were given to them
in one hand and Tennyson's *Idylls* in the other, is
there any doubt which they would read, or which
would seem to them their own intellectual possession? Malory might take his little procession of
time-stained kings, and dusty knights, and faded
ladies, back to the book-shelves, while the new public went hand in hand with the new Arthur in his
courtly finery of moral sentiment, and with the new
Guinevere in her sweet, self-conscious posing, along
the smooth highway of the nineteenth century. It is
the same impulse that leads a woman to clothe herself in the silks and laces of the period while the
gowns of her grandmother, of a plainer style, perhaps, and a stouter lining, lie in the chests that preserve and conceal them; it is the instinct that has
produced the double rose, that has given us our
summer fruits at Easter, that has forced nature and
art and science to cater to contemporary taste; it is,
in brief, the genius of modernity, without which to-
day would be as yesterday, that has made Tennyson
for the greater number of his readers the creator as
well as the re-creator of the Arthurian cycle. The
service is the same in kind that Shakespeare rendered
to his generation in immortalising old plots and versions, the difference is merely in manner and degree,
and as yet it is dangerous to venture any generalisa-
tion as to the class of minds that in the future will
accept Tennyson for their intellectual leader, since for
the present it is plain that he has driven with the

wind in draping and ornamenting the archaic simplicity of the ancient legends.

To get a suggestion of the way in which Tennyson's mind has played about its priceless material, we
need only compare certain passages from the *Idylls*
with corresponding passages from Malory's *History*,
and observe the indicative correspondences and de-
partures. We may take a part of "Lancelot and
Elaine," that being the story from which the early
"Lady of Shalott" was extracted, and one of those
in which the original is most closely followed. Beginning with "the great lamentation that the faire
maide of Astolat made when Sir Launcelot should
depart," we find Malory's version[1] very direct and
singularly free from hysterical wording :

" ' My lord sir Launcelot,' " Elaine pleads with
pathetic gentleness and sincerity, " ' now I see that
yee will depart ; faire and curteous knight, have
mercy upon mee, and suffer mee not to die for your
love.' 'What would yee that I did ?' said sir Launcelot. 'I would have you unto my husband,' said
the maide Elaine. 'Faire damosell, I thanke you,'
said sir Launcelot, 'but certainely,' said hee, 'I cast
mee never to bee married.' "

Tennyson's version runs :

" ————then out she brake :
' Going ? and we shall never see you more.
And I must die for want of one bold word.'
' Speak : that I live to hear,' he said, ' is yours.'
Then suddenly and passionately she spoke :

[1] Thomas Wright's edition of the text of 1634.

> ' I have gone mad.   I love you : let me die.'
> ' Ah, sister,' answer'd Lancelot, ' what is this ? '
> And innocently extending her white arms,
> ' Your love,' she said, ' your love—to be your wife.'
> And Lancelot answer'd, ' Had I chosen to wed,
> I had been wedded earlier, sweet Elaine :
> But now there never will be wife of mine.' "

Even while we recognise the delicacy and beauty of his rendering, we can but feel that Tennyson has too much sophisticated this passage.   He has certainly brought it well into the nineteenth century. Malory's Elaine never thought of dying " for want of one bold word " ; her concern was to let Lancelot know her trouble very plainly, and to beseech his favour ; nothing could be more delightfully simple than her reply to his question :   " ' I would have you unto my husband,' said the maide Elaine."   But Tennyson's Elaine is overcome by the thought of her temerity ; she admits that she has gone mad to dare such a confession : " ' I love you : let me die ! ' "   One gets the impression that the avowal and not the love is the dying matter.   The little Elaine of the *History* desired to die only if Lancelot should fail to reciprocate her passion.   After Lancelot had gone, and the letter had been written " like as shee had devised," then " shee prayed her father that shee might bee watched untill shee were dead."   This sad little touch is left out in the *Idyll*, and also the spirited answer to the ghostly father who " bad her leave such thoughts " ; and Elaine begins her final request with a somewhat elaborate prelude :

" ——'O sweet father, tender and true,
Deny me not,' she said—' ye never yet
Denied my fancies—this however strange,
My latest ; lay the letter in my hand
A little ere I die, and close the hand
Upon it ; I shall guard it even in death.
And when the heat is gone from out my heart,
Then take the little bed on which I died
For Lancelot's love, and deck it like the Queen's
For richness, and me also like the Queen
In all I have of rich, and lay me on it.
And let there be prepared a chariot-bier
To take me to the river, and a barge
Be ready on the river, clothed in black.
I go in state to court, to meet the Queen.' "

Save for the introductory sentence, and the fancy about the Queen which seems not quite in the guileless style of the "faire maide," this passage is very close to the original, which runs : " ' And while my body is whole let this letter be put into my right hand, and my hand bound fast with the letter untill that I bee cold, and let me be put in a faire bed with all the richest clothes that I have about me, and so let my bed and all my rich clothes be laide with me in a chariot to the next place where as the Thames is, and there let me be put in a barge, and but one man with me, such as yee trust, to stere me thither, and that my barge be covered with blacke samite over and over.' "

In the later scene also, where the barge arrives before King Arthur and the Queen, with the "faire gentlewoman" lying "as though shee had smiled," the *History* is followed very closely as to incident ;

but some additions are made which do not dignify
the story or add to its pathos. Where in the *History*
King Arthur and Queen Guinevere are speaking
together by the window, Tennyson substitutes Lancelot for the King, and puts upon the lips of Guinevere a jealous tirade that brings the poem suddenly
down almost to the level of a farce. There is plenti-
ful indication in the *History* of the Queen's jealousy,
but she is not permitted to storm and whimper at the
moment when Elaine drifts under the window, and
immediately before " the queene and all the knights "
are moved to weep "for pittie of the dolefull complaints" in the little letter, which also is robbed of
its pure simplicity, and made to convey a childish
reproach.

In the same way the *Idyll* of " Enid," inspired by
Lady Charlotte Guest's *Mabinogion*, shows a tendency
to weaken the effect of the original by superfluous
detail. The description of Enid mourning in the
summer sunshine over Geraint's loss of valour, seems,
curiously enough, more delicate and restrained in
Mabinogion than in the *Idyll* where the Greek worship of physical beauty is obtruded upon the archaic
plainness of the scene. The sense of unadorned narrative dealing with every-day life is unmistakable in
such lines as those beginning : " And Enid was without sleep in the apartment which had windows of
glass," while Tennyson's introduction of the Greek
symbols in describing Geraint's splendid strength loads
the picture, and quite destroys its charm of severity.

In "The Passing of Arthur," on the other hand, the elaboration is in the direction of fuller portrayal of character and a charming background of landscape which to the modern mind distinctly improves upon the unrelieved bareness of the early chronicle, and gives opportunity for such rememberable phrases as : "I have lived my life, and that which I have done may He within Himself make pure."

The effect upon highly cultivated minds of Tennyson's selection in making up the plot of the *Idylls* is various, and we can hardly present two more opposite, while equally brilliant, judgments than those of Mr. Swinburne and Mr. Richard Hutton. To the former, Tennyson has seemed to commit an artistic transgression, if not a crime, in eliminating from Arthur's history the youthful sin which is fastened on him in the old fables, and which creeps after him, cropping out at last in Modred's treachery. Mr. Swinburne is irresistibly attracted by this hint of Greek fatality, and would have chosen it whatever else were pushed aside. But he could not have kept it, Mr. Hutton affirms, together with the element of mystic spiritual glory which is "far the most characteristic and the most in keeping with the Christian mysticism of the San Grail legends, of the two." To Mr. Swinburne's assumption that the sin was necessary to preserve the thread of consistency in Arthur's fluctuating history, Mr. Hutton replies : "Let anyone read either Sir Thomas Malory's book, or the brief, graceful, and classical compilation of the *Legends of King Arthur*, by J. T. K., and then judge for himself whether the sin of King Arthur or his unearthly glory be the more deeply ingrained element of the two, and I suspect he will end by accepting as the overruling idea, and also as by far the better adapted for coherent treatment, the verdict of the old chroniclers, of Joseph of Exeter for example : ' The old world knows not his peer, nor will the future show us his equal ; he alone towers over all other kings, better than the past ones, and greater than those that are to be ' ; and again, another old compiler : ' In short, God has not made, since Adam was, the man more perfect than King Arthur.'[1] It is perfectly evident that this tradition of unrivalled spiritual glory was a development of elements of the story quite inconsistent with that of his great sin and shame."

Mr. Swinburne argues that "from the sin of Arthur's youth proceeds the ruin of his reign and realm through the falsehood of his wife—a wife unloving and unloved." Mr. Hutton, in refutation, quotes the conversation upon this subject between Arthur and Merlin :

"So far is Guinevere from being ' unloved ' that when Merlin asks Arthur, ' Is there any faire lady that yee love better than another ? ' he answers, ' Yea, I love Guinevere the King's daughter, Leodegrance of the land of Camelyard, which Leodegrance holdeth

---

[1] The *Memoir* shows that Tennyson himself felt his ideal Arthur justified by precisely these passages.

in his power the Table Round that yee told hee had
of my father Uther. And this demosell is the most
gentilest and fairest lady that I know living, or yet
that I ever could find.' 'Sir,' said Merlin, 'as of her
beautie and fairenesse, she is one of the fairest that
live ; *but an yee loved her not so well as yee doe, I
would finde yee a demosell of beautie and of goodnesse
that should like yee and please yee, an your heart
were not set. But there as a man's heart is set, he
will be loth to return.'* 'That is truth,' said Arthur ;—
and here not only is Arthur's passion for his queen
represented as beyond resistance, but Merlin treats
the want of love of [in] Guinevere as the root of the
calamities that were to come, and intimates that by
a happier choice these calamities might have been
avoided. And the simple truth is, that this is the
whole drift of the legends, from the date of Arthur's
marriage to the close. After Arthur's mysterious
death, Guinevere freely takes upon herself and Lancelot the whole guilt of the ruin of Arthur's kingdom.
'Through this knight and mee all these warres were
wrought, and the death of the most noble knights of
the world ; for through our love that we have loved
together is my most noble lord slaine. . . . For
as well as I have loved thee, Sir Lancelot, now mine
heart will not once serve mee to see thee ; for
through thee and mee is the floure of kings and
knights destroyed.' And her last prayer is not to see
Sir Lancelot again with her bodily eyes, lest her
earthly and disloyal love should return upon her, but

that he should bury her beside her true lord and master, King Arthur. No one can read Sir Thomas Malory's book without being struck by the complete disappearance, as it proceeds, of all trace of remorse or shame in King Arthur, and by the weight of guilt thrown upon the passionate love of Lancelot and Guinevere. Obviously, if Mr. Tennyson was to keep to the legends which cast so mysterious a halo of spiritual glory around King Arthur, he had no choice but to ignore those which connected, Œdipus-fashion, his youthful sin with the final catastrophe." [1]

As to the further charge that Arthur's exclusion from the San Grail is only intelligible on the ground of his youthful guilt, Mr. Hutton considers Mr. Tennyson's opposite view entirely justified by the legends, claiming that Arthur " looked upon the search for the San Grail as almost a disloyalty to the higher though humbler task that he had set himself and his knights —of restoring order on earth, while on the other hand, knights who, like Sir Lancelot, are stained with far deeper and more voluntary guilt than the King, even on Mr. Swinburne's view, is chargeable with, are allowed to join in the search." And he adds : " I do not know anything happier or more true in its instinct, in English poetry, than the tone Mr. Tennyson has attributed to Arthur's reluctant assent to the search for the San Grail. It is amply justified by the old legends, and it just enables the poet to express through Arthur that spiritual distrust of signs and wonders

[1] Hutton's *Essays,* vol. ii.

which, while it serves to link his faith closely with modern thought, is in no way inconsistent with the chivalric character of the whole story."

A curious defect in Tennyson's scheme is indicated by Mr. Gladstone in the following passage: "It is but a debt of justice to the Guinevere of the romancers," he says, "to observe that she loses considerably by the marked transposition which Mr. Tennyson has effected in the order of greatness between Lancelot and Arthur. With him there is an original error in her estimate, independently of the breach of a positive and sacred obligation. She prefers the inferior man; and this preference of itself implies some ethical defect rooted in her nature. In the romance of Sir T. Malory, the preference she gives to Lancelot would have been signally just, had she been free to choose. For Lancelot is of an indescribable grandeur; but the limit of Arthur's character is thus shown in certain words that he uses, and that Lancelot never could have spoken: ' Much more I am sorrier for my good knight's loss than for the loss of my queen! for queens might I have enough, but such a fellowship of good knights shall never be together in no company.' " [1]

From these fragments of the serious view of Tennyson's very serious and aspiring performance, it is interesting to turn to the criticism of one who wore his wisdom lightly:

" Oddly enough," wrote Lowell to Mr. Norton in

[1] Gladstone's *Gleanings of Past Years.*

1872, "when I got your letter about Tennyson's poem, I had just finished reading a *real* Arthurian romance—'Fergus'—not one of the best, certainly, but having that merit of being a genuine blossom for which no triumph of artifice can compensate ; having, in short, that *woodsy* hint and tantalisation of perfume which is so infinitely better than anything more defined. Emerson had left me Tennyson's book ; so last night I took it to bed with me and finished it at a gulp—reading like a naughty boy till half-past one. The contrast between his pomp and my old rhymer's simpleness was very curious and even instructive. One bit of the latter (which I cannot recollect elsewhere) amused me a good deal as a Yankee. When Fergus comes to Arthur's court and Sir Kay 'sarses' him (which, you know, is *de rigueur* in the old poems), Sir Gawain saunters up *whittling a stick* as a medicine against ennui. So afterwards, when Arthur is dreadfully bored by hearing no news of Fergus, he reclines at table without any taste for his dinner, and whittles to purge his heart of melancholy. I suppose a modern poet would not dare to come so near Nature as this lest she should fling up her heels. But I am not yet 'aff wi' the auld love' nor quite 'on with the new.' There are very fine childish things in Tennyson's poem, and fine manly things too, as it seems to me, but I conceive the theory to be wrong. I have the same feeling (I am not wholly sure of its justice) that I have when I see these modern mediæval pictures,—I am defrauded ; I do not see reality, but a

masquerade.   The costumes are all that is genuine,
and the people inside them are shams—which, I take
it, is just the reverse of what ought to be.   One special criticism I should make on Tennyson's new
Idyls, and that is that the similes are so often dragged
in by the hair.   They seem to be taken (*à la* Tom
Moore) from note-books, and not suggested by the
quickened sense of association in the glow of composition.   Sometimes it almost seems as if the verses
were made for the similes instead of being the creating of a wave that heightens as it rolls.   This is analogous to the costume objection, and springs perhaps
from the same cause—the making of poetry with
malice prepense.   However, I am not going to forget
the lovely things that Tennyson has written, and I
think they give him rather hard measure now.   However, it is the natural recoil of a too rapid fame.
Wordsworth had the true kind—an unpopularity that
roused and stimulated while he was strong enough
to despise it, and honour, obedience, troops of friends,
when the grasshopper would have been a burthen to
the drooping shoulders.   Tennyson, to be sure, has
been childishly petulant ; but what have these whip-
per-snappers who cry ' Go up, baldhead,' done that
can be named with some things of his ?   He has
been the greatest artist in words we have had
since Gray—and remember how Gray holds his
own with little fuel but real fire.   He had the
secret of the inconsumable oil, and so, I fancy,
has Tennyson."[1]

[1] *Letters of James Russell Lowell.*

The allegorical significance of the *Idylls* is sufficiently indicated in the lines to the Queen :

> "——accept this old imperfect tale,
> New-old, and shadowing Sense at war with Soul
> Rather than that gray king, whose name, a ghost,
> Streams like a cloud, man-shaped, from mountain peak,
> And cleaves to cairn and cromlech still; or him
> Of Geoffrey's book, or him of Malleor's."

This makes of Arthur a symbol, but includes no more
specific interpretations, as that the Round Table typi-
fies the Body, the three Queens, Faith, Hope, and
Charity, and so on.   It was an afterthought to dedi-
cate the *Idylls* to the Prince Consort, and a very
Tennysonian thought to liken their blameless hero to
Albert. It was done with the utmost sincerity of
feeling, and without the slightest suggestion of syco-
phancy ; but it gave unlimited opportunity to the
scoffers, who hailed joyfully the title invented by
Mr. Swinburne, of " Morte d'Albert, or Idylls of the
Prince Consort " ; and who failed to perceive with
him the " exquisite magnificence of style," and the
" splendid flashes of episodical illumination with
which the poems are vivified or adorned."

CHAPTER X.

"ENOCH ARDEN," AND THE DIALECT POEMS.

ALMOST every artist whose days have been long, has had at least a single day of simplicity. If he has valued cataracts and precipices in his choice of material, we may look among his sketches for a haying scene ; if he has been in humour for psychological novels, we shall come upon a nursery story ; if he has composed a symphony, there is ballad music somewhere among his loose sheets ; if he has made an epic, he will devise a pastoral.

It is not surprising to find that in Tennyson's good year of 1864 he followed the stately pageant of Arthur's court with the story of a fisherman. *Enoch Arden*, in comparison with *Maud* or *In Memoriam*, was certainly simple. The poet had stripped his style of its jewels and ornaments, and had striven, we learn from the *Memoir*, to use only similes " such as might have been used by simple fisher-folk." He had abjured all perplexing speculation as well, and had refrained from indulging in scientific suggestions, he had even let the superstition of the uneducated slip into his lines, and had not made his heroine more beautiful than the usual belle of a little fishing village. All this had he done when Mr. Walter Bagehot arose and selected *Enoch Arden* to illustrate his theory of the ornate in poetry! The story is simple enough, he says: "A sailor who sells fish, breaks his leg, gets dismal, gives up selling fish, goes to sea, is wrecked on a desert island, stays there some years, on his return finds his wife married to a miller, speaks to a landlady on the subject, and dies. Told in the pure and simple, the unadorned and classical style, this story would not have taken three pages, but Mr. Tennyson has been able to make it the principal, the largest, tale in his new volume. He has done so only by giving to every event and incident in the volume an accompanying commentary."

When other critics were busy pointing out either that the poem was immoral because Annie married Philip before Enoch was really dead, or that it was exceptionally pure in its delineation of self-forgetfulness and self-sacrifice, or that it was intensely natural and plain and "Saxon" in its treatment, or that it showed a perfect understanding of the feelings of sailors and the wives of sailors, Mr. Bagehot was saying that Mr. Tennyson had given us "a sailor crowded all over with ornament and illustration, because he then wanted to describe an unreal type of fancied men,—not sailors as they are, but sailors as they might be wished." Fish, he said, might be "Ocean-spoil in ocean-smelling osier," but fishermen are apt to be rather coarse and not charming at all. So it was necessary to ornament Enoch and make him the sort of man a cultivated person would choose to be if he were obliged to transmigrate into a fisherman.

The beauties of nature, said Mr. Bagehot, would not have occupied the real Enoch so much as they occupied Mr. Tennyson in thinking about tropical scenery. "He would have known little of the scarlet shafts of sunrise and nothing of the long convolvuluses. As in *Robinson Crusoe*, his own petty contrivances and his small ailments would have been the principal subject to him. 'For three years,' he might have said, 'my back was bad ; and then I put two pegs into a piece of driftwood and so made a chair ; and after that it pleased God to send me a chill.' In real life his piety would scarcely have gone beyond that." But Tennyson was quite justified, according to Mr. Bagehot's theory, in ornamenting Enoch and his surroundings. "The essence of pure art," he says, "consists in describing what is as it is, and this is very well for what can bear it, but there are many inferior things which will not bear it, and which nevertheless ought to be described in books." And a fisherman selling his wares in a small village is an inferior thing.

This, of course, is only a partial estimate of *Enoch Arden*. What probably struck Tennyson when Woolner told him the plot, and what certainly strikes the reader of the poem, is the act of self-denial by

which Enoch leaves Annie to her happiness with
Philip when he might have claimed his own again
to everyone's infinite disturbance.   This was not an
"inferior" subject, and it might have gained by a
rendering as simple as the Robinson Crusoe style.
Tennyson certainly made a tremendous effort toward
this very simplicity, although he did not attain it,
and his readers, comparing him to himself, for the
most part found him what he had tried to be.   He
was not, as Mr. Gladstone once said, so well adapted
to turning the moor into the field as to turning the
field into the garden, but at least he made of *Enoch
Arden* a beach garden, flourishing nasturtiums and
eglantine in place of the double rose and the dahlia.

A writer in the contemporaneous *Atlantic* spoke
of the witness the new poem bore to the poet's old
"faculty of penetrating to the inmost significance
both of words and of things, so that there is no waste
and so that single words in single sentences stamp
on the brain the substance of long experiences."
Take this, he says :

> "Another hand *crept*, too, across his trade,
>   Taking her bread and theirs,"

and find the " one word crowded with pathos, telling
of the weary loss of livelihood, the burden slowly
growing more intolerably irksome to the bold and
careful worker wrestling with pain, and to the fragile
mother of the new-born babe."   And the same writer

sums up his impression in the following enthusiastic passage :

"A pure manhood among the poets, a heart simple as the simplest, an imperial fancy, whose lofty supremacy none can question, a high faith, and a spirit possessed with the sublimest and most universal of Christ's truths, a tender and strong humanity, not bounded by a vague and misty sentiment, but pervading life in all its forms, and with these great skill and patience and beauty in expression,—these are the riper qualities to which *Enoch Arden* testifies."

Whether *Enoch Arden* represented to its countrymen ornateness or simplicity, ethics or drama, to foreigners it represented a typical phase of English literature, and has been put down as the essentially English poem of Tennyson's collection. For one thing it is a sea-poem, and this in itself separates it from the inland inspiration of Germany and France. Then also Enoch, the hero, is acquainted with the English watchword, Duty, and embodies the national ideal of self-control and loyalty. Stopford Brooke has put this notion into admirable words :

"Enoch," he says, "is the type of the 'able seaman' of England, nourished in the fishing-smack, and then passing from land to land through the wonders of the waves in the merchant-vessel ; and then, when wars arise, the mainstay of our navies—a type which has lasted more than a thousand years. Arden's god-fearingness is not uncommon in English seamen, but his slow-established sense of duty is common ; and so are also his sturdy endurance, his settled self-sacrifice for those ideas that his soul approves, his courage unconscious of itself, his silent love of his country—a careful, loving, and faithful picture, for which we have to honour the poet. Nowhere has he shown more convincingly the noblest side of his patriotism."

From his home at Farringford, Tennyson had constant opportunity for observation of the sea. He watched it "lazy-plunging" under the wide sky, he heard "the league-long roller thundering on the reef," and the "hollow ocean-ridges roaring into cataracts," he saw "the wild-wave . . . green-glimmering toward the summit," with "stormy crests that smoke against the sky," and noted the curious surface of the water when there came a "wrinkled sea." Concerning the felicity of this last adjective, Stopford Brooke has given as testimony a personal description of his own :

"I used to think," he says, "that the phrase 'wrinkled sea,' in the fragment called 'The Eagle,' was too bold. But one day I stood on the edge of the cliff below Slieve League in Donegal. The cliff from which I looked down on the Atlantic was nine hundred feet in height. Beside me the giant slope of Slieve League plunged down from its summit for more than eighteen hundred feet. As I gazed down on the sea below, which was calm in the shelter, for the wind blew off the land, the varying puffs that eddied in and out among the hollows and juttings of the cliffs covered the quiet surface with an infinite network of involved ripples.   It was exactly Tennyson's wrinkled sea.   Then, by huge good fortune, an eagle which built on one of the ledges of Slieve League flew out of his eyrie and poised, barking, on his wings ; but in a moment fell precipitate, as their manner is, straight down a thousand feet to the sea. And I could not help crying out :

> ' The wrinkled sea beneath him crawls ;
>   He watches from his mountain walls,
>   And like a thunderbolt he falls.' "

Tennyson's sea, however, is his picture-gallery, not his friend or his enemy.   There is to be found in his poetry no reference that indicates personal conflict with the powers of the ocean.   There is no passage that reveals the familiarity of the sailor with the element he battles against, such as the passage in Kipling's *Miracles :*

> " Uprose the deep, by gale on gale,
>   To bid me change my mind again—
>   He broke his teeth along my rail,
>   And, roaring, swung behind again."

Yet, in his letter to Dawson, Tennyson says that a simile almost identical with Kipling's was suggested to him by an old fish-wife who had lost two sons at sea.   She clenched her fist " at the advancing tide on a stormy day," and cried out : " Ay ! roar, do ! how I hates to see thee show thy white teeth."

The most interesting poem in the little volume to

which *Enoch Arden* gave a name is "The Northern Farmer, Old Style." Here, at all events, we get simplicity primeval. In fact, Tennyson, in striking this rustic note, seemed to awaken a new set of faculties within himself. Where he had been elaborately refined he became ruggedly plain-spoken ; where he had been mildly humourous, to concede the most, he became irresistibly so ; where he had picked and chosen the sweetest fruits of language, he pulled up the tubers of the Lincolnshire dialect and let them go into his lines smelling freshly of the soil. It was perhaps a whim with him, certainly not the settled tendency of his mind ; but the result was a little masterpiece. In order to realise just what the poem means, especially in America where Hosea Biglow has set the rustic type for us, it is necessary to get some idea of the class to which Tennyson's farmer belongs. The *Westminster Review*, in 1891, gave a brief account of it, from which the following extract is taken :

"These farmers were almost the last of their race. Their portraits at first sight appear to be lugubrious caricatures. Their ignorance appears so colossal as to be incredible. It must be borne in mind, however, that in their virtues, in their failings, in their mode of life and manners, and even in their speech, they differed very little from the time when their forefathers, with native grace, submitted to the yoke of the conquering Normans. Through changes—dynastic, religious, or social—they remained unchanged.

The nearest market-town formed the utmost limits to their travels.[1]

"The farm labourer was equally conservative. His ideas were almost as luminous as those of his typical ancestor, 'Gurth, the son of Beowulf, the born thrall of Cedric of Rotherwood.' Not that he acknowledged himself the 'thrall' of anybody. It was an article of his creed that 'Britons never, never, never shall be slaves.' His most treasured possession, after that of his knowledge of men and things, was that of his independence. He never dreamed of leaving his native village, and his ideas were as circumscribed as his locality. Though by nature gifted with splendid stubbornness, he yielded unquestioning obedience to the farmer. When work permitted he attended church on Sunday, and snored through the service in his humble free seat with as much devotion as the farmer in his high-backed pew. His humour was of the ruminating and ponderous kind, and manifested itself on occasion in a solemn horseplay. When opportunity occurred he proved himself a mighty man at the tankard or trencher; these were moments of supreme bliss. In an animal way he was happy. He had no ambition and therefore no discontent. Though he sometimes grumbled, and pretty loudly too, he nevertheless believed his condition to be unalterable. The agitator had not

[1] This should not surprise us, as we still have farmers in Long Island who have never been to Brooklyn or to New York, and who consider that to marry anyone "from away" is very poor policy and worse taste.

discovered him. Joseph Arch was as yet unborn, and Tom Mann had not preached the new crusade of labour.

" Yet these farmers and labourers whom Tennyson chatted with in Somersby fifty years ago were the witnesses of the beginning of a revolution in the state of English agriculture whose consequences no man then was able to foresee, which many, even now, fail to appreciate. The system of large farms was coming into vogue. They were destined to absorb all the small holdings, and to drive the sturdy yeomanry, who for generations had managed them with credit and success, into the new rising manu-facturing centres to eke out a miserable existence. The craze for large farms infected the old Lincolnshire farmer :

> ' Feyther run up to the farm, an' I runs up to the mill
> An' I 'll run up to the brig.'

The ruling passion was the acquisition of ' proputty ' by the consolidation of neighbouring small holdings into his large farm. The new system introduced new dangers. One man in every three was, as it developed, thrown out of employment. Thus ren-dered arbitrarily idle, the unemployed left their vil-lage, and flocked to the large towns. Hence the overcrowding and overcompetition, with their re-sultant complications of social and moral evil.

" Before he left home, Tennyson saw the begin-ning of these changes. He is one of the few living

Lincolnshire men who saw the now obsolete opera-
tions of sowing broadcast and dibbling beans. He
would remember thrashing with the flail—which
gave occupation to many men through the winter—
being superseded by the horse-machine, and the re-
sentment which the innovation aroused. The Lincolnshire farm labourers awoke as from sleep. Their
hatred rose to frenzy. They resorted to violence.
Machines were destroyed. The lives of their owners
were threatened. For a while terror and confusion
reigned. The red fires of incendiarism lit the midnight sky. Farmers became afraid. The machines
were guarded by night and day. The blind power
of ignorance made itself felt. At first the law seemed
powerless. The lame and toothless parish con-
stables were either unable or unwilling to arrest the
ringleaders. Ultimately, two farm labourers, aged
respectively twenty-two and twenty-four, were cap-
tured, not far from Tennyson's home, tried at the
Lincoln summer assizes in 1831, and sentenced to
death. *Both were executed.*

"The agitation subsided. It broke out again in
1848, with the introduction of the steam thrashing
machine. Even the 'Farmer, old style,' who had
stood firmly for the first machine, resented this
innovation :

> 'A kittle o' steäm
> Huzzin' an' maäzin' the blessed feälds wi' the Divil's oän teäm.'

"The opposition, however, soon died down.

'The old order' had changed. The tide of rural migration was now flowing merrily into the towns. Small holdings were fast becoming a rarity, and large farms with a minimum of labour, the rule.

"As we have already observed, the race of men from whom Tennyson drew the type of the old-style farmer is extinct. 'Nature brings not back the mastodon.' This type can never again recur."

It would be interesting to compare Lowell's Jonathan with this old Lincolnshire John. One virtue, at least, they would have in common—their overwhelming self-complacency ; keen, assertive, intelligent in Jonathan, lumbering, dull, and ignorant in John. Jonathan is a satirist with all the power of exquisite irony that lurks beneath the "Yankee" countenance and bites in the anecdote that Lowell tells of Captain Hall and the countryman :[1]

"The Captain was walking up and down the veranda of a country tavern in Massachusetts while the coach changed horses. A thunder-storm was going on, and with that pleasant European air of indirect self-compliment in condescending to be surprised by American merit which we find so conciliating, he said to a countryman lounging against the door, 'Pretty heavy thunder you have here.' The other, who had divined at a glance his feeling of generous concession to a new country, drawled gravely, 'Waal, we *du*, considerin' the number of inhabitants.'" For Lowell this stood as the type of

---

[1] Introduction to *The Biglow Papers*, Second Series.

" Yankee " humour and so it may stand for us. Place it against the slow, weighty cogitation of the Northern Farmer, when Parson says " eäsy an' freeä " :

" ' The amoighty 's a taäkin o' you to 'issén, my friend,'
        says 'eä.
    I weänt saäy men be loiars, thaw summun said it in 'aäste :
    But 'e reäds wonn sarmin a weeäk, an' I 'a stubb'd Thurnaby
        waäste."

Contrast also the somewhat partisan reverence which Jonathan shows for his own God, with the solemn irreverence of the dying farmer who criticises his Maker for His poor management :

" A mowt 'a taäen owd Joänes, as 'ant not a 'aäpoth o' sense,
    Or a mowt 'a taäen young Robins—a niver mended a fence :
    But godamoighty a moost taäke meä an taäke ma now
    Wi' aäf the cows to cauve an' Thurnaby hoälmes to plow ! "

The contemptuous remarks of Concord Bridge to " The Moniment " sound as if spoken in answer :

" I ha'n't no patience with sech swellin' fellers ez
    Think God can't forge 'thout them to blow the bellerses."

Yet Tennyson's farmer is a long way from deserving utter scorn. He has been a thorough and persistent worker, and has worked for the very love of working ; a quality already sufficiently rare, and falling suspiciously into disrepute. He has also realised a purpose :

" Dubbut looök at the waäste : theer warn't not feeäd for a
        cow ;
    Nowt at all but bracken an' fuzz, an' looök at it now—
    Warn't worth nowt a haäcre, an' now theer 's lots o' feeäd,
    Fourscoor yows upon it an' some on it down i' seeäd."

And whatever his private morals have been,—they evidently have borne some resemblance to those of his Viking ancestors,—he has been cordially faithful to his trust and to his "Squoire," and is really troubled by the necessity of dying at a moment so inconvenient :

" Do godamoighty know what a 's doing a-taäkin' o' meä ?
　　I beänt won as sows 'ere a beän an' yonder a peä ;
　　An' Squoire 'ull be sa mad an' all—a' dear a' dear !
　　And I 'a managed for Squoire coom Michaelmas thutty year."

In spite of his low estate and his pebbly dialect the poor old hard-working heathen makes an appeal to the admiration he so lavishly spent upon himself, and will live, it is easy to imagine, to be the joy and the despair of future glossologists.

　　"The Northern Farmer, New Style," is the natural sequel to the old-style farmer.　From the human point of view he is no improvement ; greed has entered into his soul and has made it a very destestable abiding place for such virtues as he possesses.　He is arguing after the fashion of the immortal Weller with his son, on the question of marriage :

" Me an' thy muther, Sammy, 'as beän a-talkin' o' thee ;
　　Thou 's beän talkin' to muther, an' she beän a tellin it me.
　　Thou 'll not marry for munny—thou 's sweet upo' parson's
　　　　lass—
　　Noä—thou 'll marry for luvv—an' we boäth on us thinks tha an
　　　　ass."

"Proputty, proputty, proputty," is the refrain, "proputty sticks," and "proputty grows," and property alone is worthy of respect.   He partially understands the sentiment of his son toward " parson's lass," for was n't he " cräzed fur the lasses " himself when he was a lad ?   But he

> "—— knaw'd a Quaäker feller as often 'as towd ma this:
> ' Doänt thou marry for munny, but goä wheer munny is ! ' "

He passes the advice on to his son with the very astute reflection :

> " Taäke my word for it, Sammy, the poor in a loomp is bad—
>   Them or thir feythers, tha sees, mun 'a beän a laäzy lot,
>   Fur work mun 'a gone to the gittin' whiniver munny was
>   got."

With these two stubborn rustics belongs the " Churchwarden " whose politic philosophy is expressed rather too openly for perfect naturalness. The Churchwarden has been a Dissenter " an' ageeän the toithe an' the raäte," but he found it was n't the " gaäinist waäy to the narra Gaäte " ; and promptly reverted to the old Church.   The Dissenters were so unkind as to retaliate in a peculiarly original fashion :

> " An' I can't abeär 'em, I can't, fur a lot on 'em coom'd to-
>   year—
>   I wur down wi' the rheumatis then—to *my* pond to wesh
>   thessens theere—
>   Sa I sticks like the ivin as long as I lives to the owd Chuch
>   now,
>   Fur they wesh'd their sins i' *my* pond, an' I doubts they pois-
>   on'd the cow."

He therefore advises the curate if he wants to find his way to a bishopric, to preach against the sins of the Baptists and let the "Quality" alone. He himself had "cottoned down to his betters,"

> "An' now by the Graäce o' the Lord, Mr. Harry, I ham wot I ham."

Again a reviewer in the *Westminster* throws a very clear and concentrated light upon the origin of "The Churchwarden and the Curate."[1] He explains that Tennyson's turncoat from his own point of view was quite sensible to return to the "owd Chuch." There was no profit in dissent. Dissenters in remote villages were, at the time of Tennyson's youth, on the losing side : "As a rule they were regarded with suspicion and disfavour. They were few in number. For the most part, the congregations that met, either in a barn, or in some humble meeting-house, comprised farm-labourers and poor cottars struggling against fate in the silent decadence of their order through the gradual absorption of small holdings by the more prosperous farmers. No Dissenter could hope to bask in the sunshine of squirely favour. To be one of the despised community was to proclaim one's self a soldier in the rabble army of discontents. It was a protest against the existing order of things—to the rural potentates the more irritating because of the immovable basis of conscience upon which it was

---

[1] Davie's "Tennyson's Turncoat," *Westminster Review*, 1894.

founded." This bred a race that was capable of a certain self-conscious nobility. "Their religion was to them dearer than life. It was the pearl of great price, and they were resolved neither to part with it nor to allow its lustre to be tarnished." There were high souls among them, "men possessed of that spiritual force which makes reformations possible and revolutions a terrible fact," but even these men were not the sort that made heaven seem attractive. They were proud to an extreme and "would undergo the severest privations rather than condescend to accept charity," they possessed the stern virtues that seldom go with sweetness and light, and these they did not possess.

"Overpowered with the continual sense of their own and their neighbour's sins, they were absorbed in the task of working out their own salvation with fear and trembling. Hence they fell into the pardonable but fatal error of identifying piety with sourness and austerity. Thus they repelled, where they would have attracted, and, like many wiser men, failed in their hope to regenerate mankind by doses of spiritual vinegar. Yet they were not dismayed. Failure became a spur to perseverance, and, confident in the righteousness of their cause, and the justice of their methods, they would have gone forth, filled with the missionary spirit which is inseparable from intense conviction, and proclaimed in the village inn, or at the corners of the streets, the glad tidings that had turned the current of their

14

thoughts to higher things. But prudence forbade. Their security of tenure was too precarious to admit of apostolic enterprise. To be turned adrift was to become a pauper, for who would employ a fiery and pestilent schismatic ? Their zeal, therefore, was perforce concentrated within narrow bounds. And it is, perhaps, the intensity born of the narrowness of these early Dissenters' views, that has kept afire the zeal which has developed into that social force whose manifestations are even now becoming notable and historic. The miserable condition of the rural population necessarily made those who had the misfortune to entertain intense political or religious convictions, prudent. Their life appeared a dull round of almost unredeemed hopelessness. Wages were barely sufficient to stave off starvation. Many of their homes, amid the most unsanitary surroundings, were, however picturesque to the casual visitor, little better than rough thatched hovels. Accommodation was meagre in the extreme. By a perverse provision of British nature, poverty and prolific families were inseparable. The hopeless and half-starved Lincolnshire labourer generally contrived to be blessed with an army of children. For sleeping-room, they were straitened to the tensest strain of poor morality's frail tenter-hooks. Education was undreamed of. As soon as a boy could walk he was set to help maintain himself. He was born to ignorance and toil as the sparks fly upward." Looking first on this picture and then upon that other of the Churchwar-

den returned to the fold, a favourite with "Quality," and in the way of temporal, if not of eternal advancement, it is easy to understand the appeal made to a flexible conscience by the estate of the latter.

Tennyson continued, at intervals, to write these dialect poems, and if they were gathered together in one volume, as they never have been, they would give a certain value and proportion to a side of Tennyson's genius that is usually neglected. They show that when he took a type of character with which he was thoroughly familiar he could lose himself in the representation. His great danger in his dramas and monodramas and dramatic conceptions lay in his tendency to read himself into every human being he drew. Without too far pushing a general characterisation, we find him insular again. It was very difficult for him to see things from different points of view, as they would be seen by people unlike himself. If one of his characters was high-minded, as Enoch Arden was, or King Arthur, or à Becket, he was apt to be high-minded in a very Tennysonian way. But these Lincolnshire people he knew too well to entertain any notion of their sharing his feelings or ways of expression. Their characteristics were so strongly marked that there was no evading them, and when Tennyson accepted them as material he seems to have let himself go in the sheer pleasure of interpretation, without any purifying, or refining, or idealising effort. The result stirs one's fancy to dreaming what would have happened if Tennyson

had been thrust out of his natural orbit into the stir and press of active life among hard-headed realists, in poverty-stricken communities. A poem like " The Northern Cobbler " indicates the power to grasp the " immanent life of things " that, according to Lowell, makes a new poet ; the power of struggling through conventions and convictions to elemental reality as it is shown, not only in beauty and holiness, but in discomfort and pain and ugliness, in vulgarity and immorality.

CHAPTER XI.

THE DRAMAS.

WHEN Tennyson, at sixty-five, decided to enter the field of drama it was naturally a surprise to his readers. In his previous work there had been little sign of the dramatic quality. *Maud* was not undramatic in a certain sense of the word ; but no one seems to have been so mad as to think of it in connection with the stage. And one of its reviewers spoke of the story in it—the plot— as so vague and so confused that a friend of his had risen from the reading, uncertain whether the heroine was dead or alive. Action, the living soul of drama, was conspicuously absent from the narrative poems, even in the metaphysical sense given to the term by Ibsen and Maeterlinck. Events followed one another with deliberation, and so did mental phases.

In the review by Mr. Henry James we find the perfect statement of this characteristic.[1] "With the poets who are natural chroniclers of movement," he says, "the words fall into their places as with some throw of the dice, which fortune should always

[1] *The Galaxy*, September, 1875.

213

favour. With Scott and Byron they leap into the verse *à pieds joints*, and shake it with their coming ; with Tennyson they arrive slowly aud settle cautiously into their attitudes, after having well scanned the locality. In consequence they are generally exquisite, and make exquisite combinations ; but the result is intellectual poetry and not passionate—poetry which, if the term is not too pedantic, one may qualify as static poetry. Any scene of violence represented by Tennyson is always singularly limited and compressed ; it is reduced to a few elements—refined to a single statuesque episode. There are, for example, several descriptions of tournaments and combats in the *Idylls of the King*. They are all most beautiful, but they are all curiously delicate. One gets no sense of the din and shock of battle ; one seems to be looking at a bas-relief of two contesting knights in chiselled silver on a priceless piece of plate."

It was then to be expected that in Tennyson's dramas we should miss the din and shock of life within and without. His customary mode of treatment when confronted by a violent action is shown in *Aylmer's Field*, where Sir Aylmer "with a sudden execration drove the footstool from before him and arose." None of Shakespeare's angry people ever kicked a footstool thus. Moreover, as Mr. James goes on to show, *Queen Mary*, the first of Tennyson's dramas in order of production, is not an edifice ; its author lacked the architectonic faculty ; there seems no adequate structure to bind together the incidents, and the incidents themselves are chosen rather to bring out the pathos of Mary's private position than to impress upon the reader or spectator the march of public events. Tennyson builded his house upon Froude and the character of the Queen is that presented by Froude[1]:

"No English Sovereign ever ascended the throne with larger popularity than Mary Tudor. The country was eager to atone to her for her mother's injuries, and the instinctive loyalty of the English towards their natural Sovereign was enhanced by the abortive efforts of Northumberland to rob her of her inheritance. She had reigned little more than five years, and she descended into the grave amid curses deeper than the acclamations which had welcomed her accession. In that brief time she had swathed her name in the horrid epithet which will cling to it forever, and yet from the passions which in general tempt men into crime she was entirely free; to the time of her accession she had lived a blameless and in many respects a noble life, and few men or women have lived less capable of doing knowingly a wrong thing."[2] A writer in the *Quarterly Review* contrasts this picture of Mary with Hume's very different judgment, which is given as follows:

"It is not necessary to employ many words in drawing the character of this Princess. She pos-

[1] I do not, of course, mean to imply that Tennyson read only Froude in preparation. The *Memoir* gives a considerable list of books that served him.

[2] Froude's *History of England*.

sessed few qualities either estimable or amiable, and her person was as little engaging as her behaviour and address. Obstinacy, bigotry, violence, cruelty, malignity, revenge, tyranny, every circumstance of her character took a tincture from her bad temper and narrow understanding. And amidst that complication of vices which entered into her composition, we shall scarcely find any virtue but that of sincerity, which she seems to have maintained throughout her whole life, except in the beginning of her reign, when the necessity of her affairs obliged her to make some promises which she never intended to perform. She appears also, as well as her father, to have been susceptible of some attachments of friendship and that without the caprice or inconsistency which were so remarkable in the conduct of that monarch. To which we may add, that in many circumstances of her life she gave indications of resolution and vigour of mind which seem to have been inherent in her family."

The *Quarterly* reviewer remarks that this delineation " does not promise a character suited to the heroine of a romantic drama," and also that Tennyson, choosing the opposite character, produced a drama, the motive of which is purely feminine : " Our attention is drawn off," he says, " from those public actions which have branded Mary's name with its execrable epithet, and pity and compassion are aroused on her behalf, for the terrible situation in which she is placed, for the suffering and loving wife, for the downfall of

The Very Reverend Dean Bradley.

From life.

the hopes of the enthusiastic and aspiring Catholic, as though it were expected that we were to waive our judgment on the Queen out of our sympathy with the woman. Thus the dignity of history is lowered for the sake of imagination and sentiment. Who would ever recognise in the passionate wife, whose nerves are always on the edge, in the pitiful and sentimental woman shrinking from the execution of Lady Jane Grey, in the hysterical mother-expectant, the dull, vindictive, and narrow-minded Princess described in the sober pages of Hume ? "

The same reviewer sums up an acute analysis of the play with the admission that it is probably the best specimen of literary drama of the time : " It is at least admirable in form," he says ; " it is better than Mr. Browning's dramatic studies, which have no form at all. It is better than the *Spanish Gypsy*, which has a hybrid form. It is better than *Bothwell*, as it has more backbone, and less of the enormous volume and verbosity, which, we think, would always prevent Mr. Swinburne from achieving success as a dramatist. Of the dramatic *spirit*, in the Shakespearian sense, the play, as we have said, has nothing."

Tennyson seems to have shared Goethe's idea of elevating the public, instead of amusing it, through the drama. We learn from the *Memoir* that " he believed in the future of our modern English stage when education should have made the masses more literary." This, perhaps, accounts for the tinge of grandiosity, the slightly supercilious and pedantic air of *Queen Mary*, in which the masses are being somewhat too obviously educated, and the poet's personal view of Mary's character is pushed to the point of dulness. The varied elements of the great popular plays are reduced to one motive—the idealisation, or, as Tennyson doubtless thought, the humanisation of Mary, and this partisanship is undertaken with so little subtlety, that the reader finds it difficult to keep up a very lively interest in his own conversion.

It should be noted that critics of authority have waxed enthusiastic over Tennyson's plays : Spedding admired them, George Eliot said "they run Shakespeare's close," Lewes agreed with her, Browning was unable to see "the shade of a fault" in *Queen Mary,* Irving thought *Becket* a finer play than *King John*, and Richard Hutton was convinced that *Queen Mary* would compare "with something more than advantage" with Shakespeare's *Henry VIII.*

"Of course," the latter critic says, "that is by no means the finest even of the historical plays of Shakespeare, nor is it probably wholly his own,—and I only mention it because it, too, contains a study of the good and of the evil qualities of the Tudor character,—but then no play of any modern poet would be likely to rank with any of the greater plays of Shakespeare. Certainly I should be surprised to hear that any true critic would rate *Queen Mary*, whether in dramatic force or in general power, below *Henry*

VIII., and my own impression is that it is a decidedly finer work of dramatic art. The morbid passions of Mary, the brief intervals of her lucid and energetic action, the gloom of her physical decay, and the despair of her moral desolation, together make up a picture which it would be impossible for anyone who can enter into it ever to forget." Were there critics like these in Shakespeare's day that *Hamlet* should believe "there is nothing good or ill but thinking makes it so"? In one point, at all events, Tennyson was not behind Shakespeare; he was equally given to incorporating in his work the very letter of his sources, and this trait is in itself a sort of commentary on the difference between the two as dramatists. Where we find in the plays of Tennyson spontaneity and vitality, we frequently discover that the essential language of the original has been bodily transferred by him. With Shakespeare, on the contrary, the passages he decides to appropriate are usually overshadowed by the richness and variety of his own fancy.

Let us take, for example, the scene of Cranmer's martyrdom in *Queen Mary*. If we turn to the account in Froude we shall find that Tennyson leaves Cranmer's passionate appeal as nearly as possible alone, and the blank verse rendering demanded singularly few changes. This is the prose version as it is given in Froude's *History* :

" 'O Father of heaven,' he prayed, ' O Son of God, Redeemer of the world ; O Holy Ghost, three Persons and one God, have mercy upon me, most wretched caitiff and miserable sinner. I have offended both heaven and earth more than my tongue can express ; whither then may I go, or whither should I flee for succour ? To heaven I am ashamed to lift up mine eyes, and in earth I find no succour nor refuge. What shall I do ? Shall I despair ? God forbid ! Oh, good God, thou art merciful, and refusest none that come to thee for succour. To thee, therefore, do I come ; to thee do I humble myself, saying, O Lord, my sins be great, yet have mercy on me for thy great mercy. The mystery was not wrought that God became man, for few or little offences. Thou didst not give thy Son, O Father, for small sins only, but for all and the greatest in the world, so that the sinner return to thee with a penitent heart, as I do at this present. Wherefore have mercy upon me, O Lord, whose property is always to have mercy ; although my sins be great, yet is thy mercy greater ; wherefore have mercy upon me, O Lord, for thy great mercy. I crave nothing, O Lord, for mine own merits, but for thy Name's sake, and, therefore, O Father of heaven, hallowed be thy Name.'

"Then rising, he went on with his address :

"'Every man desireth, good people, at the time of his death, to give some good exhortation that others may remember after his death, and be the better thereby ; for one word spoken of a man at his last end will be more remembered than the sermons made of them that live and remain.'"

And this is Tennyson's adaptation :

"————O God, Father of Heaven !
O Son of God, Redeemer of the world !
O Holy Ghost ! proceeding from them both,
Three persons and one God, have mercy on **me**,
Most miserable sinner, wretched man.
I have offended against heaven and earth
More grievously than any tongue can tell.
Then whither should I flee for any help ?
I am ashamed to lift my eyes to heaven,
And I can find no refuge upon earth.
Shall I despair then ?—God forbid ! O God,
For thou art merciful, refusing none

That come to thee for succour; unto thee,
Therefore, I come ; humble myself to thee ;
Saying, O Lord God, although my sins be great,
For thy great mercy have mercy ! O God the Son,
Not for slight faults alone, when thou becamest
Man in the Flesh, was the great mystery wrought ;
O God the Father, not for little sins
Didst thou yield up thy Son to human death ;
But for the greatest sin that can be sinn'd,
Yea even such as mine, incalculable,
Unpardonable,—sin against the light,
The truth of God which I had proven and known.
Thy mercy must be greater than all sin.
Forgive me, Father, for no merit of mine,
But that thy name by man be glorified,
And thy most blessed Son's who died for man.
Good people, every man at time of death
Would fain set forth some saying that may live
After his death and better humankind ;
For death gives life's last word a power to live,
And like the stone-cut epitaph remain
After the vanish'd voice and speak to men.
God grant me grace to glorify my God."

This passage, even with its alliterative ending, seems to us finer than the more Tennysonian passages which were most admired by Mr. Hutton ; and even of these, the parts that are closest to the original seem most significant and valuable, while with Shakespeare it is just the other way ; the more flesh he puts on his skeleton, the more he ornaments and adorns the fundamental idea, the more he compels the admiration of his students. In the speech of the dying Gaunt, which possibly was founded, Mr. Froude suggests, upon a part of Cranmer's, what a circling flight is taken about the plain text :

" O, but they say, the tongues of dying men
Enforce attention, like deep harmony :
Where words are scarce, they are seldom spent in vain :
For they breathe truth that breathe their words in pain.
He, that no more must say, is listened more
Than they whom youth and ease have taught to gloze ;
More are men's ends marked, than their lives before ;
The setting sun, and music at the close,
As the last taste of sweets, is sweetest last ;
Writ in remembrance more than things long past."

And when, as in the Duke of Norfolk's speeches, metaphor is heaped up like driftwood on a fire, apparently for the pure love of multi-coloured flame, the thought, the idea, is not, we find, retarded or tangled as in many of Tennyson's more elaborate figurings, but made clearer and given more life with every added version ; for example :

" Be advis'd.
Heat not a furnace for your foe so hot
That it do singe yourself : we may outrun
By violent swiftness that which we run at,
And lose by over-running.   Know you not
The fire that mounts the liquor till 't run o'er,
In seeming to augment it wastes it ?   Be advised."

Without dealing further with comparisons, it may be said that Tennyson's first drama was at least dignified in conception and of consistent elevation of purpose, but that it lacked variety, and equally the austerity that sometimes makes monotony seem the consummate art.

In 1876, *Harold* followed *Queen Mary*, and set

forth "the great conflict between Danes, Saxons, and Normans for supremacy, the awakening of the English people and clergy from the slumber into which they had for the most part fallen, and the forecast of the greatness of our composite race."[1] Tennyson was evidently stirred to the depths by what may be called the elemental character of his theme; but he had not the plasticity of mind or reach of imagination to throw himself back into an age of alien standards and alien manners. His warriors are pleasant gentlemen, but very different from those of Andersen's wonder-stories, who thunder with their knives or knucklebones on the table and strike on their shields, and make a tremendous noise; and his Harold of the eleventh century is very much one of ourselves in his mental and moral sophistication, and his reflective philosophy at critical moments.

Professor Jebb, in his review,[2] describes the effect of Harold's oath, made on the bones of the Norman saints:

"It becomes his avenging destiny. In his short career it is what the inherited curse was to the house of Pelops. Harold can say in the true sense which Euripides meant, 'My tongue has sworn, but my soul has not sworn.' Nothing in the play seems to us finer than the contrast between Harold's own view of his predicament and the casuistry of the

[1] Hallam Tennyson's *Alfred, Lord Tennyson.*
[2] *Times*, October 18, 1876.

theologians who seek the immediate doom of the defiled ; but beyond that doom he looks up to that Justice which shall give him the reward of the pure in spirit."

The history of this false oath is really the chief matter of the drama. Tennyson is obviously the partisan of Harold and of Saxon England, and all the dramatic necessities of battles and great public scenes dwindle to him, precisely as in *Queen Mary*, before the position of Harold toward his own conscience. In the case of the unlucky Queen, however, the prevailing sentiment was that of pity, while in *Harold* the proving of the hero's spiritual honour and essential incorruptibility becomes a national matter, in which the typical character of Tennyson's countrymen is involved. *Harold* is too meagre and too bald, too much made up of scraps and patches, to be pronounced wholly an improvement on *Queen Mary*, and yet the swifter movement and the stronger conviction give it a certain access of vitality.

If we pass over *The Cup* and *The Falcon* as unimportant interruptions of the sequence of the historic trilogy, and come directly to *Becket*, printed in 1879, published in 1884, and played in 1893, we notice a perceptible rising from the level of *Queen Mary* and *Harold ;* more suggestion of tints and tones, greater modulation, a lighter and more intelligent touch—and yet it is more than ever obvious that Tennyson's great qualities did not lie in the direction of drama built on Shakespearian lines. In the character of à Becket, whether seen from the Protestant or from the Catholic point of view, he had a subject that demanded Shakespearian faculties. A man so emphatic, so elusive, so fit for great opportunity, so capable of seeing more than one side, and apparently so incapable of seeing more than one side at one time, might well have occupied the brain that produced *Hamlet*. But Shakespeare withheld his hand, and Tennyson appropriated the vacant space. Let us see how he made use of his opportunity. In the first place, à Becket's position in the drama is that of Archbishop. He is hardly visible as Chancellor, and the double play of worldly and ecclesiastical impulse is missed. In the next place, Tennyson, as might be expected, traces à Becket's change of action to the noblest motive—that of dedication to an ideal suiting his religious position. From this we should expect —with Shakespeare—a nature fully sensible of the dignity of the clergy, and the imperial character of Rome, whereas à Becket—the St. Thomas to be— appears to look upon Rome and the clergy very much as Tennyson looks upon them across the lapse of seven centuries. Then there is the introduction of Fair Rosamund, who is so much outside the true historical narrative and so difficult to bring in, that the author has faltered in his attack upon the problem, and in place of subtly weaving the fanciful legend into the drama as a delicate underplay, has plumped it solidly down among the greater elements, to their infinite disturbance. And if we look at the whole result as a literary monument, we shall find it written, of course, in a cultivated, serious style, broken here and there by fragments of exquisite beauty, such as the duet at the beginning of the second act, and rising now and again to brief flights of passion, as in Rosamund's reply to Henry's question of what her attitude would be should à Becket excommunicate him, and in her challenge to Eleanor to meet her before God ; but totally without the immeasurable pathos of *King John*, and without the most distant approach to the magnificence contributed by Wolsey to the play of *Henry VIII*. In fact, to use a somewhat frivolous symbol, *Becket* suggests the performance of an inadequately trained acrobat, who crosses a rope at a dizzy height with terrifying uncertainty, maintaining his balance, but failing to dominate the minds of the spectators and carry them off from the danger of the situation.

The reviews managed among them to detect all the faults and most of the virtues. None, perhaps, did complete justice to the delineation of Eleanor, in whom Tennyson suggests a light and reckless humour that lifts her into the elastic element of distinction. When she enters, singing :

> " Over ! the sweet summer closes,
>   The reign of the roses is done ;
>   Over and gone with the roses,
>   And over and gone with the sun—

Here ; but our sun in Aquitaine lasts longer. I would I were in Aquitaine again—your North chills me.

> " Over ! the sweet summer closes,
>   And never a flower at the close ;
> Over and gone with the roses,
>   And winter again and the snows "—

it is possible to realise the debonair queen and gifted troubadour.

The *Memoir* records that Tennyson summoned Mr. W. G. Ward to listen to *Becket* in order to discover its effect upon the Roman Catholic mind, and that the effect was very flattering to the author, Mr. Ward indulging in exclamations of delight and amazement. In the light of this item it is interesting to observe the effect of the play upon the mind of a reviewer in the *Catholic World*.[1] Comparing it with Aubrey de Vere's *St. Thomas of Canterbury*, he says that the latter is the true portrait, and Tennyson's the unpardonably false one.

" Aubrey de Vere's conception of the motives of the martyred primate," he says, " is worthy of a Catholic poet. Tennyson grasps only faintly the Christianity [Roman-Catholicism ?] of à Becket. It does not come home to him, it does not touch him, because in his experience he has never come in contact with the inner life of a devout priest, and therefore his imagination is not equal to the task of evolving one. Of the real meaning of asceticism, he is entirely ignorant."

Again :

" It may be said that Tennyson's idea of St.

[1] Maurice F. Egan, *Catholic World*, December, 1885.

Thomas is very human, and that the poet has well depicted in rushing words a proud nature towering and neither bending nor breaking. Tennyson's Becket is well enough painted from that point of view. There are some exquisitely fine natural touches. But the poet-laureate had no right to attempt to depict the character of St. Thomas merely from that point of view. Pride and enthusiasm would never have made a Christian martyr of Thomas à Becket, and it is the full understanding of this that, leaving out other qualities, makes Aubrey de Vere the greater poet and the truer delineator of a hero whom it is almost sacrilege to misrepresent for the sake of a theatrical *succès d'estime.*"

And still again, with rising choler and no little loss of critical dignity :

"Tennyson, echoing, perhaps, some sectarian preacher, causes the pope's almoner to suggest treachery to the archbishop when the king is urging him to sign the articles against the freedom of the church. Philip de Eleemosyna tempts the archbishop to grievous sin by whispering that the pope wants him to commit it :

‘ Cannot the pope absolve thee if thou sign ? ’

This might be forgiven in a tract against popery, on the score of ignorance ; but what plea can be offered for it in the careful overwrought work of a poet whose fame is world-wide and whose knowledge ought not to be much narrower ?

"Herbert of Bosham, the archbishop's faithful friend, a devout cleric and a sensible man according to good authorities, is made to drivel :

> ' Thee, thou holy Thomas !
> I would that thou hadst been the Holy Father.'

To which Tennyson's archbishop complacently replies :

> ' I would have done my most to keep Rome holy,
> I would have made Rome know she still is Rome—
> Who stands aghast at her eternal self
> And shakes at mortal kings—her vacillation,
> Avarice, craft—O God, how many an innocent
> Has left his bones upon the way to Rome
> Unwept, uncared for.   Yea—on mine own self
> The King had had no power except for Rome.
> 'T is not the King who is guilty of mine exile,
> But Rome, Rome, Rome ! '

Was there ever an honest and faithful priest and friend so misrepresented by a poet dazzled by the glare of the footlights ?   Was ever a saint and martyr more besmeared with mock heroic pride and selfishness ? "

In Tennyson's dedication of *Becket* to the Earl of Selborne, he declares that the play is " not intended in its present form to meet the exigencies " of the modern theatre.   Irving's abridgment rendered it possible, and, in 1893, Mr. Wedmore in the *Academy* pronounced it " one of the most distinct of the Lyceum successes."   After an appreciative notice of the players who took the minor parts, he says :

"And now for the two most important of the performers—for Rosamund and Becket, as the invention of Lord Tennyson has coupled them together. They are Miss Terry and Mr. Irving. Graceful, winning, and tender, these are the words that come to one most quickly to express all that Miss Ellen Terry is—her familiar self, in fine—in the part of Rosamund. A far greater variety than Miss Terry can claim belongs to Mr. Irving, in the first place, as a man, and in the second, because he is Mr. Irving. In Becket he has added another and a quite new portrait to that accumulating group of subtle, vigorous, distinguished ecclesiastics whom, with the pencil of his own art, he has drawn in a fashion worthy almost of Holbein. Becket is a most finished picture. His bravery and fidelity—faithful first to the secular arm, faithful then to the spiritual,—his obstinacy even, his occasional tenderness, his firmness, and his ,piety—all these qualities or characteristics by the most refined methods Mr. Irving contrives to express. No performance of his has been more dignified, more expressive, yet more wisely restrained. Among his recent successes this is certainly one of the most conspicuous. As actor he does his large part toward making the play not only acceptable but thoroughly enjoyable. As manager he bestows upon it such further advantage as a piece may gain when the resources of the Lyceum treasury and of the Lyceum good taste are lavished upon its production. Things greater in themselves—greater as poetic pro-

Henry Irving.

(As " Becket.")
From life.

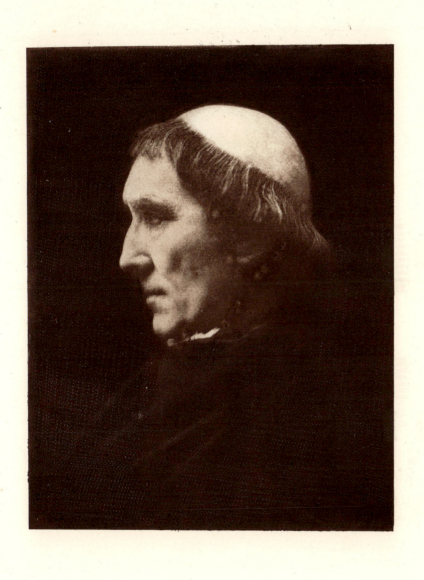

ductions—have, of course, been seen, but seldom anything more creditable. Seldom has somewhat limited literary material been applied to better effect."

If devotion of one art to another, the contribution of a plastic science to rather a stiff medium, counts at all in the way of friendship, Mr. Irving has obviously earned his rank among Tennyson's good friends.

The Promise of May is now usually called "that unfortunate play," and when it was produced the *Saturday Review* demonstrated that it was not a play at all. It trampled upon the prejudices of freethinkers, and lifted up Lord Queensberry in his seat at the theatre to declare, apropos of Edgar's comments upon marriage : "These are the sentiments that a professing Christian has put into the mouth of his imaginary freethinker, and it is not the truth." Nevertheless, Tennyson nowhere else came so near writing an original drama. It is hardly probable that he evolved the plot entirely from his inner consciousness ; but he certainly had his own idea of the characters, and although they are like shapeless twigs torn from the living tree, there is sap in them. The farm labourers and Farmer Dobson have plenty of fresh colour, and even Edgar shows an effort toward coördination of impression, although his villainy is so transparent as almost to be ludicrous. Lowell tells us that "every age says to its poets, like a mistress to her lover, 'Tell me what I am like,'" and in *The Promise of May* Tennyson seems to have made a clumsy little

caricature of certain phases of the life he knew. It
is grotesque, it is incredible, it is so badly worked
out as to seem positively cheap in method, but there
are lines of genuine resemblance ; it has an air of
struggle toward undiscoverable truth.　No actor
could make Edgar interesting ; he is not only vulgar
and bad, he is irremediably dull ; his mind is malari-
ous like a stagnant pool, and the flies and insects that
hover over it in the form of thoughts, are merely attracted to it without forming any essential part of it ;
but in his relation with the two village girls Tennyson caught a glimpse of the strangeness of human
nature, and set it down without sentimentalism.
And then, as he was seventy-three years old and too
fixed in his tendencies of mind to break a new road,
he passed on to *The Foresters* and the familiar legends
of Robin Hood, to make what the *Athenæum* called
a picture play.

The figures of *The Foresters* are those of the old
ballads roaming " merry Sherwood " in a peaceable
fashion, without the smiting off of heads, and the
" ferly strife " of the old ballad company.　Tennyson
here has shown in a thoroughly modern fashion how

> " In summer when the shaws be sheen
> 　　And leaves be large and long,
> 　It is full merry in fair forest
> 　　To hear the fowlès song;
> To see the deer draw to the dale
> 　　And leave the hillès hie
> And shadow them in the leavès green
> 　　Under the greenwood tree."

Robin Hood, the hero, is also a modern version of him whose "merry sportis" the "vulgar pepyll" sang before the fourteenth century, but he and his men correspond in outward appearance to Drayton's description, and so does Marian.   Robin

> " —— to his mistress dear, his loved Marian,
> Was ever constant known, which, whereso'er she came,
> Was sovereign of the woods, chief lady of the game";

and Tennyson's Robin is equally constant, but he has a vein of Elizabethan self-consciousness which shows itself in such philosophy as he utters when he is alone in the wood :

> " —— My lonely hour !
> The king of day hath stept from off his throne,
> Flung by the golden mantle of the cloud,
> And sets, a naked fire.   The King of England
> Perchance this day may sink as gloriously,
> Red with his own and enemy's blood—but no !
> We hear he is in prison.   It is my birthday.
> I have reign'd one year in the wild wood.   My mother,
> For whose sake, and the blessed Queen of Heaven,
> I reverence all women, bad me, dying,
> Whene'er this day should come about, to carve
> One lone hour from it, so to meditate
> Upon my greater nearness to the birthday
> Of the after-life, when all the sheeted dead
> Are shaken from their stillness in the grave
> By the last trumpet."

These serious moments are not, however, permitted to overweight the delightful fragility of the picturesque romance. The fitness of Robin Hood's story to English drama has been shown through many a century. Bishop Latimer, in 1549, told of coming to a town to preach upon a holy day, and finding the church locked :

" I tarried there half an houre and more," he said, " and at last the keye was founde, and one of the parishe commes to me and sayes, Syr, thys ys a busye day with us, we cannot heare you ; it is Robyn Hoodes Daye. The parishe are gone abroad to gather for Robyn Hoode, I pray you let them not. I was fayne there to geve place to Robyn Hoode." And this the Bishop thought " no laughyng matter," but " a wepynge matter." [1]

When *The Foresters* was produced at Daly's theatre and the New York public " went abroad to gather for Robin Hood," there was similar enthusiasm, and Professor Jebb, who was on his way to Baltimore, wrote back that he was " a highly compressed and squalid object in a back seat amid a seething mass of humanity." It is curiously consistent with the grace and lightness of Tennyson's octogenarian song, that this final essay in drama should be so delicate, so complete, so suited to the exigencies of that stage which he had not seriously studied, and so perfectly in harmony with English sentiment and taste.

[1] Taken from R. H. Stoddard's Preface to *Ballads and Romances*.

CHAPTER XII.

"TWILIGHT AND EVENING BELL."

WHILE Tennyson was engaged upon the enterprises of his later years, he was leading a secluded but very interesting life. On the anniversary of Shakespeare's birthday, 1868, he laid the corner-stone of Aldworth, his new home in Surrey, where he was henceforth to spend his summers and rid himself of the distressing malady of hay-fever, and the distressing interruption of inopportune visitors. There he had two summer-houses, one for the west wind and one for the east, from which he could look on cornland and woodland, groves and granges, and where he could hear the cries of many birds. He kept his love of long tramps, and from the *Memoir* we learn that "to plant new trees, and to watch the growth of what were already planted, continued to be unfailing sources of pleasure to him." There is a charming account of Garibaldi planting the "Wellingtonia" in the Farringford garden, and we hear of many interests connected with the management of the two estates. Both at Farringford and Aldworth a large hospitality was exercised, not only toward those "fortunate persons" whom Tennyson, like Lucy Percy, valued by nature, but toward the humblest individual who came in sincerity with adequate reason. Hallam Tennyson tells an amusing story, for example, of an American who worked his way across the sea on a cattle-ship for the honour of reading *Maud* to its author, who indulged him, but suffered from the reading, and then paid his way back to America. Toward his servants Tennyson seems to have been always considerate and generous, and they remained with him after the English fashion for terms of many years. With the dumb creatures of his household he was also gentle and kind. It is well known that he was a passionate anti-vivisectionist, and we hear of one occasion when he stole a chicken from his own larder at midnight to comfort a new dog.

In his immediate family there were few changes. In 1886, his younger son, Lionel, died as he was returning from India :

> "Beneath a hard Arabian moon
> And alien stars."

With this great exception Tennyson's personal life seems to have flowed gently enough in its quiet channel, his home remaining a fair and peaceful place, inhabited by accordant spirits. His fragile wife outlived him, so that for him the long felicitous companionship remained unbroken to the end ; and the dedication of the last book of his life reveals anew

Aldworth, Blackdown.

the brightness of his fortune in his most intimate experience :

> " I thought to myself I would offer this book to you,
> This, and my love together,
> To you that are seventy-seven,
> With a faith as clear as the heights of the June-blue heaven,
> And a fancy as summer-new,
> As the green of the bracken amid the gloom of the heather."

Three times during his life Tennyson was offered a baronetcy and declined it, preferring his plain title. In 1883 the question of a barony was broached. Tennyson seems not to have liked the idea, but finally, by Gladstone's advice, consented to it. He certainly had no foolish pride about it, and the fact that it was the Queen's pleasure had probably as much as any argument to do with moving him toward consent. His relations with the Queen had always been singularly simple and happy. Some of her letters to him were almost like the newsy pages that one expects from home,—for example, the letter describing the wedding of the Princess Beatrice,—and Tennyson on his side mingled sympathy and personal affection with his reverence and loyalty. In an extract from the Queen's private journal, given in the *Memoir*, is found a very characteristic speech that shows the temper of his mind toward the royal lady :

"When I took leave of him," the Queen records, "I thanked him for his kindness, and said I needed it for I had gone thro' much, and he said, 'You are so alone on that terrible height ; it is terrible.' "

But whatever his motive for accepting what was proffered as an honour, it was not a mean one ; and Tennyson was very far indeed from ever parading his title. The delightful story is told of him that once when the conversation turned upon the House of Lords, he suddenly exclaimed :

"I was just going to say what I would do if I were a lord, and then I remembered that I was one." [1]

It was, however, impossible that such a step should be taken without sharp criticism from the press ; and slurs, with answering defence, were numerous enough. The most dignified form of the argument against the gift of the Peerage is fairly represented by the *Spectator,* which held that the honour is not one suited to "spiritual" merit ; that so temporal a gift is not really an honour at all when considered as the reward of poetic genius. It says :

"Our own view is that a Peerage is an appropriate distinction only for those who in some degree already wield and deserve political influence, and not as a mark of popular reverence for any qualities, whatever they may be, which justly deserve reverence. That Tennyson would be a great ornament to the House of Lords we are far from denying. But he will be an incongruous ornament,—such an ornament as a wreath of roses round the brow of the Governor of the Bank of England, or a spiritual smile on the countenance of a London Lord Mayor."

The *Saturday Review,* on the other hand, con-

[1] "Aspects of Tennyson," *The Nineteenth Century.*

sidered that no "spiritual" or temporal genius could enter the House of Lords without receiving at least as much honour as he conferred. And, very likely, at the foundation of this sentiment was the fear which Bagehot expressed in saying that "the danger of the House of Lords certainly is that it may never be reformed. . . . If most of its members neglect their duties ; if all its members continue to be of one class, and that not quite the best ; if its doors are shut against genius that cannot found a family, and ability which has not five thousand a year,—its power will be less year by year, and at last be gone."

What the *Saturday Review* said is this :

"The English House of Lords is not more unique by its method of constitution than it is by its merit of performance. It has not been more prompt to resist the madness of the people than it has been to face the *vultus instantis tyranni ;* not more sure in moderating the thoughtless excesses of democracy than it has been in staying the whims of a *chambre incroyable.* The measure of any politician may be taken directly from his attitude towards the House of Lords—the most august, the most peculiar, the most beneficial, the most irreplaceable of the elements of the English Constitution." And the admission of Tennyson on literary grounds (although his descent warranted it) doubtless seemed an appropriate step to take toward keeping the "Upper Chamber" continuously august and beneficent.

Being in, Tennyson was not at all inclined to shirk his duty. Seventy-five years old and "oppressed with gout," he went up to London in behalf of the Redistribution Bill, and wrote a little poem to Gladstone, showing him his choice between two channels, one leading over a cataract, the other streaming "about the bend," and urging him to choose the "bend." How much influence he had in the matter, prosaically or poetically, it is impossible to say ; but the course of the Franchise and Redistribution Bills went in the direction he wished, and Gladstone received his congratulations.

In 1886, *Locksley Hall Sixty Years After* was published, and the excited young lover of the first *Locksley Hall* is heard again as " an old white-headed dreamer," philosophising upon, and chastising the generation. The poem drew from Mr. Gladstone a most interesting review of national life during the middle years of the century. He pointed out that while it was well " to be reminded, and in tones to make the deaf man hear, of city children who 'soak and blacken soul and sense in city slime' ; of maidens cast by thousands on the street ; of the sempstress scrimped of her daily bread ; of dwellings miserably crowded, of fever as the result " ; and of many other shameful defects in civilisation ; nevertheless the case was far better than when the first *Locksley Hall* was written. Slavery had been abolished, the criminal code had been reformed, " laws of combination and contract, which prevented the working population from obtaining the best price for their labour," had been repealed ; "the lamentable and demoralising abuses of the Poor Law " had been swept away ; the scandals of labour in mines, factories, and elsewhere had been removed or reduced, good schools had been put within reach of the poor, means of husbanding savings under the guarantee of the State had been provided, cheap communication through the post had been established for all classes, taxes had been reduced to those " paid to the State for the needful purposes of government, and nowhere to the wealthy classes of the community for the purpose of enhancing the prices of articles produced for their account."   Labouring-people were working fewer hours for increased wages, with which they could " purchase at diminished rates almost every article, except tobacco and spirits, of which the price can be affected by the acts of the Legislature."   And after citing many more improvements in the social order, he continues :

" And the sum of the matter seems to be that upon the whole, and in a degree, we who lived fifty, sixty, seventy years back, and are living now, have lived into a gentler time ; that the public conscience has grown more tender, as indeed was very needful, and that, in matters of practice, at sight of evils formerly regarded with indifference or even connivance, it now not only winces but rebels : that upon the whole, the race has been reaping, and not scattering ; earning, and not wasting ; and that, without its be-

ing said that the old Prophet is wrong, it may be said
that the young Prophet was unquestionably right."[1]

Undoubtedly the second *Locksley Hall* was dark-
ened by the natural pessimism of Tennyson's nature,
which one could hardly expect to see dissipated by
the advance of age. Unlike the imaginary victim in
Matthew Arnold's poem on *Growing Old*, Tennyson
never knew what it was to "feel but half, and
feebly," what he felt. As much as in his youth he
saw the world with "heart profoundly stirr'd"; and
there is an amount of touching truth in his stanzas :

"Nay, your pardon, cry you 'forward,' yours are hope and
    youth, but I—
Eighty winters leave the dog too lame to follow with the cry,
Lame and old, and past his time, and passing now into the night ;
Yet I would the rising race were half as eager for the light."

It was his misfortune that when moved to verbal
castigation, he developed a petulance of expression
that was very far from poetic. Addressing the

"Authors—atheist, essayist, novelist, realist, rhymester,"

who have painted "the mortal shame of nature with
the living hues of Art," his poetry loses its charming
refinement, without gaining the dignity of real irony.
These stanzas, for example, are not what one expects
from a trained intelligence :

"Rip your brothers' vices open, strip your own foul passions bare ;
    Down with Reticence, down with Reverence—forward—
        naked—let them stare.

[1] "Locksley Hall and the Jubilee," *The Nineteenth Century*, January, 1887.

Feed the budding rose of boyhood with the drainage of your
    sewer ;
Send the drain into the fountain, lest the stream should issue
    pure.

Set the maiden fancies wallowing in the troughs of Zolaism,—
Forward, forward, ay and backward, downward too into the
    abysm.

Do your best to charm the worst, to lower the rising race of
    men ;
Have we risen from out the beast, then back into the beast
    again ? "

An example of this old Lincolnshire trick of laying about him with words is found in a letter to Sir Henry Taylor describing an evening spent with Tennyson:[1]

"Alfred talked very pleasantly that evening to Annie Thackeray and L. S. He spoke of Jane Austen as James Spedding does—as next to Shakespeare ! . . . Alfred has grown, he says, very much fonder of you since your two last visits here. He says he feels now he is beginning to know you and not feel afraid of you, and that he is beginning to get over your extreme insolence to him when he was young and you were in your meridian splendour and glory. He was very violent with the girls on the subject of the rage for autographs. He said he believed every crime and every vice in the world was connected with the passion for autographs and anecdotes and records ; that the desiring of anecdotes and acquaintance with the lives of great men was treating them

[1] *Autobiography of Sir Henry Taylor.*

like pigs, to be ripped open for the benefit of the public ; that he knew he himself should be ripped open
like a pig ; that he thanked God Almighty that he
knew nothing of Jane Austen, and that there were no
letters preserved either of Shakespeare or of Jane
Austen ; that they had not been ripped open like
pigs. Then he said that the post for two days had
brought him no letters, and he thought there was a
sort of syncope in the world as to him and to his fame."

Among the poems published in the 'eighties was
"Rizpah." When Swinburne wrote of this poem he
gave the same rein to his approbation that he elsewhere gives to his disapproval. After an ecstatic
prelude he proceeds :

"Some indeed may probably be found to object
that pity is here strained and racked into actual and
intolerable anguish—that terror here darkens and
condenses into sheer physical pain and horror : and,
doubtless, of no contemporary writer can it be so
truly said—nor can it be said more truly of any writer
in time past—that he has 'created a new shudder' ;
a pang of piercing and dreadful compassion which
cleaves, as it were, the very core of 'the spirit of
sense' in sunder. But here is one more proof—and
a proof beyond all price and beyond all question—
that passion and imagination are justified of their
children. Were it not so, the very crowning glory
of this most pathetic and terrible poem would be
frightful rather than terrible, and unbearable rather
than pathetic."

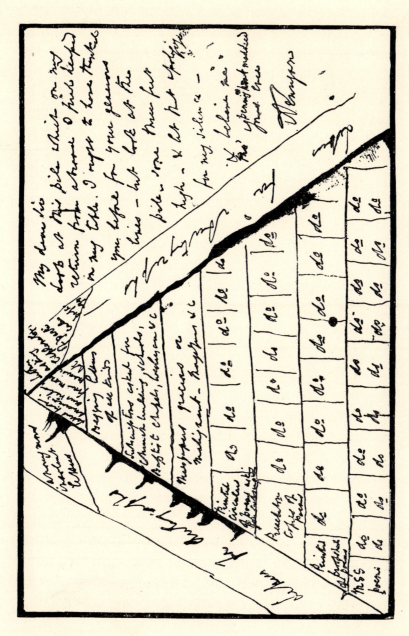

LETTER FROM TENNYSON TO W. C. BENNETT

Tiresias, which was not published until 1885, resulted from a visit made in 1876 to FitzGerald, who was then "an old vegetarian philosopher sitting among his doves at Woodbridge." In a letter Fitz-Gerald wrote of the meeting : "Tennyson, a man of Genius, who, I think, has crippled his growth by over-elaboration, came suddenly upon me here six weeks ago, and, many years as it was since we had met, there seemed not a Day's Interval between." The dedication of *Tiresias* to FitzGerald describes Tennyson's own essay in vegetarianism :

> " And once for ten long weeks I tried
> Your table of Pythagoras,
>   And seem'd at first 'a thing enskied'
>   (As Shakespeare has it) airy-light
>   To float above the ways of men,
> Then fell from that half-spiritual height
>   Chill'd, till I tasted flesh again
> One night when earth was winter-black
>   And all the heavens flash'd in frost ;
> And on me, half-asleep, came back
>   That wholesome heat the blood had lost,
> And set me climbing icy capes
>   And glaciers, over which there roll'd
> To meet me long-arm'd vines with grapes
>   Of Eschcol hugeness ; for the cold
> Without and warmth within me, wrought
>   To mould the dream ; but none can say
> That Lenten fare makes Lenten thought,
>   Who reads your golden Eastern lay."

FitzGerald wrote to Fanny Kemble that Tennyson looked " much the same, except for his fallen locks," as twenty years before. " We went over the same old grounds of debate," he said, "told some of the old stories, and all was well. I suppose I may never see him again." He never did, nor did he live to read the dedication, and the later edition of *Tiresias* gives some beautiful supplementary lines, full of mourning for the friend who had been so consistently severe a critic :

> " The tolling of his funeral bell
>   Broke on my Pagan Paradise,
> And mixt the dream of classic times
>   And all the phantoms of the dream,
> With present grief, and made the rhymes,
>   That miss'd his living welcome, seem
> Like would-be guests an hour too late,
>   Who down the highway moving on
> With easy laughter find the gate
>   Is bolted and the master gone.
> Gone into darkness, that full light
>   Of friendship ! past, in sleep, away
> By night, into the deeper night !
>   The deeper night ? A clearer day
> Than our poor twilight dawn on earth—
>   If night what barren toil to be !
> What life, so maim'd by night, were worth
>   Our living out ? Not mine to me,—"

Among the poems of the later years were also "Vastness," a singularly noble composition, and "The Revenge, A Ballad of the Fleet." The latter was, it will be remembered, one of the national poems that drew Swinburne's praise, and has at the present moment a contemporary interest. The opening lines show its place among the ballads made to stir the British blood :

" At Flores in the Azores, Sir Richard Grenville lay.
And a pinnace, like a flutter'd bird, came flying from far away:
'Spanish ships of war at sea ! we have sighted fifty-three!'
Then sware Lord Thomas Howard : ''Fore God I am no
 coward !
But I cannot meet them here, for my ships are out of gear,
And the half of my men are sick. I must fly, but follow quick.
We are six ships of the line; can we fight with fifty-three?'"

These poems were the good ripe fruit of the tree ; fit to nourish and refresh. They hung among blossoms and leaves, for Tennyson's genius continued to bud and flower when everyone looked for the changes that come with the seasons. And the final phenomenon was the one that always touches the heart as the sight of a pale apple-blossom after the frosts, or the springing of a single garden flower to decorate the Christmas ground. It had been with Tennyson a green winter, and when he was eighty years old he offered *Demeter and Other Poems* to the wondering public. The slender little volume can hardly be criticised from any usual standpoint. Among its contents " Merlin and the Gleam " stands out conspicuous as an autobiographical outline, and the short-breathing lines have in them a solemn suggestion of the close :

" And broader and brighter
 The Gleam flying onward,
 Wed to the melody,
 Sang thro' the world ;
 And slower and fainter,
 Old and weary,
 But eager to follow,
 I saw, whenever
 In passing it glanced upon

> Hamlet or city,
> That under the Crosses
> The dead man's garden,
> The mortal hillock,
> Would break into blossom ;
> And so to the land's
> Last limit I came—
> And can no longer,
> But die rejoicing."

The poem with which the volume ends is also one of potent and haunting significance. Like a prophesy it sounded to the waiting world :

> " Sunset and evening star,
> And one clear call for me !
> And may there be no moaning of the bar,
> When I put out to sea."

There are very few instances on record of such sustained felicity as this ; and its charm is singular. That Tennyson, who so much loved the stately harmonies of mental existence, whose sense of order and fitness was so persistent, should have been granted a physical decline so beautiful, and a farewell so equal to his earlier performance, is one of our compensations for the jarring irregularities of human fate.

When on Thursday, October 6, 1892, the end came, there was nothing to interrupt the effect of beauty and harmony. "There were no artificial lights in the chamber, and all was darkness save for the silvery light of the moon at its full. The soft beams of the light fell upon the bed and played upon the features of the dying poet like a halo of Rembrandt." Outside were the woods and rolling ground about Aldworth. Toward the last he wandered and dreamed of walking in his garden with Gladstone, showing him his trees. Shakespeare's *Cymbeline* was the last book in his hand, and he had opened it at the passage :

> " Hang there like fruit, my soul,
> Till the tree die,"

and that took place of which Swinburne wrote :

> " So when night for his eyes grew bright, his proud head pillowed on Shakespeare's breast,
> Hand in hand with him, soon to stand where shine the glories that death loves best,
> Passed the light of his face from sight, and sank sublimely to radiant rest."

Mr. Pickford has quoted in illustration of this tranquil death-scene these verses of Leopardi, which came to him, he says, as he lay awake in the moonlight of the same lovely night[1] :

> " Intatta luna, tale
> È lo stato mortale.
> Ma tu mortal non sei,
> E forse del mio dir poco ti cale.
> Pur tu, solinga, eterna peregrina
> Che sì pensosa sei, tu forse intendi,
> Questo viver terreno,
> Il patir nostro, il sospirar, che sia ;
> Che sia questo morir, questo supremo
> Scolorar del sembiante,

[1] In *Notes and Queries.*

E perir della terra, e venir meno
Ad ogni usata, amante campagnia." [1]

After the moonlit night was over, and the great
frame of Tennyson had to be taken out of the charming home in which he had so happily and so sanely
dwelt, his coffin was borne away on one of his own
waggons, the horse was led by his old servant, and
the pall that covered him was "woven by working
men and women of the North, and embroidered by
the cottagers of Keswick."

In Westminster Abbey, where he was laid by
Browning's side, immediately under Chaucer's tomb,
and near the bust of Longfellow and the monument
of Dryden, a vast number gathered to do honour to
his memory. "The 'power and presence' that was
alive in the Abbey," says a writer in the *Spectator*,
"was very different from that which is convention-
ally associated with the burial of the dead. The
sense of solemnity was there, but not the sense of
sorrow, for though this or that man may misunder-

---

[1] Inviolate moon, such is
The mortal condition.
But thou art not mortal,
And perchance for my speech thou carest but little.
Yet thou alone and forever a pilgrim,
Pensively wandering, thou perchance knowest
What is this earthly life,
What is this suffering, what is this sighing,
What is this dying and this supremest
Pallor of countenance,
This perishing, waning, relinquishing
All of our loving and constant companionship.

This does not pretend to be a metrical translation, but gives, I think, the sentiment of the lines.

stand and misread his own heart, the instinct of a mass of men does not err. We were not there to mourn some 'mighty poet in his misery dead,' some 'young Marcellus of our tongue,' some hope of the nation cut off before his time, and carrying with him to the grave the unfulfilled promise of high deeds in song. Rather we of the English kin, whether here or in America, or in other English lands over sea, had gathered to honour the memory of a great Englishman, and to thank God for a great achievement, and a life well spent. In every heart was something of the feeling that inspired Milton when he wrote :

'Nothing is here for tears, nothing to wail
  Or knock the breast, no weakness, no contempt,
  Dispraise, or blame ; nothing but well and fair,
  And what may quiet us in a death so noble.'

. . . .

"Most appropriately, and, we may add, most naturally, an American envoy took his place among the great statesmen and men of learning who acted as pall-bearers, in order to represent that portion of the English kin which lives under another flag than that which covered the coffin of Tennyson. The men of the rest of Greater Britain were represented by their fellow-subjects, but it would have been a matter of deep regret if our kinsmen in America had taken no share in the ceremony of Wednesday. As it was, the right of America to share in honouring the poet's memory was fully admitted and a precedent was created which we trust will never be forgotten when any great Englishman is laid in the Abbey or St. Paul's."

During the impressive services two of Tennyson's songs, *Crossing the Bar* and *The Silent Voices*, were sung, the latter to music of Lady Tennyson's own composing, and Tennyson lay at last in state among his peers, "'*le père là-bas dans l'île*' was gone."

CHAPTER XIII.

ECHOES.

IMMEDIATELY a great strain of eulogy arose.
Those who had known Tennyson in person recalled how simple he had been and how sincere.
"His charm," said Theodore Watts, "lay in a great
veracity of soul—in a simple single-mindedness so
childlike that unless you had known him to be the undoubted author of his exquisitely artistic poems, you
would have supposed that even the subtleties of poetic
art must be foreign to a nature so devoid of all subtlety
as his." Others recalled his generosity toward people needing a "lift," and his temperate judgments
of the work of fellow poets. Others still remembered his magnificent physical presence, how at
seventy he outwalked a man of forty and was gleeful to see the latter ignominiously resting ; and how
at eighty-two he climbed a difficult gate and "literally ran" down a hill. In an article on the various
portraits of Tennyson, Theodore Watts declared that
his face was one of the few that do not gain by "the
artistic halo which a painter of genius always sheds

over his work."[1]   And he noted for readers of a time
when memory of the poet's physiognomy should
have faded, the curious expression of the eyes which
suggested to him "the 'song-smith' of the northern
Olympus, Bragi, the son of Odin and Frigga, described in the Elder Edda, whose eyes were 'both
old and young.'"   He noted also the line of hair,
"which indeed may almost be called tresses," upon
the cheek and neck, so finely given in the portraits
by Watts, and the colour of the skin, which was not,
he said, really of a dark complexion, but was deeply
tanned by the sun.   And he found his personal impression of Tennyson's aspect most truly rendered
by the photograph by Mayall, hanging at Aldworth.
The impression made upon a very large number of
persons by Tennyson's death is given in a paper contributed to the *Speaker*.   It is an impression of the
heart, not of the intellect, and is interesting because
it is representative :

"You ask me," the writer begins, "why I, a
middle-aged business man, with, as you phrase it,
'more than enough to do on my own account,'
should have travelled two hundred miles and given
up a day and a half of precious time merely in order
to witness the poet's funeral."   Then, recalling Thackeray and Dickens, both dead, the writer quotes Tennyson's own line,

" Three dead men have I loved and thou art last of the three,"

and proposes through his own experience to illustrate

[1] *The Magazine of Art*, 1893.

Alfred, Lord Tennyson, 1888.

From life.

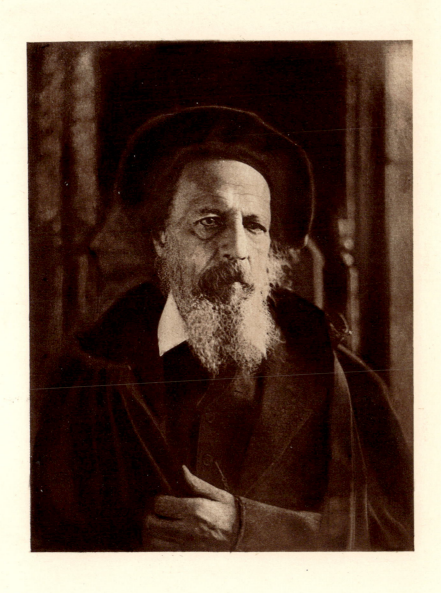

Tennyson's hold upon the men and women past the middle years, and sufficiently prosaic to the outer view, who thronged the Abbey on the day of the funeral.

"Tennyson has been my friend and companion these forty years," he says, "in the sense in which he has been the friend and companion of thousands of other men, for my personal knowledge of him was hardly greater than that which I had of Thackeray and Dickens. As I look back on those forty years of work and endurance, I see hardly an episode or an hour in which this man on whose coffin I looked to-day, was not with me—a friend, a teacher, and a guide. In what varied moods he has found me during these years of pilgrimage, and how fully he has responded to each! When first I came by the great railway from the North to London, it was the lines in *Locksley Hall*[1] which sprang to my lips as I leaned from the carriage window to catch the earliest reflection of the lights of the wonderful city in the evening sky. It was *Maud* and *Enoch Arden* on which I fed myself when the moment of romance came to me, as it does to all of us once at least, and the chord of self, smitten by the hand of Love, 'passed in music out of sight.' It was in *The Princess* that I found the picture of the ideal woman I had sought for and won at last. And then came the long evenings of happy married lovers, when the same volume

[1] " Eager-hearted as a boy when first he leaves his father's field,
And at night along the dusky highway near and nearer drawn
Sees in heaven the light of London flaring like a dreary dawn."

had two readers instead of one, and we went hand in hand through the flowery paths by which our poet led us. In my heart I thanked him for those far-off hours of a joy almost divine, when I stood in the Abbey to-day. But it was later—a few brief months later—when the poet came to me in another guise, and stretched forth his hand as a brother, and held me up, and made me face the world again. . . . I had read *In Memoriam* before ; I have read it many times since ; but it is only when one reads it by the hearth that has suddenly become cold, in presence of the empty chair, the empty bed, that its inner meaning is borne in upon the soul."

In this frank avowal of sentiment it is easy to trace the nature of Tennyson's service to the multitude ; his sublimation of their usual thoughts about the strange facts of their existence ; his imaginative version of every-day life. Such is the undoubted source of his influence over the ordinary school-taught mind ; but it needs to be capped by the recognition which Mr. Traill has made of its separateness from Tennyson's true poetic gift : "When we talk of Tennyson's 'popularity,'" he says, "intending thereby to describe that wide and increasing influence which he exercised for upwards of forty years over the minds of educated Englishmen, let us not forget that in this connection we are not really speaking of him as a poet at all. Let us not forget that, though to have yielded such a power is a good and a great thing,— is, if you like to think so, a better and a greater thing than to have been the greatest of poets,—it is not the same thing, and in short, that the influences in question are of something not primarily and essentially connected with Lord Tennyson's poetic gift at all."

To Mr. Edmund Gosse this popularity, this mass of humanity attending the public services at Westminster, this excitement of critics suddenly declaring that poetry had died with Tennyson, this over-wrought sentiment in the minds of the people, seemed a perilous sign. " I think," he wrote," of the funeral of Wordsworth at Grasmere, only forty-two years ago, with a score of persons gathering quietly under the low wall that fenced them from the brawling Rotha ; and I turn to the spectacle of the 12th, the vast black crowd in the street, the ten thousand persons refused admittance to the Abbey, the whole enormous popular manifestation. What does it mean ? Is Tennyson, great as he is, a thousand times greater than Wordsworth ? Has poetry, in forty years, risen at this ratio in the public estimation ? The democracy, I fear, doth protest too much, and there is danger in this hollow reverence.

"The danger takes this form. It may at any moment come to be held that the poet, were he the greatest that ever lived, was greater than poetry, the artist more interesting than his art. This was a peril unknown in ancient times. The plays of Shakespeare and his contemporaries were scarcely more closely identified with the man who wrote them than

Gothic cathedrals were with their architects. Cowley was the first English poet about whom much personal interest was felt outside the poetic class. Dryden is far more evident to us than the Elizabethans were, yet phantasmal by the side of Pope. Since the age of Anne, an interest in the poet as distinguished from his poetry has steadily increased; the fashion for Byron, the posthumous curiosity in Shelley and Keats, are examples of the rapid growth of this individualisation in the present century. But since the death of Wordsworth it has taken colossal proportions, without, so far as can be observed, any parallel quickening of the taste for poetry itself. The result is that a very interesting or picturesque figure, if identified with poetry, may attract an amount of attention and admiration which is spurious as regards the poetry and of no real significance. Tennyson had grown to be by far the most mysterious, august, and singular figure in English society. He represented poetry, and the world now expects its poets to be as picturesque, as aged, and as individual as he was, or else it will pay poetry no attention. I fear, to be brief, that the personal as distinguished from the purely literary distinction of Tennyson may strike, for the time being, a serious blow at the vitality of poetry in this country." [1]

From this dark prophecy, which in half a dozen years has not been contradicted, Mr. Gosse passes on to show how alien to Tennyson's own spirit were

[1] Article on Tennyson in *The New Review*.

the lamentations with which his surrender of the poetic field to his successors was greeted.

"The ingratitude of the hour towards the surviving poets of England," he says, "pays but a poor compliment to the memory of that great man whose fame it professes to honour. I suppose that there has scarcely been a writer of interesting verse who has come into anything like prominence within the lifetime of Tennyson who has not received from him some letter of praise, some message of benevolent indulgence. More than fifty years ago he wrote, in glowing terms, to congratulate Mr. Bailey on his 'Festus'; it is only yesterday that we were hearing of his letters to Mr. Rudyard Kipling and Mr. William Watson. Tennyson did not affect to be a critic—no man, indeed, can ever have lived who less *affected* to be anything—but he loved good verses, and he knew them when he saw them, and welcomed them indulgently. No one can find it more distasteful to him to have it asserted that Tennyson was, and will be, 'the last of the English poets,' than would Tennyson himself. It was not my good fortune to see him many times, and only twice, at an interval of about twelve years, did I have the privilege of hearing him talk at length and ease. On each of those occasions, however, it was noticeable with what warmth and confidence he spoke of the future of English poetry, with what interest he evidently followed its progress, and how cordially he appreciated what various younger men were doing. In particular, I hope it is not indiscreet to refer to the tone in which he spoke to me on each of these occasions of Mr. Swinburne, whose critical conscience had, it must not be forgotten, led him to refer with no slight severity to several of the elder poet's writings. In 1877 Mr. Swinburne's strictures were still recent, and might not unreasonably have been painfully recollected. Yet Tennyson spoke of him almost as Dryden did two hundred years ago to Congreve :

> ' And thus I prophesy—thou shalt be seen
> (Though with some short parenthesis between)
> High on the throne of wit, and, seated there,
> Not mine (that's little), but thy laurel wear.'

It would never have occurred to this great and wise man that his own death could be supposed to mark the final burning up and turning to ashes of these prophetic bays."

When we come to the appeal made by Tennyson's poetry to the small number of judicial minds that were uninfluenced by personal emotion, we find it singularly independent of the long poems. A volume could be made up of the shorter pieces ranking with " Morte d'Arthur," " Ulysses," " Tithonus," and the songs in *Maud*, that would arouse enthusiasm of a purer flame, perhaps, than could be awakened by the *Idylls of the King*, or *In Memoriam*, or *The Princess*. They are not the " popular " poetry that comes naturally to the lips when Tennyson's name is mentioned, that is quoted in essays on literature, and

repeated at school exhibitions; but they form the
ballast that steadies the critical impression of the
work as a whole. And what variety is in them; how
much they contain of the essence of pure poetry!
Tennyson's experience of life was not compressed:
unlike Musset, unlike Keats, he had not a single
hour full to the brim of emotion; but a life slowly
developing through more than eighty years. Some
of his later poems are infinitely more beautiful than
most of his earlier ones; some of the earlier—the
" Ulysses," for example—have a maturity of quality
never exceeded. But we must follow the entire
course, from " Claribel" to " The Dreamer," if we
would get the range of his best; and if part of the way
lies through the commonplace, the exquisite serenity
and purity of the end brings unusual compensation.
Age is not often permitted to express itself as with
Tennyson, and one of the rarest pleasures to be
found in reading his collected work is to trace the
larger interests and calmer view in the poems written
after the limit of threescore years and ten, when ordinarily, if all is not labour and sorrow, all is vague-
ness and inertia. At the time of his death a poem
was written about him, giving a new reading to the
old saying, " Whom the gods love die young," by
finding youth still blooming in his age. And so it
was in one sense; but it is still more satisfying to remember that his age was not like real youth, but was
the true age of man, the normal, conscious, vigorous age of a sane mind in a sane body; the ripening

of the spirit without the loss of self-expression, and without the flitting of the precious individuality. This health and persistence, so noticeable in his genius, showed equally in his character. His friends seem to have experienced no falling off, no waning of personal attractiveness ; there was no temptation to think that it was well for the body to decline since mind and spirit had sunk. Jowett, who had written in 1862, "I sometimes think that merely being in the neighbourhood of Alfred keeps me up to a higher standard of what ought to be in writing and thinking," found the loss that came thirty years later almost heavier than he could bear.

When the authoritative biography of Tennyson appeared in 1897, after four years of careful preparation by the present Lord Tennyson, an immense satisfaction was felt by the literary public. There was nothing in the published material to change the prevailing impression of Tennyson's greatness of character and dignity of life ; and the fulness of the account, and the nature of the testimony brought by old friends and private letters and records, precluded the idea that any reservations or omissions had been made which could seriously mar that noble impression. It was found that with rare and admirable taste Lord Tennyson had left his "sources" to speak in the main for themselves. What he added was merely the affectionate tribute of a son to a father. The story is naturally not particularly rich in adventure ; there was but one real adventure to record,—the visit to the Spanish insurgents,—and upon the subject of this romantic episode little is said. Neither are there any details of spiritual and personal crises, such as are revealed by the letters of men like John Addington Symonds and Robert Louis Stevenson. If Tennyson had his intense hours of mental stress, we shall never hear of them. Nor is there very much of the indescribable pungency that lingers in the faintest reminiscence of Thackeray and the barest anecdote of Charles Lamb. In his youth Tennyson was poor ; but there are no details of picturesque poverty. The one love affair is the enduring passion for his wife, but, though the period of long waiting offered a capital chance for fine writing, it is disposed of in the fewest possible words. In fact there is nothing in Tennyson's biography to excite the fancy of the reader. For this very reason the book is fascinating. It is like a Doric temple in its unimpeachable severity. We see the poet steadily employed with his art, never entirely distracted from it, or finding contradictory outlets for his genius. What he cared for was what furthered and harmonised with the making of poetry. His friends were chosen upon the high level of his own intellectual capacity. To some of them he looked up ; to few of them can he have looked down. There were no degradations of taste or of principle ; it was a wholly moral life in the sturdiest sense of the word. Nor was it lacking on the human side. Single sentences spoken of his wife or to his children, or, curiously enough, to his Queen, reveal the fire and

impulse at the core of Tennyson's nature, "too deep
for sound and foam." His talk, in the main, was
about subjects of permanent importance; he was
ready always to hear of the advance of science in
any field. Human progress was the most poetic fact
with which he could occupy his mind, although his
efforts to clothe it in poetic language did not always
accomplish his object. The most interesting and
unique feature of the biography is the collection of
reminiscences at the end, contributed by old friends,
some of them already dead, all of them at the season
of the yellow leaf. These also follow the general
plan adopted, which excludes anything like trivial
gossip or inconsequent detail. They add, however,
an appreciable amount to one's realisation of Tennyson's good-fellowship with his friends, and of his
kind, engaging ways when he was at home in mind
and spirit. We hear of his humour, of his teasing,
of his grumbling, of his strength and his weakness,
of his shyness and frankness; most of all, of his
"loveableness." The Duke of Argyle contributes an
anecdote of singular charm.

"The first words I heard him utter," he says,
"remain indelibly impressed upon my memory. On
being introduced to him at an evening party in the
house of Lord John Russell, I said, perhaps with
some emotion, 'I am so glad to know you.' Not in
the tone or voice of a mere conventional reply, but
in the accents of sincere humility, he answered,
'You won't find much in me—after all.'"

This reply indicates the one fact absolutely necessary to remember in forming a fair estimate of Tennyson's character,—his essential humility. He never indulged in any cant about it ; but no one can read his familiar letters without realising how little he was satisfied with himself and his achievement in comparison with the great best to which he continually aspired. The fact that he pitched his ideals so high, and tried for perfection in all the ways he knew, accounts for his success in poetry. Others have had more of the divine spark ; many others have had stronger personal views and clearer insight, but very few have been strong enough to sustain such dangerous facility as his by unwavering devotion to the highest standard of performance. In the biography are eighty-three poems hitherto unpublished ; and while in the main they are of high excellence compared to the average poetical effusion, they bear witness to Tennyson's good judgment in rejecting them. He supplied certainly one half the requirement which, Mr. Henry James has told us, is made by any artistic performance, whatever the instrument. He supplied "the perfect presence of mind, unconfused, unhurried by emotion," the "clear and calculated" application of the idea. Had he carried out the rest of the formula, had the ideas themselves been conceived by him "in the glow of experience, of suffering, of joy," there could never have been two words about his greatness as an artist. Among his unpublished poems is one beginning :

"Art for Art's sake ! Hail, truest Lord of Hell !
Hail, Genius, Master of the Moral Will !"

But, in spite of the uninterrupted supremacy of the Moral Will in his mind, was there ever a better example than he himself offers of " art for art's sake," as most of us understand the phrase ? Did he not tame and subdue his noble talent in working outside his own experience, because he so much loved the work and so little realised the necessity to genius of an individual conception ? And this, too, is a part of his integral humility. Had he more heartily believed that there was much within himself to be sought and found and expressed, had he insisted upon drinking from his own glass, believing it to hold the wine best suited to him, we might have had a Musset plus a Tennyson. And as it is, we may follow M. Taine's example, dismiss our critical analyses, and " prefer " our Tennyson.

CHAPTER XIV.

"CONTEMPORARY POSTERITY."

LOWELL says that posterity is seldom wont to judge a writer by his best rather than by the average of his achievement, and if this is true of posterity it is doubly true of that substitute for posterity,—the criticism of alien minds. In fact it is doubtful if our best is ever really known to the foreigner, and *vice versa*. Everyone who has read it must remember Hamerton's description of the scholarly Frenchman who knew most of the great English authors "even down to the close critical comparison of different readings," but could not write or speak English in a manner tolerable to an Englishman. "His appreciation of our authors," said Mr. Hamerton, "especially of our poets, differed so widely from English criticism and English feeling that it was evident he did not understand them as we understand them. Two things especially proved this : he frequently mistook declamatory versification of the most mediocre quality for poetry of an elevated order ; whilst, on the other hand, his ear failed to perceive the music of the musical poets, as Byron

and Tennyson.　How *could* he hear their music, he
to whom our English sounds were all unknown?
Here, for example, is the way he read 'Claribel':

> ' At ev ze bittle bommess
> 　Azvart ze zeeket lon
> At none ze veeld be ommess
> 　Aboot ze most edston
> At meedneez ze mon commess
> 　An lokez dovn alon
> Ere songg ze lintveet zvelless
> Ze clirvoic-ed mavi dvelless
> 　Ze fledgling srost lispess
> Ze slombroos vav ootvelless
> 　Ze babblang ronnel creespess
> Ze ollov grot replee-ess
> Vere Claribel lovlee-ess.' "

Against this disadvantage of imperfect comprehension may be placed, however, the advantage of
sufficient aloofness to command the whole view.
The perspective for which we have to wait a century,
or a couple of generations at least, the foreign critics
obtain by virtue of modes of thought, and, more particularly, modes of feeling, quite different from our
own.　They are not cheated into admiration or affection by the sense of kinship—the faults of the writer
under their consideration wound them not at all, nor
do his virtues reflect credit in the slightest degree
upon themselves.　They are quite free to take an
impartial view, and the view is therefore apt to be
interesting, whether we agree with it or find it as
objectionable as we are prone to find the national
dishes of other countries.

George Frederick Watts, R.A.

From life.

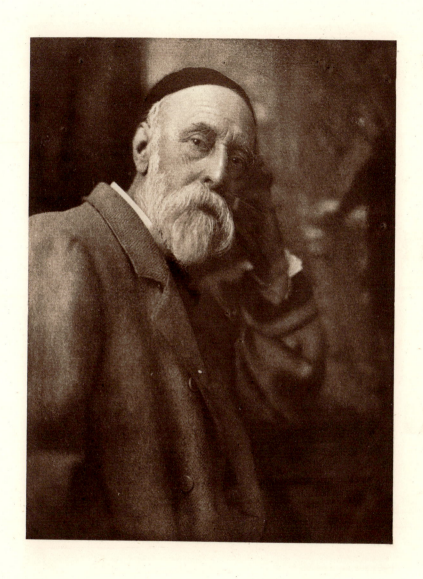

As early as 1847, Tennyson's poetry was attracting critical attention in France. Writing of the 1842 collection, M. Forgues, in the *Revue des Deux Mondes*, finds that Tennyson "to no greater degree than John Keats, to no greater degree than Samuel Coleridge," fulfils to his mind the "first conditions of all fame that shall be at once universal and durable."

"Deprive his verse of its voluptuous melody, its merit of scholarly archaism," he says, "and you will already have done it irreparable harm, for Tennyson is creator only in details of style. Finder of words rather than of ideas, he borrows willingly and without overmuch discrimination, the commonplace theme upon which he loves to spend the richness of his harmonic combinations. Whether through inability or veritable disdain, he, preoccupied chiefly with the lyric effect, hardly reveals a glimpse of the inner drama, of the human fact from which emanate, laughing or sorrowful, sympathetic or scornful and bitter, the effusions of his thought. With him the reality is confounded, amalgamated, with the dream; it takes on vague proportions, a supernatural character. Nothing precise or palpable is discoverable. In these Eolian poems, the women are the sylphs, the passions, the entities of the Germanic mind, mere musical abstractions; the description,—often admirable,—a mirage about to vanish.

"From time to time, it is true, English realism brings light into this vapoury chaos, and in a fashion sufficiently bizarre. The wandering will-o'-the-wisp

becomes a lantern omnibus; by the side of the singing syren is heard the squawking goose, and you
have hardly quitted the fanciful country, the en-
chanted isle of the Lotophagi, when you find yourself
on a cross-road in the company of simple travellers
who have come afoot to wait for the mail coach:
tremendous discords which cannot fail to throw the
reader's mind into some degree of embarrassment."

Among the several poems chosen by M. Forgues
for translation is "The Sisters," and it rather upsets
the general idea of French sensitiveness to find him
translating the third stanza with omissions. The
original, he says, shows "a Shakespearian naïveté
which in French is neither tolerable nor tolerated."
One point that he makes is interesting: "Upon occasions," he says, "Dickens's prose and Tennyson's
verse offer striking resemblances. The thoughts have
an air of belonging to the same family; the very
words take on an analogous physiognomy or harmony. To be convinced, compare the account in
The Old Curiosity Shop of Nelly's funeral with the
'New Year's Eve,' or the 'Dirge,' or any other elegy
in which the poet is filled with the spectacle of
death and burial. The comparison is in this instance
the easier that Dickens has written in irregular blank
verse the passage to which we refer our readers."

M. Milsand, writing in 1851, probably before *In
Memoriam* reached him, said with more judgment
than prophetic power:

"M. Tennyson has *l'haleine courte*, he is incapable of a prolonged effort. Vast combinations should not be expected from him, but he will not attempt that which he cannot do. His talent obeys his nature with docility, and the mind loves to linger over his works, delighting to look upon a planet which shines because it remains admirably within its orbit. That which is true of all superior men may be said of him : that the faculties which they have not are as useful to them as those which they possess. If the chords of his instrument quickly cease to vibrate, it is to that very quality that they owe their exactitude ; it is that which renders them always ready to respond to the least breath."

After the publication of the 1864 edition of the *Idylls of the King*, M. Taine elaborated his comparison between Tennyson and Musset. His estimate of the former is so well known that it will only be necessary to recall two or three significant passages. *Maud* is the only poem that calls out enthusiastic admiration ; *In Memoriam*, as we have seen, is dismissed with a few words that contain something very like a sneer. *The Princess* is " a fairy tale as sentimental as those of Shakespeare." In the *Idylls* "Tennyson has renewed the feelings and the language ; and his pliant soul takes all tones in order to give itself all pleasures. This time he has become epic, antique, and ingenuous like Homer, and like the old *trouvères* of the *Chansons de Geste*." (How unlike surely no one could have known better than M. Taine.)

If we sum up the criticism we are strongly impressed by the fact that, while M. Taine was writing of Tennyson, he was thinking of Musset, of how different he was, how superior, how much more French, how much more real ! In the final paragraph, all the critic has not said positively of the English poet he says negatively in extolling his contemporary : " We feel pity ; we think of that other poet, away there in the Isle of Wight, who amuses himself by dressing up lost epics. How happy he is amongst his fine books, his friends, his honeysuckles and roses ! No matter. De Musset, in this very spot, in this filth and misery, rose higher. From the heights of his doubt and despair, he beheld the infinite, as we behold the ocean from a storm-beaten promontory. Religions, their glory and their decay ; the human race, its pangs and its destiny ; all that is sublime in the world, appeared to him there in a flash of lightning. He felt, at least this once in his life, the inner tempest of deep sensations, giant dreams, and intense pleasures, the desire of which enabled him to live, and whose lack forced him to die. He was no mere dilettante ; he was not content to taste and enjoy ; he left his mark on human thought ; he told the world what was man, love, truth, happiness. He suffered, but he invented ; he fainted, but he produced. He tore from his vitals with despair the idea which he had conceived, and showed it to the eyes of all, bloody but alive. That is harder and lovelier than to go fondling and gazing upon the ideas of

others.   There is in the world but one work worthy
of a man, the production of a truth to which we de-
vote ourselves, and in which we believe.   The people
who have listened to Tennyson are superior to our
aristocracy of townsfolk and bohemians, but I prefer
Alfred de Musset to Tennyson."

M. Montégut, in 1866, with *Enoch Arden, and
Other Poems* for his theme, brings the same charge,
but more directly as well as more delicately, against
Tennyson's general style.   "The sentiment of
beauty," he says, "may, and too often does, create
in a poet a state not unlike barrenness.   Mr. Tennyson
has more than once suffered this experience ; a certain absence of heat is felt in him, a too great tranquillity ; sometimes, also, a sort of powerlessness to
express what is purely moral as perfectly as that
which is purely beautiful.   We shall not reproach
him for having always ignored the strong but somewhat rude sympathies of the political partisan, since
for the high-born soul there is ordinarily too much
hate and too little love in these robust sympathies,
whose fire and salt too often amount to obstinacy
and harshness.   Nor shall we reproach him for ignor-
ing the strong conviction of the partisan philosopher
which savours too much of pedantry for so delicate a
soul ; but what we could wish added to his talent is
more heat, a stronger grip, a more ardent curiosity,
something, in short, of that impetuous admiration
and that passionate sympathy with which the great
poets of all times have been inspired by the richness

18

and potency of the human soul, with which, for example, Robert Browning, his own neighbour and colleague and rival before Apollo, has been inspired."

The volume under discussion, however, reveals Tennyson's power of bending to meet humble realities, and it is more praiseworthy, M. Montégut declares, in one of Tennyson's nature to stoop to what is humble than to rise to what is noble. "In fact, where is the great merit," he says, "in comprehending and loving what is noble when one so well comprehends and loves what is beautiful? To pass from one of these worlds to the other is hardly to change the sphere. The magician who evokes the beautiful Helen can with the same formula summon the valiant Achilles; the poet who has just written 'A Dream of Fair Women' can, without putting any constraint upon his imagination, follow with 'Morte d'Arthur,' and the epic *Idylls of the King* may succeed the aristocratic talk of *The Princess* with no need for a change of tone on the part of the author. There is transition, but the passage is easier than from the beautiful to the humble; and if it is not difficult to describe a knight after having described a lady, and to become absorbed in a noble soul after being interested in a beautiful face, quite another effort is required, after the intoxication of these fine sights, to delight in describing the person of a sailor burnt and browned by the sun and rain, to take pleasure in the skeptical jargon of an English farmer, or to glean with difficulty the seeds of poetry hidden beneath a rustic roof. This, however, is what has been done by Alfred Tennyson, the correct and polished singer of aristocratic elegance, the lettered classicist, the ingenious imitator of the old masters. Far from turning away from these humble realities, he has sought them out, and they have rewarded him, for he owes to them one of his most incontestable titles to fame, the idyll of familiar and domestic life." In rehearsing the merits of the poems, M. Montégut struggles manfully and with wonderful success against the difficulties of "The Northern Farmer," confessing that it took him half a day to translate the dialect into ordinary English, and quoting the first stanza with malicious glee in foreseeing the bewilderment of his readers. *Enoch Arden* seems to him as simple as it seemed ornate to Mr. Bagehot, and "Aylmer's Field" makes no appeal. "Sea Dreams" is frankly given up ; but the one fine sentence which almost justifies the poem is extracted :

> " Forgive ! How many will say, 'forgive,' and find
> A sort of absolution in the sound
> To hate a little longer."

And when M. Montégut reaches "Tithonus" he reads into it a very suggestive meaning which can certainly by the exercise of imagination be found there.

"In his lamentation the old husband of Aurora expresses to us one of the most painful sentiments that can weigh upon the heart in a timeworn society : the sentiment born of the discord between a task incessantly renewed, and forces too wearied to sustain the burden laid upon them by the exigences of civilisation.　The work to be accomplished returns each morning, young as the dawn ; and, each morning, the souls charged with its accomplishment waken with the lassitude of Tithonus.　It is immortal age beside immortal youth.　Ah ! how much more equal was the union in the old times ! "

In conclusion, M. Montégut permits himself a cautious glance into the future, and declines to prophesy whether the new volume is really the inauguration of a new style, or whether it is chance, or a passing essay to be at once abandoned.　The wisdom of this caution the later years have shown.

When *Queen Mary* was published, and before it was acted, M. Léon Boucher discussed it at considerable length, finding it typical of such dramatic genius as remained in England, hunted from the stage into the study.　Tennyson, among others, he says in his article, has " desired to attempt in his turn a career that is not without its dangers, and he has not feared to risk his fame on this throw of the dice.　He has wished to show the young critic who reproaches him with being the commonplace echo of aristocratic salons and a lady's poet, that his voice can find virile accents upon occasion, and that the gift of supreme grace is not in his case incompatible with strength.　For some years it has been said that the Laureate's poetry has had its day, that his rose-water knights are no longer in fashion, and that the future belongs to Mr. Browning's difficult and profound enigmas, or to the sonorous hymns in which Mr.

Swinburne loves to sing the myths of antiquity, the forces of nature, and the triumphs of liberty. The statue raised by the admiration of his readers to the author of *Idylls of the King* has been found, it is said, to have feet of clay; the slightest blow would overturn it. Mr. Tennyson has been meditating upon this; abandoning legend for history, and the heroes of the Round-Table for the characters of Shakespeare, he has composed his drama of *Queen Mary*, which has been the literary event of the past year on the other side of the channel. The surprise was natural enough, for nothing in Mr. Tennyson's previous work indicated the new direction just taken by his talent at a time of life when it is not usual to change one's route. What is difficult at the moment is to determine whether the success has been as great as the attempt was bold; this the near future must decide, if, as we are told, the Laureate's drama is destined to pass from the book to the stage."

After a minute examination of the play, in which its best and its worst points are well brought out, M. Boucher continues:

"Has a fold of Shakespeare's mantle fallen upon Mr. Tennyson's shoulders? This is the question *Queen Mary* has started in the world of criticism. What seems clear is that the author would have spared his judges much expenditure of ink if, in place of calling his work a drama, he had given it the more flexible and less compromising title of dramatic poem. If by a drama is meant, as certain critics have defined it, a definite action with a beginning, a plot, and a denouement, *Queen Mary* hardly justifies its title. Strongly to desire marriage, to espouse an unamiable prince, to live very unhappily with him, to seek in the persecution of heretics an insufficient consolation, and to die in bed of a fever, constitute a variety of things, undoubtedly, and while they may be brought well together, the result is not, properly speaking, dramatic action. There is rich enough matter for romance ; but tragedy is sought in vain in this succession of events. In all dramas it must be felt, however feebly, that there is a plot, a progression in interest ; in one word, a crisis. There is nothing of the kind in *Queen Mary.* Why the personages go and come, entering and departing, why they are there, even, and what they are doing, is a mystery. They are there by the poet's wish, that is all. A series of pictures are unfolded without other connection than that of chronological succession. There are no skilfully prepared surprises, no ingenious combinations, no stirring catastrophes. All these people talk and recount ; they do not act at all, having nothing to do. We recognise that a hidden art has presided over the disposition of the acts and the scenes, but it is an art quite different from that which we must ask from writers who work for the stage. Shakespeare, it will be said, did not do otherwise. With this great master there are no *coups de théâtre*, or rigorous chains of circumstance. He is content to follow the order of events and fill the frame that history has placed

for him. It is true that in this respect Mr. Tennyson
has shown himself an apt pupil. He has not limited
himself to reproducing the scenic arrangement of the
historical plays of his model ; he has sought to obtain
that mingling of the familiar and the sublime which
gives to these plays such a puissant reality. He has
brought into his drama a current of trivial gayety and
popular jocularity. Thus Elizabeth, reproaching an
envoy of the queen for appearing in her presence
without attending sufficiently to his dress, says to
him :

> '—— God hath blest or cursed me with a nose—
> Your boots are from the horses.'

Such also is this criticism made by an old woman
upon the punishment of Cranmer and the policy of
Mary :

"'Ay, Joan ; and Queen Mary gwoes on a-burnin'
and a-burnin', to get her baaby born ; but all her
burnin's 'ill never burn out the hypocrisy that makes
the water in her.'

"But this imitation of the Shakespearian forms on
the part of the modern poet is only a way of trick-
ing the eye of the reader ; the resemblance stops
there. With the author of *Richard III.* and *Henry
VIII.*, all is action ; with the author of *Queen Mary*,
all is recital or portraiture. The method is entirely
different. Shakespeare puts his characters under
the light of their public life. He does not go out
of his way to guess what history has not revealed

to him. He clings closely to the chronicles, taking
scoundrels or saints, heroes or cowards, princes,
lords, and clowns, as they are furnished to him, without troubling himself about anything more than to
make them seem natural. And such is the power
of his genius, that he seems in all his plays to have
created rather than to have resuscitated them. Mr.
Tennyson, on the contrary, peers into the intimate life of his characters like an antiquarian. He
sees in them not living beings, but historic figures
which he must reconstruct with the greatest care.
He calls analysis to the aid of imagination, he descends into the conscience of his queen and into that
of his bishops ; he inquires the most secret motives
of their acts ; he becomes an erudite historian ; forgetting to be a creator and a poet. The result, therefore, is not happy. We see how these heroes have
been manufactured, and recognise in them only
puppets more than usually well dressed. If, unfortunately, we have read M. Froude, all illusion disap-
pears. We continually find ourselves recalling faces
that we have seen before. When Elizabeth speaks
of old Gardiner, of his ' irritable forelock which he
rubs,' of his ' buzzard beak and deep-incavern'd eyes,'
we know whence came the portrait. In the poetically emphatic language of Cardinal Pole, in his endless tropes and his biblical allegories, we feel the
style of the legate's Latin letters quoted by the historian. The same could be said of Lord Paget and of
Lord Howard, and of Philip and of Simon Renard,

The Very Reverend Dr. Butler.

(Master of Trinity, Cambridge.)
From life.

and especially of Mary herself ; all have been painted with the poet's eyes fixed on the history-book ; all have their germ in Mr. Froude's beautiful prose. And indeed, is Mr. Froude not the one to whom Mr. Tennyson should have dedicated his volume ; saying something like this : 'This book is yours, I give it to you ; without you it would not have been made'?"

To this limited group of French representatives we will add one more name.   M. Filon, in 1885, contributed to the *Revue des Deux Mondes* a long article introduced by the announcement: "The Tennyson cult is organised ; it has its rites, its initiates, its legends ; it has even its skeptics and its atheists, whose manifestations vary from smile to insult. A legion of commentators has commenced to portion out his works.   Some seek the poetic system ; most of them detach the dogma and the moral lesson ; others study what is obscure and delight in what is unintelligible.   In the distance a heavy step is heard ; the Germans are approaching.   But the prey is living.   The hour of the Teuton scholiast has not yet sounded.   In France, Tennyson is studied as a classic, and the committee on public instruction has by a judicious selection placed *Enoch Arden* and the *Idylls of the King* upon our programmes.   The moment seems to have arrived for offering to the public an all-around view that shall serve as a clue to this work which is luxuriant, mysterious, varied of aspect, and difficult of access to foreigners."

After a careful examination of most of the more important poems, M. Filon sums up his impression of Tennyson's poetic quality :

"Nathaniel Hawthorne," he says, "encountering Tennyson, in 1857, at the Manchester Exhibition, tried in vain to define his impression. 'All that I can say,' he wrote to a friend, 'is that he has an un-English and at the same time not an American look.' [1]

"This phrase was striking, and came back to us as we were trying to characterise some of the features of Lord Tennyson's literary physiognomy. We are tempted to apply to the talent what has been said of the man. Certainly he has the qualities and defects of his race. He is English when he loves the fields and the sea ; he is English in his scorn of the Celt, in his hatred of Rome ; English in patriotism and in pride. But we believe that he will never by future historians of literature be considered a representative of the Saxon genius in the same way as Shakespeare or Dickens. Taste with his compatriots is only distaste. We do not despise this mental disposition ; aversion to that which is unclean and unhealthy is always a safeguard and often an inspiration. But something more must be recognised in Lord Tennyson : the choice of elements, the art of composition, the science of proportion, and, throughout, the exquisite feeling for sound and form. An after-touch is an artistic effort, an erasure—with due deference to

---

[1] The actual phrase is : " Un-English as he was, Tennyson had not, however, an American look."

those who boast of pouring themselves forth upon paper like a torrent—is a sign of intelligence. How many after-touches and erasures in Tennyson! We could show him, for example, three times remaking that passage in *The Princess* where he has simply to bring before us three men letting themselves slip from the top of a rampart like spiders hanging from the end of their thread. This scrupulousness is an honour to the writer. The molten metal flows from a cast and is of no value ; a thousand strokes of the hammer are necessary to give to the forged object its form and its price.

" As to the harmony of words, Tennyson possesses it, not as a *Parnassian*, not as a virtuoso of cæsura and rhyme, but by instinct, through genius. His verse imitates everything—the neighing and galloping of horses, the dry murmur of guitar-strings, the tearing sound of the clarion, joyous or drawling vibration, bells, echoes waning and dying, the grating sound of the wave grinding the pebbles on the strand, all the sounds of living nature from the growl of thunder to the burring of the grasshopper. In his plays he bends to his use the alliteration of the old Saxons, at the same time borrowing from the prosody of the Greeks their scholarly flexions. Sometimes he gives richness and amplitude to his song by composite words which he brings together or unlinks at will ; sometimes he originates velvety gamuts of marvellously adjusted monosyllables. Our professors have recommended to our admiration the famous line:

'Le jour n'est pas plus pur que le fond de mon cœur.'

What would they have said if someone had told them that one of the most melodious stanzas of *In Memoriam* counts in eight lines but two dissyllabic words, and fifty-eight words of one syllable without ceasing to caress the ear! Sometimes the meaning of these lines is vague. What matter! A false shame keeps us from admitting that in poetry, as in music, the charm is often in inverse ratio to the precision. Tennyson, like Mendelssohn, has his 'songs without words,' in which words are not so much intellectual signs as musical notes. It is with these vague, delicious modulations that three or four generations of young men and women have already sung lullaby to their dreams.

"If we admire the great artist, we reserve the best of our sympathy for the sincere thinker. Literary sincerity! who troubles himself about it to-day? In criticism, to serve one's coterie or injure one's neighbour, one leans always to one side or the other; in romance, one swells, one lashes oneself into aping passion; the historian recounts the past, thinking of the present, often of the future. We leave aside political eloquence, which lives on lies. The furious search after novelty, the need of advertisement, the prejudice of systems, party spirit, scholastic servility, or fear of the rabble; we do not undertake to say which of these causes has most contributed to the reign of falsehood; but we do state that, since Diderot, nearly all our great writers have been great

liars as well. To say only what one has himself
thought and felt, and nothing more : the author who
will seriously abide by this plain rule will make a
revolution in literature such as Descartes made in
science. That is why we love the sincerity of Lord
Tennyson. It makes the moral value of his work,
the identity of his talent in the midst of multiple
transformations ; and through it, after many imitations and essays, he has conquered his originality."

Ten years later, and three years after Tennyson's
death, this appreciative critic reviewed in an article
on "Le Théâtre Anglais Contemporain" the sum of
Tennyson's dramatic production.

"Mr. Archer," he says, "remarks that Tennyson,
who was so fortunate in his poetic life, lacked fitness
for his career as a dramatist. He wrote his plays too
late and too soon : too soon for the public and too
late for his talent. He was, in truth, sixty-six years
old when he published *Queen Mary*, the first in date
of his six dramatic pieces. That was twenty years
ago, and the education of the audience was far from
being as advanced as it is to-day. It was not their
fault if they brought to the poet a taste somewhat
spoilt by the success of *Our Boys* and *Pink Dominoes*,
and a soul closed to the higher delights of the imagination. The players did their duty by the Laureate
and even a little more than their duty ; it is criticism,
—and, here, I shelter myself under the authority of
the most eminent member of the society of critics,—
it is criticism that has decided the repulse given to

Tennyson's dramas, and if it did not precisely con-
demn him unheard, it at least heard him under the
dominion of a preconceived idea.   I shall borrow Mr.
Archer's acute expression : the critics 'expected to
be disappointed'; they came for that alone.   Why
should an old man enter upon a new career, and one
for which youth itself has need of all its powers ?
What has possessed him to discover in himself fresh
faculties at an age when ordinarily one can only re-
peat oneself ?   Has a man any right to be good at
two trades ?   Is there not against this sort of thing a
'law of cumulation' tacitly acknowledged by the
critics, and applied by them with pitiless severity ?
For the success of this logic it was necessary that
Tennyson should fail in drama : so he failed.

   " But, as this repulse was not just, he recovered
from it, and his drama, even when it is commonplace, even when it is bad, belongs to the living
drama.

   " I have fallen into the common mistake.   In the
course of the first articles which I had the honour of
inserting in this *Review*, I spoke of Tennyson, in
1885, as if the tomb had already closed over him.
Perhaps I was correct in saying that in the garden of
the poet upon which winter had descended, certain
flowers would not flourish.   But what was not then
apparent to me, and what to-day is manifest to me
and to many others as well, is that the last age of
the poet has preserved some of his early graces, and
has developed before our sight qualities unknown to

his youth. To the end he remained in touch with the soul of the humble. Furthermore, he has shown himself a master in the art of giving poetic and vivifying expression to the social and religious discussions by which we are moved. He has used in the service of the stage a historic and a dramatic sense of the highest order, and, if these two gifts sometimes work injury to each other, to the point of paralysing each other, their combination at a fortunate moment has furnished us with fragments of dramatic masterpieces.

"I shall consider his plays not in chronological order, but in the order of their importance. The slightest of all is *The Falcon*. The scene is laid in some vague region of a half-fantastic Italy ; with no indication of place or century. It is a well-known tale by Boccaccio ; but a purified and simplified Boccaccio. A poor gentleman, Federigo, entertains a respectful and hopeless love for the beautiful and wealthy widow, the Lady Giovanna. His last possession, his pride, his joy, and, also, his one means of gaining a livelihood is an admirable falcon which he himself raised for the chase. One morning the Lady Giovanna, unaware of her neighbour's poverty, invites herself to breakfast without ceremony. Federigo, whose larder is empty, has his favourite bird killed and served to the lady. But it is the falcon for which she has come to ask him, to satisfy the whim of a sick child. Federigo is forced to confess the sacrifice inspired by his hospitality and love, and the Lady

Giovanna is so touched by it that she falls, and forever, into his arms. When *The Falcon* was presented to the public in 1879, at St. James's, John Hare, who is a manager of excellent taste and also an admirable actor, used respect and love in the mounting, giving it a poetically realistic setting. Federigo and the Lady Giovanna were taken by the Kendals, and those who have seen Madge Robertson in this rôle remember how much she suggested a picture by an old master, in a German or an Italian museum. From the plastic point of view she has, in creating Giovanna, given a pendant to her Galatea. But neither the charm of the scenery, nor the perfection of the acting, nor the music of the lines could insure long life for the play. Just a few hundred chosen spectators enjoying this light thing for an hour, enthusiastic for an evening. Then on the morrow cockneyism takes possession of the hall and asks for its usual pleasures again. The critics made common cause with the cockneys, but for a reason less foreign to art. They said that if there be any ' motive' to *The Falcon*, it is apparently Federigo's sacrifice. But this motive, slender as it is, has not been developed. Two words apart with his servant, an order in an undertone, and that is all that leads up to and justifies the condemnation. More deceptive than the breakfast offered to the Lady Giovanna is the menu presented by Lord Tennyson to his audience, consisting as it does only of delicate *hors d'œuvres*, too meagre for those robust appetites.

" *The Promise of May* has had a worse fate than *The Falcon*. The play unreservedly collapsed. A certain part of the public—with the famous Marquis of Queensberry at its head—pretended to believe that the poet spoke through the mouth of his hero, where he denounces with so much bitterness and in a disquieting jumble of words, the principles and prejudices upon which society is built.[1] These people were certainly decifient in patience and intelligence. The argument against Harold's negative theories was not lacking. When he has finished declaiming upon the subject of the evil brought to mankind by religions, Dora points out to him (somewhat feebly, it is true) the benefits it has received from them. After he has prophesied the approach of the universal dissolution of the marriage bond, she replies to him simply, but not without emotion and grace[2]: 'And yet I had once a vision of a pure and perfect marriage, where the man and the woman, only differing as the stronger and the weaker, should walk hand in hand together down this valley of tears to the grave at the bottom, and lie down there together in the darkness which would seem but a moment, to be wakened again together by the light of the resurrection, and no more partings for ever and ever!' And when Harold breaks off for her a spray

---

[1] Here M. Filon has fallen into error, as the Marquis of Queensberry did not assume that Tennyson was exploiting his own views, but that he was misrepresenting the views of the agnostic party.

[2] She does not "reply to him," but soliloquises in her room.

19

of apple-blossoms,[1] this farmer's daughter looks sorrowfully at the devastated branch : 'Next year there will be no apples there.'[2]   That is touching symbolism, and it is agreeable to find a poet refuting the. ethics of the feeling by which flowers are plucked only to prevent the birth of the fruit and to destroy the seed of the future.

"By such detail was Tennyson's thought revealed, and they should have gained him the indulgence of the hissers : but these would not listen to reason.   Such misconceptions are only possible with a play that is not its own defence.   But, unfortunately, *The Promise of May* is such a play.   There are to be found in it some traces of those idyllic gifts which gave to the little poems of Tennyson's youth so much charm, together with that comprehension of the rustic mind which never abandoned him, and a bitter eloquence, a vein of moral and social satire, currents of which flowed through the second part of *Locksley Hall, Sixty Years After*.   But when it comes to the action, the poet is deplorably weak, childish, almost silly.   This Harold who in the beginning poses as the type of nihilist whom nothing can agitate or terrify, falls finally into such stammering disorder that one is ashamed for him.   If Tennyson wished us to regard the marriage of this sad seducer with the sister of his victim as a satisfaction to

[1] He breaks them off for Eva, and it is Eva, not Dora, who answers him.   Fortunately M. Filon's contempt for accuracy does not extend to essentials.
[2] " You have robb'd poor father of ten good apples," is what she really says.

morality, he is gravely mistaken, and the little that remains of the play vanishes with this repulsive denouement.[1]

"The relative success of *The Cup*, at the Lyceum, astonishes me less than it has astonished Mr. Archer. I shall not seek the principal cause in Ellen Terry's grace or in the magnificent decoration of the temple of Diana. *The Cup* has certain qualities which are made to please the average public. The subject is taken from Plutarch's tales of *The Virtues of Women*, and from one episode which already had drawn into tragedy a Frenchman, a German, and an Italian. Perhaps, without precisely knowing it, Tennyson took something of the tone of his original author and of the manner of his forerunners. He has been this time less English, less Shakespearian, and less himself than in his other works. The dialogue is rapid and stirring ; the characters do not yield themselves to poetic fantasies, they develop no theories, they express emotions that have nothing complicated or strange about them. One of them, Synorix, is interesting. Apart from the Don Juan-ism which too much modernises him, this ambiguous type, half barbaric, half Roman, whose intelligence has been refined but whose passions have not been eradicated by civilisation, is an exceptional creature, a kind of monster, who knows his intellectual superiority and his moral deficiency ; uniting these two sentiments in a melancholy which is not without grandeur.

[1] It will of course be remembered that Harold does *not* marry Dora.

The attraction of this character has been the source of Tennyson's failure with the play ; he has departed from the motive that Plutarch offered him, and that impressed Thomas Corneille and Montanelli, the latter making use of it with talent and success in spite of a florid style. This motive is the action of Camma, the widow of the Galatian tetrarch whom Synorix, with the aid of the Romans, had killed and succeeded in power. Synorix loves her and wishes to marry her. Camma cannot consider this odious marriage, but pretends to consent. After the sacred rite, she is to touch with her lips the cup that Synorix drinks from before the altar of Diana. She makes him drink of death from this cup, and does the same herself. In order that this culmination should awaken no objection in our mind, we must be made to hate Synorix as Camma hates him. But Tennyson seems to have made every effort to diminish the horror of his character. He has given him the prestige of a noble sadness, the excuse of a great love, has in some sort obliged him to kill his rival as a method of legitimate defence. He has completed the effect by showing us in Camma's first husband an unintelligent and brutal individual who poorly justifies the regrets and sacrifice of the young wife. Add to this the fact that if the real motive lies in the hidden drama passing in Camma's soul, we know nothing of it until the last scene. A *coup de théâtre* does not make a play, and Mr. Archer is undoubtedly right in preferring Montanelli's work to that of Tennyson.

In spite of its faults, however, I believe that *The Cup* will again find, as in 1881, a favourable reception with the public. It decidedly suggests our own tragedies by the dignity, the decency, the seriousness undisturbed by any comic element, by that identity in the characters, that continuity of tone, and that unity of action, which, whatever one may say, pleases the mind better than the most faithful imitation of the contrasts and incoherences of life can please it.

"If he had written only *The Falcon*, *The Cup*, and *The Promise of May*, Tennyson would hold but a very small place among dramatic writers. If he is to live on the stage, it is through his three historic dramas : *Queen Mary*, *Harold*, *Becket*.

"These dramas, it was said, were very inferior, even before their birth, to the historic dramas of the Elizabethan age, the style and character of which they so faithfully imitate. In fact, the *Histories* of Shakespeare and of his contemporaries were shaped in the Chronicles, which keep the vivacity of personal impression and the warmth of life itself almost as much as Memoirs. Tennyson, on his part, took his dramas from history so called ; but history is like a serious and scientific person who dissects life to study it the better ; who discusses instead of narrating, and puts modern judgments in the place of ancient passions. This objection is plausible, but that is all. In the first place, the definition given to history is true, perhaps, of the work of a Guizot, a Hallam, or a Lecky, but would ill apply to a Carlyle, a Michelet, or a Taine. In reading Freeman, and particularly Froude, was Tennyson further from direct contact with the soul of the past than Shakespeare in going through the often cold and languishing pages of Holinshed? And, again, were Froude as sententious and frozen as he is on the contrary picturesque and impassioned, Tennyson would have counteracted this defect by his own qualities. It is the time to render full justice to his delicacy and to the veritably incomparable power of his historic sense. An historical drama, if I understand the words, contains history and drama. But, among the authors of historical dramas in this century, who has been an historian and at the same time a dramatist and a poet?

" It is not a question of the historical critical sense, —in no wise involved in this matter,—but of the gift, accorded to few, of the imaginative sense able to make live again the emotions of a century sleeping in the dust. Michelet thus saw the torture of Jeanne d'Arc, Macaulay the trial of Warren Hastings, Carlyle the taking of the Bastille and the battle of Marston Moor. A hundred times more precious is their intellectual vision than the eyesight of a Holinshed or an Ayala.

" This rare gift was one of Tennyson's privileges, and in him it took that feminine acuteness that refined all his poetic faculties. For proof, take all the by-play of his historic pieces, all not essential, all accessory action, detail of manners, minute traits of character, fragments of history—for instance, the story of the marriage of Philip and Mary, that of the torture of Jane Grey by Bagenhall in *Queen Mary;* and in *Becket* the sarcasms launched at the Roman Church by Walter Map, the spiritual precursor of the bitter and sombre Langland. A Bulwer, a Tom Taylor, can cut out little bits from a chronicle, or frame historic sayings in his prose; can he, as Tennyson does, compel us to see states of soul, and plunge in the depths of the ancient life?

“I am well aware that this is not all; that it is, indeed, nothing if the poet cannot add dramatic force to this power of intimate evocation. Is there a drama in *Becket*, in *Queen Mary*, in *Harold?* My answer—juror-fashion—is: to the first question, No; to the second and third, Yes.

“True, *Becket*, in the summer of 1893, attained brilliant success, but three fourths of that success were due to Irving. Those to whom the great actor has long been familiar know to what degree he is Episcopal, Pontifical, hieratic. Mediæval asceticism is a mode of being which his artistic personality fills most exactly, in which it ensconces itself at greatest ease. It was worth a long journey and hours of fatigue to watch that symbolic game of chess in which the struggle of bishop and king foretokened the whole play; or that striking dialogue in which Becket recounts to his confidant his tragic anguish and his prophetic dreams; or that stormy discussion at Northampton where the Archbishop first signs the famous 'constitution' and then retracts; or that assassination scene which follows history step by step, and where, moreover, pure pantomime would have sufficed. They who saw Irving, mitre on head and cross in hand, fall stricken on the steps of the altar while faint waves of the monks' chant floated down from the church above, mingled with the cries of the people battering at the portal and the rumblings of thunder with which the vast and un-just basilica quivered to its foundations, have ex-perienced emotion as powerful as any spectacle has ever yielded.

"Nevertheless the drama is missing, for a drama is a situation evolving through transformation, it is action in movement. The duel of the King and the Prelate is, in the play as in history, only a confused series of indecisive encounters. The metamorphosis of the soldier-courtier into the martyr-bishop is hardly indicated by the poet. And what can be said of the amorous idyl annexed to the play, in defiance of his-tory and of the drama itself? All Ellen Terry's tact could not save the insipid Rosamond. The compli-cations as to the mysterious retreat of the young wo-man smack more of farce than even of melodrama; and as to the amusing details with which the episode is relieved, their comedy is so flat and on so low a plane as to be slightly nauseating. I pass that feature in silence rather than incur the pain of subjecting a man of genius to ridicule, but I cannot help blaming Tennyson for his irreparable error in compromising

Becket by his equivocal adventure, and in giving him the custody of the King's mistress at the very moment he was with such boldness holding the King in check.

"The same criticism cannot be directed to the *Queen Mary* nor to the *Harold*. In the first, the psychologic human drama, half submerged but never wholly hidden by history, lies in the development of the character and the mournful fate of the wretched Queen ; it lies in the path, first strewn with flowers and then paved with sharp stones and thick with thorns, along which she moves, in so few years, from a prolonged youth to premature age, from enthusiastic joy to lonely, accursed, and despairing agony and death. As Queen, she dreamed of the grandeur of her realm, and left it smitten by the national disgrace of the loss of Calais. As a Catholic, she sought to restore her religion, and far from succeeding she opened between her people and Rome an abyss which the centuries have not closed. As a woman, she loved a man of ice, a living rock by whom her heart was wounded and broken. Before her death she knew the wreck of all her plans, and read scorn and disgust in the eyes of him to whom in propitiation she had offered human sacrifices.

"This is the drama Tennyson has sketched if not fully accomplished in *Queen Mary*. That which forms the subject of *Harold* stands out in full light in striking relief. It is the struggle of religious faith with patriotism and ambition. All the sentiments

aroused on the one part and on the other are indicated with superiority worthy of the master in the
successive scenes at the court of William while Harold
is a prisoner there. After policy has spoken by the
lips of the old Norman Lord, comes the sublime
scene in which Wulfnoth, Harold's younger brother,
describes to him the slow torture of the prisoner, the
living dead man, forever cut off from love, from the
sight of fields and sea and sky as from the society of
men, his very name vanishing from their memory,
eaten out by forgetfulness as his body in his cell
is eaten by the hateful vermin of the earth. When
Harold has yielded, it is a touching thing to see him
bow, with Edith, before Christian fatalism, sacrificing
to his kingly duty, as the atonement for his violated
oath, his own happiness. The dilemma changes,
and its two new aspects are personified in two women, whose rivalry is in no wise banal, and never
suggests those vulgar outbreaks of jealousy to which
the theatre has too much accustomed us. Edith
surrenders to Aldwyth, the living hero ; dead, she
claims him again with a nobility and pride in her
accent that thrill us.

"Thus the legacy of the great lyric poet to the
theatre of his country consists of two dramatic
works—I cannot venture to call them *chefs-d'œuvre*
—surrounded by a vein-stone of history, in itself material of extraordinary value. There comes a pious
hand to disengage the two dramas and set the air cir-
culating about their essential lives ; there comes a

great actor who comprehends the character of Harold and embodies it, a great actress who devotes herself with passion to the character of Mary, and without effort Tennyson takes his place among the dramatists."

When we recall Tennyson's not too exuberant affection for the French, it seems a little odd that they should have been on the whole so much more appreciative of him than the Germans. Perhaps appreciative is not just the word. The Germans translated him with characteristic thoroughness, and some of the translations went through so many editions that we can hardly consider him put down as a negligible author in that country. But when he took his place in the *Litteratur Geschichte* it was not a very enviable place. Bleibtreu, for example, denies that he was a poet "in the higher and highest sense of the word," and finds that while his roses are without thorns they are also often as scentless as the gorgeously coloured Bengal rose.

"The most noteworthy of his personal experiences," he says, "is that he spent his youth among the Lincolnshire moorland, which he sketched in a masterly fashion in 'The Dying Swan,' for example, while his later life was spent in the paradise of the Isle of Wight, the physiognomy of which stands out in 'The Gardener's Daughter'; since for so great a landscapist such retreats in which to study are veritably important events. The measureless adoration which is paid to these national poets leads necessarily to contradiction, the more that *Enoch Arden* with truly English perspective is neglected, and the tiresome ' Day-Dreams,' ' Vision of Sin,' and so forth, are emphasised. There is a good deal of truth in Professor Austin's bitter attacks against him, and the comparison of his Pegasus to a thorough-bred racer without a sign of wings is sufficiently striking. But whether Shakespeare and Byron would drive him ' out of Elysium to ' the garden that he loves is un- likely. Especially would the latter, whose name was the unavailing war-cry on the lips of the Convulsive Poets, honour in Tennyson the tasteful artist who unites Wordsworth's absorption in Nature with the classic word-painting and chiselled form of *Childe Harold*. In reality, Tennyson beheld Nature solely with the eyes of a landscape painter. There is nothing of Shelley's mystical symbolising of Nature. Of the godlike idea of *Erscheinungsform* he knows nothing. He is the true poet of the century, transcen- dentalism has no charm for him. With his landscape painting is united the sense of historic costuming, which together with his absorption in the woman- soul he shared with Victor Hugo. ' Simeon Stylites,' ' Lucretius,' ' Ulysses,' are original cabinet-pieces of this sort. Originality, the prime characteristic of genius, he certainly possesses only in limited quantity. He has copied many styles, and in the process he has fused them all into one Tennysonism. Nor does his philosophic sense spring from anything but his going back to and living in the time of the Minnesingers.

Tennyson's Memorial, Beacon Hill,
Freshwater.

Heavenly and earthly bards are the fountains of his reflection, as with Wolfram von Eschenbach."

Wülker says that all the lyric poets of our time hark back to Tennyson, but "in spite of his gift Tennyson has struck out no new path. The age of Queen Victoria, so epoch-making in romance, is for lyrics only a period of beautiful after-bloom. Tennyson's poems are above Byron's in point of agreeable sound, and can only be likened to Shelley's. His thoughts are not always new, but the form in which he gives them is nevertheless peculiar to himself. A true Englishman, he is as far removed from Byron's cosmopolitanism as from Shelley's polytheism. He does not care to go frequently into distant times and alien countries, and if he does it once as in the *Idylls of the King*, the figures bear a very modern stamp, and therefore stand very close to the people of the present time."

In Engel's *Geschichte der Englischen Litteratur*, the direct question of Tennyson's entrance into that "little society" in which there is no crowding, is plainly faced.

"One question must be asked," the critic declares, "concerning every poet who is considered 'great' by his countrymen: What new thing has he said to the world at large or even to his own country alone? For Tennyson it may be answered in this way: he has given substantial aid in the formation of the new romanticism in England, and he has given to the lyric many new forms. The romanticism of

Tennyson and of his followers lies in the revival of the King Arthur fables. Now that this romanticism is entirely dead, we can regard them as merely a pretty play with a subject already tested ; as unspontaneous, unreal poetry. Not even Tennyson's mastery could infuse life into the forms of Arthur, Lancelot, Guinevere, etc. This new English romanticism seemed in essence not quite so artificial as the coquetting with classic mythology that went on in the eighteenth century, or the rioting in Oriental gorgeousness characteristic of the early part of the nineteenth. Nevertheless not one stanza of Tennyson's many Arthur-poems will live. . . . Of his many volumes very little, perhaps only here and there one of his little songs, will survive ; but with the English people the memory of him as a noble man and a poet of fine feeling will outlive his work."

In Italy Tennyson's fame was spread by Signor Bellezza's *Life*, which must be, we imagine, a very interesting contribution to the mass of Tennyson literature. As it could not be procured in time to serve the purposes of this chapter, we shall have to content ourselves with a few fragments culled from a review in the *Athenæum*,[1] and in themselves quite significant of the critical attitude of the writer :

"The metre which the Laureate prefers is the iambic, as best adapted to the patient and minute elaboration, and to the systematic distribution of parts in which he delights. This metre is the base

[1] October 13, 1894.

of the heroic stanza, rhymed and unrhymed, and it is the measure in which all the masterpieces of English literature were written : *The Canterbury Tales, Paradise Lost,* Pope's *Essays and Satires,* Dryden's *Fables,* Shakespeare's *Tragedies, The Faëry Queen, The Revolt of Islam, The Excursion, Don Juan,* and *Childe Harold.* Occasionally, as in *Locksley Hall,* Tennyson adopted the trochaic measure to express the tumult of passion and the raging of the elements ; while in *Maud* he drew marvellous effects from alternated anapæsts.

". . . But for better appreciation of the minute and delicate care which our poet devoted to form, we must enter, so to speak, the workshop of his art, examine closely the devices and details, and observe the methods and the infinite elaboration by which he attains perfection in word and phrase. His is a language which has been fused into harmony by a thousand refinings, and consequently ' to analyse a work of Tennyson's it is always necessary to observe all the minutiæ of form.' One of these peculiarities of form is his use of monosyllabic words. One of the most inspired stanzas of *In Memoriam* contains in 8 verses only 2 dissyllabic words, while 58 are monosyllables. Of the 197 words in one of the stanzas in *Maud* (XVIII. 8), 164 are monosyllabic ; the third stanza of the youthful ' Rosalind' consists of 122 words, of which 104 are monosyllabic and only 18 polysyllabic. . . .

" Frequently, to give perspicuity and effectiveness

to his thought, the poet resorts to compound words, notably in the *Idylls*, to which this device lends a certain archaic colour in harmony with their subject. The following examples are taken from the *Idylls:* bee-chen (!) ; furze-cramm'd ; bracken-rooft ; wide-wing'd ; death-dumb ; autumn-dripping ; slender-shafted ; heather-scented ; silver-misty ; wan-sallow ; satin-shining ; gloomy-gladed ; May-blossom ; hawk-eyes ; tip-tilted ; topaz-lights ; livid-flickering ; green-glimmering ; sallow-rifted ; passion-pale ; love-royal ; tenderest-touching ; dark-splendid ; jacinth-work ; many-knotted ; many-cobwebb'd ; tiny-trumpeting ; ruby-circled ; stubborn-shafted ; dusky-rafter'd ; newly-fallen ; and so forth.

"Sometimes he abuses this expedient, and indulges in certain monstrous combinations, which tend to affectation and awkwardness, even when they do not enfeeble or obscure the idea which he desires to make more clear and impressive. A good example is the adjective ' lily-cradled,' which he applies to the bee to indicate that it was cradled in the lily. Another is ' brain-dizzied,' in ' The May Queen'; the *Idylls* contain a number of these vicious combinations, as ' bridge-broken,' ' tip-tilted,' ' knee-broken,' ' head-stock,' ' kitchen-vassalage,' etc."

INDEX.